DEBATING GENDER IN
EARLY MODERN ENGLAND, 1500–1700

EARLY MODERN CULTURAL STUDIES

Ivo Kamps, Series Editor

PUBLISHED BY PALGRAVE

DEBATING GENDER IN EARLY MODERN ENGLAND, 1500–1700

Edited by
Cristina Malcolmson
and Mihoko Suzuki

A version of Chapter 7 appears as "The mat(t)er of death: the defense of Eve and the female Ars Morendi" in *Women, Death and Literature in Post-Reformation England* by Patricia Phillippy published by Cambridge University Press.

DEBATING GENDER IN EARLY MODERN ENGLAND, 1500–1700
Copyright © Cristina Malcolmson and Mihoko Suzuki, 2002.

First published 2002 by
PALGRAVE MACMILLAN™
175 Fifth Avenue, New York, N.Y. 10010 and
Houndmills, Basingstoke, Hampshire, England RG21 6XS.
Companies and representatives throughout the world.

PALGRAVE MACMILLAN IS THE GLOBAL ACADEMIC IMPRINT OF THE PALGRAVE MACMILLAN division of St. Martin's Press, LLC and of Palgrave Macmillan Ltd. Macmillan® is a registered trademark in the United States, United Kingdom and other countries. Palgrave is a registered trademark in the European Union and other countries.

ISBN 0-312-29457-3

Library of Congress Cataloging-in-Publication Data
Debating gender in early modern England, 1500–1700 / edited by Cristina Malcolmson
And Mihoko Suzuki
    p.   cm — (Early modern cultural studies series)
    Includes bibliographical references and index.
    ISBN 0-312-29457-3
    1. English literature—Early modern, 1500–1700—History and criticism.   2. Feminism and literature—England—History—16th century.   3. Feminism and literature—England—History—17th century.   4. English literature—Women authors—History and criticism.   5. Women and literature—England—History—16th century.   6. Women and literature—England—History—17th century.   7. Sex role in literature.   8. Women in literature.   I. Malcolmson, Cristina.   II. Suzuki, Mihoko, 1953–   III. Series.
    PR428.F45 D43   2002
    820.9'00082—dc21   2001056140

A catalogue record for this book is available from the British Library.

Design by Letra Libre, Inc.

First edition: August 2002
10 9 8 7 6 5 4 3 2 1

Printed in the United States of America

CONTENTS

ACKNOWLEDGMENTS

We would like to thank everyone who made this volume possible: first and foremost, our contributors, as well as all those who attended the 1999 Shakespeare Association of America seminar in San Francisco on "Women Writers and the Pamphlet Debate about Gender"; Susan Frye, Frank Palmeri, Jyotsna Singh, Hilda Smith, and Georgianna Ziegler at the Folger Shakespeare Library. Thanks also to our editor Kristi Long, the series editor Ivo Kamps, Roee Raz and Meg Weaver at Palgrave; Erin Chase at the Huntington Library; Marsheila Ksor, who prepared the index; and Yvette LaChapelle at Bates College. Finally, we acknowledge the financial assistance of Bates College and the University of Miami for indexing and permission fees.

ABOUT THE
CONTRIBUTORS

SANDRA CLARK is Reader in Renaissance Literature at Birkbeck College, University of London. Among other works, she is the author of *The Elizabethan Pamphleteers: Popular Moralistic Pamphlets, 1580–1640* (London, 1983), and *The Plays of Beaumont and Fletcher: Sexual Themes and Dramatic Representation* (Hemel Hempstead, 1994). She has edited *Amorous Rites: Elizabethan Erotic Verse* (London, 1994), *Shakespeare Made Fit: Restoration Adaptations of Shakespeare* (London, 1997), and *The Penguin Shakespeare Dictionary* (London, 1999). She has written articles on Shakespeare and on the pamphlet debate on gender.

ELIZABETH CLARKE is Reader in English at Warwick University. She is director of the British Academy-funded Perdita Project for early modern women's manuscript writing. She published a book on George Herbert in 1997 with Oxford University Press. A collection of essays edited with Danielle Clarke, *The Double Voice: Gendered Writing in Early Modern England*, came out in 2000 with Macmillan (published in the United States with St. Martin's Press).

MELINDA J. GOUGH is Assistant Professor of English and Women's Studies at McMaster University, and is a 2001–02 Fellow at the National Humanities Center. Author of Renaissance Women Online's Introduction to *Swetnam the Woman-hater*, she has published a series of related articles on the Renaissance enchantress in epic, popular drama, and the masque ("Tasso's Enchantress, Tasso's Captive Woman," *Renaissance Quarterly* 2001; "Jonson's Siren Stage," *Studies in Philology* 1999; and "'Her filthy feature open showne' in Ariosto, Spenser, and *Much Ado About Nothing*," *SEL* 1999). Her work in progress includes a book on Queen Henrietta Maria.

CRISTINA MALCOLMSON is Associate Professor of English at Bates College. She is the author of *Heart-Work: George Herbert and the Protestant Ethic* (Stanford, 1999) and *George Herbert: A Literary Life* (forthcoming from Palgrave), and the editor for *Longman Critical Readers: Renaissance Poetry* (1998). Her essays on the gender debate include "'What You Will': Social Mobility and Gender in *Twelfth Night*" in *The Matter of Difference* (1991); and "'As Tame as the Ladies': Politics and Gender in *The Changeling*" (*ELR* 1990). She is now working on a study of Robert Boyle and Margaret Cavendish.

NAOMI J. MILLER is Associate Professor of English Literature and Women's Studies at the University of Arizona. Her publications on early modern women writers and gender include *Changing the Subject: Mary Wroth and Figurations of Gender in Early Modern England* (Kentucky, 1996), which received an Honorable Mention for Best Scholarly Book from the Society for the Study of Early Modern Women (EMW), as well as a collection of essays on Wroth, coedited with Gary Waller, *Reading Mary Wroth: Representing Alternatives in Early Modern England* (Tennessee, 1991). Most recently, she has coedited, with Naomi Yavneh, an interdisciplinary collection of essays, *Maternal Measures: Figuring Caregiving in the Early Modern Period* (Ashgate, 2000), which received the Best Collaborative Project Award from EMW.

SUSAN GUSHEE O'MALLEY is a Professor of English at Kingsborough Community College, City University of New York (CUNY), and a Professor of Liberal Studies at the CUNY Graduate School and University Center. Her *"Custom Is an Idiot": Jacobean Pamphlet Literature on Women* will be published by the University of Illinois Press in 2003. Her books include *Defences of Women: Jane Anger, Rachel Speght, Ester Sowernam and Constantia Munda* for Scholar Press in the *Early Modern Englishwoman* series, a scholarly edition of Thomas Goffe's *The Courageous Turk* (Garland Publishing), and *The Politics of Education* (SUNY Press).

PATRICIA PHILLIPPY is an Associate Professor of English and Coordinator of the Program in Comparative Literature at Texas A&M University. She is the author of numerous essays on early modern women's writing and *Women, Death and Literature in Post-Reformation England* (Cambridge, 2002).

KATHERINE ROMACK is an Assistant Professor of English at the University of West Florida where she teaches early modern literature and feminist studies. Her essay, "Margaret Cavendish, Shakespeare Critic," appeared in Dympna Callaghan's anthology *The Feminist Companion to Shakespeare* (Blackwell, 2000) and she is currently completing a book on women and political representation in the Interregnum.

LISA J. SCHNELL is an Associate Professor of English at the University of Vermont. Among her published pieces are articles on Aphra Behn and Aemilia Lanyer. She is also, together with Andrew Barnaby, the author of *Literate Experience: The Work of Knowing in Seventeenth-Century English Literature* (Palgrave, 2002).

MIHOKO SUZUKI is Professor of English at the University of Miami. She is the author of *Metamorphoses of Helen: Authority, Difference, and the Epic* (Cornell, 1989) and *Subordinate Subjects: Gender, the Political Nation, and Literary Form in England, 1588–1688* (forthcoming in the series *Women and Gender in the Early Modern World*, Ashgate, 2002). She is editor of two forthcoming volumes in Ashgate's *Early Modern Englishwoman* series, on Mary Carleton and Elizabeth Cellier, and is at work on a collection of women's political writings in seventeenth-century England, coedited with Hilda L. Smith.

RACHEL TRUBOWITZ is Associate Professor of English at the University of New Hampshire. She has written essays on a variety of early modern topics, including seventeenth-century women prophets and Renaissance motherhood. Her most recent publications are "'I feel / The Link of Nature draw me': The Reformation of Death in Adam's Lament," in *Imagining Death in Spenser and Milton*, ed. Bellamy, Cheney, and Schoenfeldt (Palgrave, 2003).

SERIES EDITOR'S FOREWORD

Once there was a time when each field of knowledge in the liberal arts had its own mode of inquiry. A historian's labors were governed by an entirely different set of rules than those of the anthropologist or the literary critic. But this is less true now than it has ever been. This new series begins with the assumption that, as we enter the twenty-first century, literary criticism, literary theory, historiography, and cultural studies have become so interwoven that we can now think of them as an eclectic and only loosely unified (but still recognizable) approach to formerly distinct fields of inquiry such as literature, society, history, and culture. This series furthermore presumes that the early modern period was witness to an incipient process of transculturation through exploration, mercantilism, colonization, and migration that set into motion a process of globalization that is still with us today. The purpose of this series is to bring together this eclectic approach, which freely and unapologetically crosses disciplinary, theoretical, and political boundaries, with early modern texts and artifacts that bear the traces of transculturation and globalization. We know that the complex processes of cultural exchange and influence can be studied locally and internationally, and this new series is dedicated to both.

Feminist scholarship has long acknowledged the effects of cross-cultural and continental forces on the relationship between the sexes in early modern England. In the 1980s, for instance, Joan Kelly asserted that later English writers defending women used arguments remarkably similar to those offered in Christine de Pizan's *Book of the City of Ladies,* a text written on the brink of the fifteenth century in France. *Debating Gender in Early Modern England, 1500–1700,* confronts this issue head on, arguing that English women writers may have had greater access to continental authors than was hitherto thought possible. Cristina Malcolmson, for instance, claims that de Pizan's text was available to anyone who could enter the Royal Library. *Debating Gender* thus enters the politically charged fray of contested early modern gender relations through a consideration of contemporary continental influences as well as of classical antecedents of the controversy.

From there *Debating Gender* broadens its focus on the *querelle des femmes* to a thoroughgoing consideration of its class-marked manifestations in both manuscript and print cultures. Elizabeth Clarke writes on the politics of gender, class, and manuscript as they relate to the work of Anne Southwell. Lisa J. Schnell shows that although the writings of Rachel Speght and Esther Sowerman appeared in print and were imbedded in popular culture, they still could not escape the shaping imprint of class. Essays by Patricia Phillippy, Rachel Trubowitz, and Naomi J. Miller challenge familiar binary oppositions such as masculine/feminine and public/private to gain a nuanced understanding of the impact of the debate on representations of the maternal and the family. Sandra Clark and Susan O'Malley push for the provocative possibility that some male-authored pamphlets and ballads were at least as successful in marketing women's causes as were manuscripts or printed texts written by women.

These and other essays in this collection address questions crucial to the ongoing mapping of women's history: what light can the debate over women's "proper" subject position in the early modern period shed on a historical understanding of female authorship? How did their lack of rhetorical training and a cultural prohibition against women assuming voices of authority in the public sphere affect women's performance in the debate? Did the debate make any difference for women's role and experience within their own families? Did the debate help to frame the ideology of the English nation during the first period of English geographic and mercantile exploration?

Always insisting on extraordinary specificity in all of its essay, Cristina Malcolmson and Mihoko Suzuki's *Debating Gender* relentlessly shies away from the "easy" generalizations about the historical conditions and circumstances of women's lives that sometimes prevent us from appreciating the uniqueness of individual lives. The editors and authors of this collection—all of whom are in one way or another bound up with the progress of feminist scholarship—are keen to determine ways in which male authors have significantly influenced women, are not afraid to acknowledge that women writers did not always support each other, and that the early modern debate on gender roles had both an enabling and a debilitating effect on the women who became involved with it.

Ivo Kamps
Series Editor

INTRODUCTION

Cristina Malcolmson
and Mihoko Suzuki

This book contributes to the growing scholarship on women, women writers, and the construction of gender ideology in early modern England by considering these topics in the context of the *querelle des femmes*—the debate about the relationship between the sexes that originated on the Continent during the Middle Ages and the Renaissance, in works such as Boccaccio's *Concerning Famous Women* (c. 1380), Christine de Pizan's *The Book of the City of Ladies* (from 1405), and Cornelius Agrippa's *Declamation on the Nobility and Preeminence of the Female Sex* (1509). The debate found its particular flowering in Jacobean England in what is called the Swetnam controversy, which revolved around Joseph Swetnam's extraordinarily popular *The Arraignment of Lewd, idle, froward, and unconstant women* (1615) and the three pamphlets that responded to Swetnam's misogynist attacks. This collection of essays begins by contextualizing the debate in terms of its Continental antecedents and elite manuscript circulation in England; then moves to consider popular culture and printed texts from the Jacobean debate and its effects on women's writing as well as the discourse of gender; and concludes with the uses and ramifications of the debate during the Civil War and the Restoration. Thus this volume, while following on and building upon previous collections of essays on women and gender, will differ from them by focusing attention on the implications of the gender debate for 1) women writers and their literary relations, 2) cultural ideology and the family, and 3) political discourse and ideas of nationhood.[1]

The volume originated in a Shakespeare Association seminar on "Early Modern Women Writers and the Pamphlet Debate about

Gender" held in April 1999. The session included as contributors and participants a number of the writers whose work has determined the course of scholarship about the debate, which began in earnest only in 1984. It was clear from the discussion that most believed that, amongst early modern scholars, there was still not general recognition of the significance of the debate, its influence on canonical writers like Milton, and its complex meaning for women writers. In the discussions on women writers, there was general agreement that looking for an essentialized woman's view was problematic for a number of reasons. Nevertheless, there was disagreement about the implications of this conclusion. Some maintained that identifiable women writers in the debate should be considered both for their defenses of women and for their implication in class, national, and racial positions that complicated any attempt to label them as progressive. Others argued that the gender of the writer was insignificant, and that pro-woman positions taken in the debate could be viewed as genuine contributions to social change. The energy of the discussion matched the increased interest on this topic in both the scholarship and pedagogy of early modern English literature, history, and cultural studies encouraged by the wider availability of texts from the debate.[2]

The debate has previously been studied as a rhetorical practice in the schools, the means by which a proto-feminism was formulated, and as the context for the outpouring of pamphlets and other literature related to Swetnam's *Arraignment*. Women writers have been considered in terms of upper-class female coteries, the prohibition on female speech, in their relation to canonical male writers, and more recently, in terms of the problems posed by projecting modern feminism backward. When critics do consider the debate and women writers together, they either dispute the appropriateness of using modern feminism as a model or refer to the influence of an overarching but rarely defined tradition. Little specific work has been done to determine what influence particular writers had on others.[3]

The essays in this collection address the literary tradition posited by Joan Kelly in her influential article "Early Feminist Theory and the *Querelle des Femmes*, 1400–1789" (1984):

> The feminists of the *querelle* . . . created an intellectual tradition. . . . As yet no one knows the full extent and effectiveness of that tradition. It is clear that feminist writers drew strength and arguments from their predecessors. . . . Establishment of which authors were incorporated by

later ones or were referred to by women readers would be useful. These works were unmistakably written on behalf of women, and in reading them, I felt they were also written for women, but we need to discover who their readership actually was as well as the networks of women who supported such projects.[4]

Kelly's essay is groundbreaking but dated. She wrote before the emergence in the 1980s and 90s of important controversies among scholars of early modern women: 1) Is the term "feminist" appropriate for these early writers? 2) To what extent can links only among women explain the intellectual tradition of pro-woman defenses? 3) Was the debate a male rhetorical institution that sought to enforce the subordination of women, writing or not?

We, like Kelly, are looking for an answer to the following question: Why do writers defending women in seventeenth-century England, like Aemilia Lanyer and Anne Bradstreet, reproduce the same arguments as Christine de Pizan, writing in France in 1400?[5] Yet the answers do not fit into Kelly's schema. Malcolmson claims that Christine de Pizan's *Book of the City of Ladies* was available to those who could enter the royal libraries, including Lanyer, but that the authorship of the work by a woman was unclear. Clarke argues that aristocrat Anne Southwell had to develop a kind of language outside the tradition of the debate in order to defend women without undertones of misogyny. As Lisa J. Schnell's essay in this collection and the work of others have made quite clear, several pro-woman texts in the debate were written by men and/or supported by the commercial production of printed pamphlets, not by "networks of women" joined in a shared feminist goal. Malcolmson, Clarke, Trubowitz, and Romack argue that the debate was not supportive of the interests of women, while Clark, O'Malley, Phillippy, and Suzuki argue that pro-woman defenses advanced the position of women, whether these arguments were written by women or by men, in manuscript or print.

More importantly, this collection seeks to take a third position in these controversies. Even if pro-woman arguments in the early modern period cannot be termed feminist, and even if links among women do not explain the literary influences on these writers, scholars nevertheless need to study these links among women to discover a more accurate model of influence, which moves beyond that offered by Kelly. Studies of the literary relationships between women are more precise when they acknowledge that 1) in particular cases, male writers were major influences on women;[6] 2) women writers did not always agree or support each other, especially when they were of different classes; and 3) it is possible that the early modern debate on gender had either an empowering or debilitating effect on the women who responded to it, depending on the specific instance. The authors in this volume do not always agree in their responses to these issues, but their essays contribute to the more accurate, because more specific, picture of women's literary history that this collection seeks to establish.

For instance, four essays in the collection consider the role of the works of Rachel Speght in women's literary and political history. Educated and middle class, Speght wrote the only response to Swetnam clearly by a woman. This and her other works, a dream narrative in verse and a poetic *ars moriendi,* have recently elicited a great deal of attention among scholars and in the classroom. Here, Schnell argues that Speght's work did not produce the female solidarity that she sought, and her literary ambitions were defeated by her nonelite status and the commercial system that fueled the Swetnam controversy. Clarke maintains that Speght found her way out of the debate by developing language free of the emphasis on the witty commonplace. Phillippy argues that Speght's *Mortalities Memorandum* is a triumph not a defeat, since it turns the knowledge and experience of mourning into a written work that authorizes gendered authorship. Finally, Suzuki suggests that Speght's answer to Swetnam, like the other pro-woman responses, actively contributed to political change by "galvanizing women's identity as a subordinate group with common interests."

We believe that these questions cannot be addressed if attention is focused exclusively, as it has been, on the texts and dates of the Swetnam debate (1615–22). This collection seeks to widen our scope by including the origins of the debate in the medieval church and the schools, as well as the fading out of the debate in the Civil War period (according to Romack) and its afterlife during the Restoration and beyond (according to Suzuki). Only with this widened view can we evaluate how the debate contributed to or impeded political action. This wider view also brings into focus the theoretical questions at stake: How is gender differentiated along class lines in this material? What do the texts of the debate reveal about gender as performance rather than essence? What did gender mean then as opposed to now?

The volume also poses new questions: How did the shift from manuscript to print, from elite to popular culture, change the terms of the debate? How did it promote the interrogation of essentialist subject positions, allowing male writers to write from and in sympathy with the subject position of women? What difference did the debate make for women's experience within the family and their aspirations beyond it? How did the debate help set the terms for the construction of the English nation in the first period of English imperialism? And, finally, what are the ramifications of the debate in twentieth-century scholarship of early modern England?

The first section, "Manuscript and Debate," considers the potential influence of early and Continental versions of the debate on English writers as well as the significance of manuscript culture. In "Christine de Pizan's *City of Ladies* in Early Modern England," Cristina Malcolmson questions the assumption that Christine de Pizan is the precursor of all later women writers by providing evidence of only limited knowledge of her works in England in the sixteenth and seventeenth centuries. Christine's clear popularity in late-fifteenth-century England, when many translations of her works were printed and attributed to her, extended into the later Tudor courts through the existence of manuscripts in the royal libraries, including the *Livre de la cité des dames,* and through tapestries representing the *Cité des dames* in Princess Elizabeth's rooms. Nevertheless, authorship of the manuscript of the *Cité des dames* is unclear, and the English translation and publication of *The Boke of the Cyte of Ladyes* (1521) attributes authorship to Bryan Anslay, the translator. Finally, evidence is provided that William and Margaret Cavendish brought back into England the valuable Harley manuscript collection in which Christine explicitly identified herself as author, and which includes the *Cité des dames.* The essay claims that the *Cité des dames* influenced Margaret's protests against institutional restrictions on women, her equally strong sense that women preachers and petitioners were anathema, and her insight into the debate about women as a male game that hindered actual progress for women.

In "Anne Southwell and the Pamphlet Debate: The Politics of Gender, Class, and Manuscript," Elizabeth Clarke considers an aristocratic writer rarely analyzed in relation to the debate and still largely available only in manuscript. Clarke discusses Southwell's familiarity with coterie society, her knowledge of classical rhetoric, including commonplaces, mock encomium, and paradox used in the debate, and her aversion to print. But Clarke also argues for a similarity across class lines between Southwell and the middle-class Rachel Speght, who both eventually adopted a rhetoric quite distinct from the gamesmanship of the witty commonplace. Although Southwell probably was published in print in the volume associated with the Overbury scandal, *A Wife, now the Widdow of Sir Thomas Overbury,* and did write manuscript poems characteristic of the debate, she later eschews both print publication and the satiric "flouting" linked with commonplace culture. Clarke concludes in terms that look forward to Katherine Romack's essay that Southwell and Speght shared with Civil War women writers a commitment to actual change rather than the endless repetition of commonplaces that limited those who wrote in the discourse of the debate.

The next section, "Print, Pedagogy, and the Question of Class," addresses similar questions, but primarily in terms of middle-class and popular culture. These essays contribute to a growing body of literature on the differing significance of print for male and female writers, and for those of various class positions, especially in relation to the developing commercial economy in the cities. In "Muzzling the Competition: Rachel Speght and the Economics of Print," Lisa J. Schnell studies the Swetnam controversy as an episode in that economy, through analysis of the printing histories of treatises by Swetnam, Speght, Sowernam, and Munda. In contrast with Clarke's linking of the aristocratic Southwell and the middle-class Speght, Schnell focuses on class difference and argues that whether or not Sowernam was a man, Sowernam marks herself primarily as a writer of a higher class, and humiliates Speght for her inexperience and naiveté, not only about class decorum, but also about the profit motive and purposes of entertainment governing the print industry. Schnell examines Speght's later work *Mortalities Memorandum, with a Dreame Prefixed* as a response to Sowernam's attack, and argues that the *Memorandum* demonstrates why "reading the gender controversy of the seventeenth century as an early example of feminist unanimity bears so little fruit."

Melinda J. Gough calls attention to the value of including nonelite writers and genres in courses on early modern literature, as well as the pitfalls of studying Shakespeare alongside aristocratic women writers in "Women's Popular Culture? Teaching the Swetnam Controversy." Including popular culture on syllabi disrupts the tendency of students to idolize Shakespeare as a genius untouched by other forms of entertainment, the habit of rejecting the paired woman writer as inferior aesthetically, and the search for an essentialized woman's voice, either speaking out or silenced. Gough describes courses that emphasize the cultural agency of nonelite women by interrogating the modern notion of an author and demonstrating the early modern practice of collaboration and intertextuality. Gough outlines an intriguing unit in which students debate the positions of Swetnam and Sowernam and then consider the participation and influence of women in performances of *Swetnam the Woman-hater,* an anonymous play performed at the Red Bull in the 1620s. Using recent scholarship and contextual material provided by *Renaissance Drama by Women,* the unit allows students to imagine the influence of women patrons (like Queen Anne), women investors (like Susan Baskerville), and nonelite women in the audience in determining the reception of not only this play, but also plays like *Taming of the Shrew.*[7]

The essays by Sandra Clark and Susan Gushee O'Malley in the section on "Women's Subjectivity in Male-Authored Texts" consider the possibility that ballads and pamphlets written by men may have been as successful in promoting the interests of women as manuscript culture or works by female authors. Both Clark and O'Malley call attention to the importance of print production and distribution, and the possibilities this economy opened for a female readership. In "The Broadside Ballad and the Woman's Voice," Sandra Clark places these texts in the context of the pamphlet debate; she argues that despite the assumption of male authorship, these texts can be expressive of a woman's subject position in targeting female consumers and a female audience. Moreover, the performative nature of ballads made possible and encouraged female transmission of these texts. Paired ballads took the form of debating both sides of issues such as marriage and courtship, and so the ballads voicing the woman's point of view critique and subvert the dominant patriarchal perspective. Clark thus argues against those who consider the pamphlet debate to be a monolithic patriarchal textual production that ventriloquizes women's voices purely as a rhetorical game or for financial gain; rather, she sees evidence in the broadside ballad of possibilities for manifesting slippages and gaps in the ideology of patriarchal marriage.

In "'Weele have a Wench shall be our Poet': Samuel Rowlands' Gossip Pamphlets," Susan Gushee O'Malley argues that the pamphlet form was both part of the new entertainment market geared toward the middle classes and yet also especially suited for considering questions about women. She explores the production of pamphlets at the time, and gives examples of official reaction against their circulation. The popular gossip pamphlets of Samuel Rowlands (*Tis Merry when Gossips meete,* 1602, and *A whole crew of kind Gossips,* 1609) exploit the comedy of citizen women drinking in a tavern apart from men, yet also, in later editions, represent these women as intelligent and witty enough to publish a pamphlet and write a poem exposing the foolishness of their husbands. Although O'Malley concludes that Rowlands probably used this scenario to "satirize women who drink together in taverns away from their husbands," she also claims that these gossip pamphlets might have been read very differently by women, drawn to the image of female camaraderie that results in publication. Contemporary writers like Rachel Speght, Aemilia Lanyer, and Dorothy Leigh may have enjoyed the idea of gossips printing a pamphlet, and applauded the independence of these female characters.

The next section, on "Generic Departures: Figuring the Maternal Body, Constructing Female Culture," includes essays by Patricia Phillippy, Naomi J. Miller, and Rachel Trubowitz, all of which place the pamphlet debate in the context of other genres and literary forms, and thereby question the commonly accepted hierarchized binary between the "public" and the "private," gendered "masculine" and "feminine." Patricia Phillippy's "The Ma(t)ter of Death: The Defense of Eve and the Female *Ars Moriendi*" argues that Rachel Speght and Alice Sutcliffe strategically translate the feminine, familial, and private ritual of mourning into the masculine literary form of the *ars moriendi*, which enables their entrance into public discourse and into print. Here, as in the essays in the preceding two sections, the importance of the print medium is brought to the fore. Juxtaposing these female-authored texts to Phillip Stubbes's account of his wife's death, Phillippy finds that Speght and Sutcliffe, writing in a predominantly masculine genre, seek to construct their gendered presence as authors. Speght dedicates her work to her godmother, and Sutcliffe to female patrons; in both instances, however, the woman's voice is not understood in terms of biological essentialism, but as one that is socially and culturally constructed. Paradoxically, this understanding manifests itself in the figure of Eve—a strategic figure for the pamphlet debate in staging the defense of women—and her body, which represents the historicized and contingent notion of the origin of both death and maternity. As such, the figure of Eve offers a means of self-authorization for the female authors of these texts, as well as a defense of women's desire for knowledge and their accomplishments in education.

In her "'Hens should be served first': Prioritizing Maternal Production in the Early Modern Pamphlet Debate," Naomi J. Miller juxtaposes the texts in the pamphlet debate to male-authored conduct books and female-authored mothers' advice books, examining the strategic uses of the rhetoric of maternity in each. Miller finds in these texts contradictory and competing notions of maternity—either debased and caricatured on the one hand, or celebrated and idealized on the other. In this rhetorical battleground, the trope of production and consumption becomes an important focus: whether women are consumers and wasters of male-produced goods and services or producers and contributors as mothers who not only give birth to children but educate them into "culture." (Significantly, many of the ballads Sandra Clark discusses tend to blame *men* as improvident spendthrifts.) Arguing for a double sense of production as both biological and cultural, Miller sees the female authors as interrogating the conventional hierarchized and gendered binary between biological reproduction (by mothers) and textual production (by male writers), an interrogation that enabled women to resist at once their confinement in the private sphere and the injunction against female authorship—just as the trope of maternity in the figure of Eve grounds Speght and Sutcliffe's textual productions in Phillippy's account.

The last essay in this section, Rachel Trubowitz's "Cross-Dressed Women and Natural Mothers: 'Boundary Panic' in *Hic Mulier*," also serves as a bridge to the final section on politics and the nation, for Trubowitz negotiates the political uses to which the representation of motherhood was put in the construction of the early modern English nation. Like Phillippy and Miller, who enrich our understanding of the pamphlet debate through recovering its relationship to other kinds of textual production, Trubowitz reads *Hic Mulier* through domestic guidebooks (including defenses of breast-feeding), travel narratives, and ethnography. She argues that the "invention of motherhood"—with its attendant affirmation of the transmission of unadulterated Englishness through breast-feeding—served as a guarantor of the integrity of the English nation in the period of its first imperial expansion. Trubowitz thereby maps the breakdown of the opposition between "nation" and the "family," most saliently in the figuration of England as the "mother country"—with the attendant scapegoating of what is considered foreign and "deviant," both outside and within the nation, a scapegoating that found its target especially in Catholics and Jews. In the attraction to and repulsion from the cross-dressed woman expressed in *Hic Mulier*, she diagnoses a "boundary panic" that also manifests itself in the demonizing of the proto-racialized Other. By contrast with Miller's focus on women's empowerment through the maternal "good" breast, here the "bad" breast of the sexualized transvestite whore prevails, as the figure that defines the limits of the social order.

Extending Trubowitz's engagement with "Politics, State, and Nation," the final essays, by Katherine Romack and Mihoko Suzuki, examine the effects of the gender debate on the political discourse of the seventeenth century and beyond. Katherine Romack's "Monstrous Births and the Body Politic: Women's Political Writings and the Strange and Wonderful Travails of Mistris Parliament and Mris. Rump," like many of the preceding essays, marks the importance of the explosion of print culture in giving women entry into public discourse, especially during the midcentury Civil War and Interregnum. She notices, however, a departure from the defensive rhetoric of the pro-woman pamphlets to a new kind of rhetoric of enthusiasm among women prophets and writers such as Elizabeth Poole—a millenarian and apocalyptic rhetoric that disrupts the traditional ordering of gender and its relationship to politics. While Poole deploys the trope of childbirth to legitimate her address to the army and as member of the body politic, the satires against women that proliferated in the latter part of the Interregnum seek to stabilize that disruption by expelling the "monstrous body" of the woman—and its products—to preserve the health of the commonwealth. Here the obsessive policing of the deformed female body and the representation of women as defective and anomalous subjects, recalling the earlier contest over maternal figuration that Miller and Trubowitz discuss, seek to undermine women's bid for political involvement.

Mihoko Suzuki's "Elizabeth, Gender, and the Political Imaginary of Seventeenth-Century England," like Romack's essay, is also interested in the extended afterlife of the early Jacobean debate. Suggesting that Elizabeth's celebrated rule was an important subtext of the pamphlet debate on gender, here she focuses on what she calls the "Elizabeth-effect" in mapping the uses to which Elizabeth Tudor was put in the century after her reign and even beyond. Suzuki sees the representations of Elizabeth throughout the seventeenth century as countering misogynist constructions for women writers such as Anne Clifford, Aemilia Lanyer, Elizabeth Cellier, and Elinor James, who sought to justify legal, political, and authorial rights for women. Yet just as Romack noticed a chiastic relationship between republican males whose democratic vision and practices did not extend to women, so Suzuki sees a similar discrepancy in the uses parliamentarians made of Elizabeth to promote their own cause while disparaging ordinary women's claims to participate in politics and public affairs. What was then at stake can be gauged now in the historiographical split between those twentieth-century historians who acknowledge the democratic achievements of the English Civil War and Revolution and those who minimize them: the latter not coincidentally belittle Elizabeth's achievements through satiric emphasis on her gender (recalling Romack's satires, which sought to debase women's political activity). Such contemporary examples indicate that we in the beginning of the twenty-first century are far from being able to pronounce the early modern gender debate as settled once and for all.

NOTES

1. Recent collections include *Women, Texts and Histories 1575–1760*, ed. Clare Brant and Diane Purkiss (London: Routledge, 1993); *Women and Literature in Britain, 1500–1700*, ed. Helen Wilcox (Cambridge: Cambridge University Press, 1996); *Feminist Readings of Early Modern Culture: Emerging Subjects*, ed. Valerie Traub, M. Lindsay Kaplan, and Dympna Callaghan (Cambridge: Cambridge University Press, 1996); and *Maids and Mistresses, Cousins and Queens: Women's Alliances in Early Modern England*, ed. Susan Frye and Karen Robertson (New York: Oxford University Press, 1999).

2. Texts from the debate are printed in *Half Humankind: Contexts and Texts of the Controversy about Women in England, 1540–1640*, ed. Katherine Usher Henderson and Barbara F. McManus (Urbana: University of Illinois Press, 1985); the series *The Other Voice in Early Modern Europe*, University of Chicago Press, and *The Early Modern Englishwoman: A Facsimile Library of Essential Works*, Ashgate Publishing.

3. Linda Woodbridge considers the debate as rhetorical practice in *Women and the English Renaissance: Literature and the Nature of Womankind, 1540–1620* (Urbana: University of Illinois Press, 1984). Constance Jordan argues for a proto-feminism in the early modern period in *Renaissance Feminism: Literary Texts and Political Models* (Ithaca: Cornell University Press, 1990). Ann Rosalind Jones analyzes the responses to Swetnam's *Arraignment* in "Counterattacks on 'the Bayter of Women': Three Pamphleteers of the Early Seventeenth Century," in *The Renaissance Englishwoman in Print*, ed. Anne M. Haselkorn and Betty S. Travitsky (Amherst: University of Massachusetts Press, 1990), 45–62; and "From Polemical Prose to the Red Bull: the Swetnam Controversy in Women-Voiced Pamphlets and the Public Theater," in *The Project of Prose in Early Modern Europe and the New World*, ed. Elizabeth Fowler and Roland Greene (Cambridge: Cambridge University Press, 1997), 122–37. Diane Purkiss challenges the prevailing reading of the debate through the lens of feminism in "Material Girls: The Seventeenth-Century Woman Debate" in *Women, Texts and Histories 1575–1760*. On upper-class female coteries, see Mary Ellen Lamb, *Gender and Authorship in Sidney Circle* (Madison: University of Wisconsin Press, 1990); Barbara Lewalski, *Writing Women in Jacobean England* (Cambridge: Harvard University Press, 1994); and Louise Schleiner, *Tudor and Stuart Women*

Writers (Bloomington: Indiana University Press, 1994). Wendy Wall (*The Imprint of Gender: Authorship and Publication in the English Renaissance,* Ithaca: Cornell University Press, 1993) and Barry Weller and Margaret Ferguson (Introduction to *The Tragedy of Mariam,* Berkeley and Los Angeles: University of California Press, 1994) focus on the prohibition of female speech. For women writers in their relation to canonical male writers, see "Teaching Judith Shakespeare," *Shakespeare Quarterly* 47 (winter 1996). Those who argue against projecting feminism backward include Margaret Ezell (*Writing Women's Literary History,* Baltimore: Johns Hopkins University Press, 1993), and Margaret Ferguson ("Moderation and its Discontents: Recent Work on Renaissance Women," *Feminist Studies* 20:2 [1994], 349–66). See also Ferguson's forthcoming *Dido's Daughters: Literacy, Gender and Empire in Early Modern England and France* (University of Chicago Press, 2002). Those who read the debate in light of a woman's tradition include Elaine Beilin (*Redeeming Eve: Women Writers of the English Renaissance,* Princeton: Princeton University Press, 1987) and Betty Travitsky ("The Lady Doth Protest: Protest in the Popular Writings of Renaissance Englishwomen," *English Literary Renaissance* 14 [autumn 1984], 255–83).

4. *Women, History and Theory: The Essays of Joan Kelly* (Chicago: University of Chicago Press, 1984), pp. 94; 109, n. 108.

5. Thanks to Susan Frye for this point.

6. See Susanne Woods, *Lanyer: A Renaissance Woman Poet* (New York: Oxford, 1999) on Lanyer's links with Spenser, Shakespeare, and Jonson.

7. S. P. Cerasano and Marion Wynne-Davies, eds. *Renaissance Drama by Women: Texts and Documents* (London: Routledge, 1996).

PART I

MANUSCRIPT AND DEBATE

CHAPTER 1

CHRISTINE DE PIZAN'S *City of Ladies* IN EARLY MODERN ENGLAND

Cristina Malcolmson

In the study of women writers in early modern England, Christine de Pizan is everywhere and nowhere. Whereas she presides as first feminist over her descendants, and her *City of Ladies* is used as a model for their work as well as for that of scholars today,[1] research has not yet clarified the extent to which her works could have been known in England during the sixteenth and seventeenth centuries.[2] In this essay, I hope to demonstrate that the Tudor courts were familiar with the idea of a "city of ladies" in a limited but definite way, and that manuscripts of her works including the *Livre de la cité des dames* were available in the royal libraries. Therefore Elizabeth I and others associated with the court, including Aemilia Lanyer, could have read Christine's text. I will also argue that William and Margaret Cavendish owned the important Harley manuscript collection of Christine's work. This account of Christine's legacy is formulated as an alternative to the search for "sisterly precursors" developed by critics like Gilbert and Gubar.[3] Instead of offering a refuge from the "anxiety of authorship," Christine's work and the concept of the "city of ladies" most likely provided the Tudor courts with an unidentified, generic defense of women and a compendium of rhetorical strategies.

Entries in the debate about women are best approached not as statements of personal opinion, pro or con, but as a discourse situated within the institutions of the university and the church. The debate's focus on questions about women rather than men determined from the outset the prejudicial nature of its deliberations. As Linda Woodbridge notes, the formal controversy about women was in large part an intellectual game associated with the teaching of rhetoric and oratory in the exclusively male universities. Students argued on both sides of a question in order to develop their logic and linguistic skills. Woodbridge claims that the published entries in the debate were not primarily expressions of passion, but exercises "in bestowing originality on a rhetorical set piece."[4] Howard Bloch and Daniel Kempton argue that clerical authority in the university and church produced a commentary about women focused on virtue and vice, in which the figures of the exceptional "virago," faithful wife, obedient daughter, and virgin martyr did little to undermine the principles of medieval misogyny.[5] From this perspective, women writers were not free agents, independently using the debate to produce feminist statements of protest; they reproduced ideologies about gender inherent to the debate.

The marginalized position of women in relation to the debate, outside the university and church, gave them some ability to disrupt its terms. Christine experienced a loss of position that gave her a special insight into the power that marginalized her.[6] But this critical perspective was inherently complicated by her strong desire to enter and remain within the very elite that she analyzed. We might say that Christine, and those women writers influenced by her works, wanted to be produced by the debate: that is, labeled as learned, wise, cultured, and equipped with the verbal dexterity that normally brought patronage to men. The debate helped them to emerge as writers because it taught them the rules of performative display; their own critical perspective helped them to analyze with acuity the institutions that made it very difficult for them to acquire the rewards of success.

Christine was included among the courtly elite during her early adult years, but she lost this comfortable position suddenly. She was the daughter of a learned man from Italy who became an astrologer and medical adviser to the French king Charles V in 1365, and she was later married to a royal secretary. However, her father lost favor at court with the death of Charles V in 1380, and he and Christine's husband died between 1387 and 1390. When Christine was twenty-five, she was suddenly responsible for three children, her widowed mother, and a niece. From the outset Christine was excluded from the university training that gave men opportunities for promotion. Nevertheless she turned to writing for financial support and the patronage that could provide the social benefits associated with the elite. Through her writing, Christine eventually won the admiration of the learned and the court, and also managed to support her family for forty years.[7]

This life history can illuminate why Christine wrote entries in the debate about women, and how these entries may have influenced women writers in early modern England. In their works, they protested against their exclusion from the schools and the rewards of education. But these books were also requests for recognition, perhaps including money and patronage. To some extent, Christine and early modern women writers argued for the value of women for the same reason that men did, to display their verbal skill.

MANUSCRIPTS IN THE ROYAL LIBRARIES

Scholars of the early modern period have not recognized that there was a French manuscript of Christine's *Livre de la cité des dames* in the English royal libraries throughout this time (Royal MS. 19 A.XIX). However, it is without authorial attribution; therefore "Christine," or x̄p̄ine, as it appears, may have been understood as only the character, not the writer, of the work. But there were also several other manuscripts of works by Christine in the libraries, and one manuscript included a written note on the cover identifying the text as "A boke of chyvalrie and of fayttes of armes made by x̄p̄yne of pyse in frenshe." This notation, which was apparently added to the original manuscript, suggests that the note writer felt that knowledge of Christine's identity was beginning to fade. If someone who had access to the various royal libraries had taken the trouble, it would have been possible to recognize that the several works there that included the character Christine were written in French by Christine de Pizan, but the manuscript of the *Cité des dames* alone does not provide this information.[8]

The presence of this manuscript is made even more significant by the tapestries indicated by the inventories of Henry VIII taken after 1537, which list "6 peces" representing "the Citie of Ladies" hanging in the "guarderobe" of Lady Elizabeth and Prince Edward. A guarderobe or gardarobe was a dressing room near the bedchamber that housed clothes as well as other precious items. The inventories suggest that the idea of a "city of ladies" had significant currency. Many tapestries in this inventory covering all the royal homes represent stories popular in the debate about women, including the stories of Esther, Susanna, and Judith. A tapestry illustrating the "city of dammys" was also purchased for King James V in Scotland in 1538. This suggests that such tapestries were not uncommon, and that they were considered appropriate for royal homes.[9]

There is also evidence that the *querelle des femmes* was a popular ritual within the early Tudor courts. There were several copies and translations of Boccaccio's *De Mulieribus Claris,* one of Christine's sources, in the royal libraries.[10] George Boleyn, Anne's brother, owned a manuscript of Jean LeFèvre's old French translation of Matheolus' *Lamentations,* the very misogynist text that depresses the character Christine at the beginning of the *Cité des dames* and that the rest of the book is meant to answer. Several courtiers have written inscriptions in this manuscript, including someone named Wyat, possibly Thomas, whose own poetry considers rather savagely the pro-woman position within courtly love.[11] This manuscript and the inscriptions in it demonstrate that the *querelle* was alive and well in the Tudor courts in the rituals of manuscript circulation, and that Boleyn and others may have noticed Christine's text and its dramatic critique of Matheolus.

Furthermore, knowledge of Christine's works could have derived from the Woodville family, responsible for the presence of several of her manuscripts in the royal libraries after 1461, and still active in court affairs until at least 1523. In 1425, the duke of Bedford, regent of France, bought the complete libraries of the French kings Charles V and VI. One manuscript in these libraries was the famous Harley manuscript of Christine's works, which included the *Cité des dames,* and which identifies Christine as author quite explicitly. The duke's wife, Jacquetta of Luxembourg, acquired this manuscript and later left it to her son from her second marriage, Anthony Woodville. Woodville translated and had printed by William Caxton some of Christine's works in the late fifteenth century. Anthony died in 1483, and the Harley manuscript was taken to the Continent sometime before the death of its new owner, Louis of Bruges (d. 1492).[12]

Edward IV, the husband of Anthony's sister, was also intrigued by French manuscripts. Edward's stay with Louis, Seigneur de la Gruthuyse, at Bruges in 1470–71, and Louis' visit to England in 1472 developed Edward's interest in acquiring a "long series of manuscripts of French Chronicles and romances, written and illuminated in Flanders."[13] Edward IV had learned about the patronage and collecting of "ornamental books" from the French monarchy and aristocracy.[14]

However, Royal MS. 19 A.XIX of the *Cité des dames* was probably present in the royal libraries even before 1472. It most likely be-
longed to the father of Edward IV, Richard, the third duke of York,
who died in 1468. Richard's fetter-lock and white rose appear in the
border of folio 4 of this manuscript. The insignia of Edward IV's father, as well as the listing of the manuscript in a 1666 catalogue of
the royal library, suggest that the manuscript was present there from
some time around Richard's death in 1468 until that library was
transferred to the national collections in 1757, and eventually to the
British Museum.[15]

Henry VII, married to the daughter of Elizabeth Woodville, knew
Christine's works, since, according to Caxton, in 1489, the king
asked the printer to translate the *Livre des faits d'armes et de cheva-
lerie* in order to educate gentlemen, and Caxton's translation refers
directly to "Chrystyne of Pise" as the writer.[16] Certainly Henry VII
would have been aware of other manuscripts in his library by Christine. Henry VII was present in the court with Catherine of Aragón,
wife to Henry VIII, for eight years before his death in 1509, and
there is a story that he took pity on her homesickness when she first
arrived, and introduced her to the royal library.[17] She herself had
been urged to learn French by Margaret Beaufort, Henry VII's
mother, who had received Christine's *Epistle of Othea* as a gift from a
woman friend.[18] Such details make it probable that, among the older
members of the Tudor and Woodville families, Christine was well
known.

Perhaps this knowledge was passed along to Henry VIII and his
wife Catherine of Aragón. Richard Grey, the third earl of Kent (d.
1523), son to Anne Woodville, may also have known of Christine's
works. In the printer's preface, the earl of Kent is asked to be a patron to the 1521 translation of the *Cité des dames* by printer Henry
Pepwell. Nevertheless, by this time, it was possible to publish the text
without any attribution to Christine.

The presence of the French manuscript of the *Cité des dames* in
the royal libraries has important implications, unnoticed by students
of this period and of Christine de Pizan. It becomes possible that any
member of the royal family who knew French, including Elizabeth
as princess or queen, could have read this text.[19] Manuscripts were
always considered valuable, and it seems likely that those interested
in the libraries would be drawn to the manuscripts. This French
manuscript of the *Cité des dames* is not huge in size, like the volumes
of the Harley collection, made to be read out loud from a lectern,
but rather small enough for one person to read comfortably in a

chair. Although there were librarians and catalogues after 1492, I have found no evidence that members of the court were excluded from the collection.[20] Certainly the debate about women had moments of great popularity during this period, as it did in the 1540's and in the 1590's. At these times, court conversations may have included references to this manuscript of the *Cité des dames* and to the tapestries, but perhaps without consideration of Christine as author.

THE 1521 TRANSLATION

Many scholars have studied the 1521 printing of an English translation of the *Cité des dames*, called *The Boke of the Cyte of Ladyes*. For this essay, it is important to note a few points. First, whereas Christine's name is scrupulously included in earlier English translations, *The Boke* attributes authorship to its translator Bryan Anslay. Second, its translation and publication seem to be related to Catherine of Aragón's campaign for her daughter Mary to be the successor to the throne. Third, knowledge of Christine's work outside the court would have been quite limited, since the 1521 translation was published without attribution and never reprinted.[21]

As many have argued, the printer Henry Pepwell and the translator Anslay may have produced the work to appeal to Queen Catherine, who was beginning to marshal the humanist program to educate her daughter Mary for the position of monarch of England.[22] Henry VIII saw the birth of his illegitimate son Henry Fitzroy in 1519 as providing a possible successor. Catherine opposed this plan through her education of Mary, which included commissioning from Juan Luis Vives his *De Institutione Christianae Feminae* (Antwerp, 1523) and inviting him to England to serve as Mary's tutor. Already by July of 1521, Catherine was seeking Vives' support.[23] Therefore the publication of *The Boke of the Cyte of Ladyes* in October was the first in a series that promoted the education of women and, indirectly, the legitimacy of female monarchs (Vives, *De Ratione Studii Puerilis*, 1523; Erasmus, *Christiani Matrimonii Institutio*, 1526; Richard Hyrde, translator, *Instruction of a Christian Woman*, before 1528).

Within the court, the concept of a "city of ladies" would have been a powerful method to counteract arguments against female sovereignty and support Catherine's interests. Defenders of Mary may have appealed to arguments in favor of women rulers in the French manuscript of *Cité des dames*, and to the printed translation.[24] If the tapestries had arrived by 1521, they could also have been used to support this purpose. The concept of a "city of ladies" does nothing to undermine class prejudice or the traditional models of female morality. But it does imply that a female ruler can fulfill the duties of the office, and that she will need active defense against misogynist detractors.

Throughout the sixteenth and seventeenth centuries, knowledge of a "city of ladies" was largely a court phenomenon. However, nonelite writers with access to the royal libraries could have read the manuscript of Christine's *Cité des dames*. Aemilia Lanyer, for instance, may have been permitted to use the library through the auspices of her father, a royal musician; Lady Susan Wingfield, in whose household in Greenwich "on the banks of Kent" Lanyer served when young; or her lover Lord Hunsdon, serving as Lord Chamberlain after 1583.[25] Queen Elizabeth was another possible patron in this regard: in *Salve Deus Rex Judaeorum,* Lanyer refers to the time when "great *Elizaes* favour blest my youth. . . ." For this reason, Lanyer may also have seen or heard about the tapestries in Elizabeth's gardarobe. Although there is little evidence of the direct influence of Christine's work on *Salve Deus,* far more explicitly shaped by Agrippa's *Declamation on the Nobility and Preeminence of the Female Sex,* nevertheless the idea of a "city of ladies" seems quite prominent, especially in Lanyer's series of dedications to "vertuous ladies" and references to biblical women, as well as in the female-centered estate at Cookham.[26]

THE HARLEY MANUSCRIPT
AND THE CAVENDISH FAMILY

I will argue here that Margaret Cavendish knew Christine's *Livre de la cité des dames.* Both Christine and Cavendish wrote within court or aristocratic culture, which gave Cavendish access to the conversational *querelle des femmes* and to Christine's manuscripts. Neither writer questions the moral terms of the debate, focused so firmly on female chastity. Their calls for change were largely limited to the area of education and did not clearly extend to all women or beyond the interests of Christine's "ladies."[27] Cavendish was especially hungry to learn the rules of rhetoric in part to participate more successfully within aristocratic society. Nevertheless, her standpoint outside the schools gave her a special insight into the uselessness of the debate in meeting the needs of women and moving society toward an acknowledgment of their intellectual powers. The following passage from Cavendish's *Sociable Letters* will clarify these points:

> Thus, Madam, the Sages Discoursed, but they perceiving I was very Attentive to their Discourse, they ask'd my Opinion, I answered, they had left no Room for another Opinion, for the World was Eternal or not Eternal, and they had given their Opinions of either side; then they desired me to be a Judg between their Opinions, I said, such an Ignorant woman as I will be a very unfit Judge, and though you be both Learned, and Witty Men, yet you cannot Resolve the Question . . . wherefore said I, the best is to leave this Discourse, and Discourse of some other Subject that is more Sociable, as being more Conceivable: Then they Laugh'd, and said they would Discourse of Women, I said I did believe they would find that Women were as Difficult to be Known and Understood as the Universe. . . . [28]

In this account, which might or might not be autobiographical, the speaker reveals the process of exclusion that the educated enforce when they "discourse" in front of the uninitiated. After "the Lord N.N." and the other "Sages" in his company pretend to include the woman listening to them as an equal, she exposes their gesture as condescension. Although she satirizes the ritual of disputation taught in the schools as arbitrarily assigning two sides to every question, she also refuses to argue the issue, which in itself would reveal her lack of training in a practice at once intellectually questionable and the indisputable sign of privilege.[29] Her reaction is not taken as serious satire, however, but as entertainment, the only possible role for the excluded, since they can never break into or imitate the codes of speech that signal "serious" thought. As if in order to appease their auditor, the sages offer to "Discourse of Women." Her answer just as keenly lays bare the power play in their offer as well as in the centuries-old *querelle des femmes*. To invite women to write entries in the debate begs the only question that really matters: who has been trained in the schools and who has not. The woman writer in this passage rather pointedly informs the company that the "Discourse of Women" bears no relationship and never could bear any relationship to her experience or that of other women, since its only purpose is to validate the credentials of educated men. The company, characteristically, responds with laughter:

> I said I did believe they would find that Women were as Difficult to be Known and Understood as the Universe, but yet I thought they would find them more Sociable, at which Expression they made themselves very merry: but being my near Relative Friends, I took their Mirth in good part. . . . (#111)

The woman's resentment at being situated as an object of amusement is only barely under the surface here, as Margaret Cavendish offers up the word that defines her volume, *Sociable Letters*. Being sociable requires including others, as opposed to this group of discoursers who exclude by arguing topics that they themselves can never understand. As her writer put it earlier in this letter, "wherefore said I, the best is to leave this Discourse, and Discourse of some other Subject that is more Sociable, as being more Conceivable." This is not an instance of confessing to be or playing dumb, but rather an assertion that the pseudo-scientific discourse that had preceded was more a matter of self-display than serious inquiry. The woman's critique is however dismissed as a confession of intellectual inferiority, and the men offer instead to talk about women. But this letter writer does not want women to be a sociable "topic," something pleasant to discuss, but to be seen as "sociable" themselves, that is, as originators and initiators of conversation. Men may never understand anything substantial about women despite mastery of the "Discourse of Women," but men could actually listen to what women have to say. Such a possibility is eliminated in this case, as the men "made themselves very merry" at the writer's expense. Her willingness to take "their Mirth in good part" may be the result not only of familial affection but also of the knowledge that few sources of education apart from listening to her husband's friends were available to her.

"HENRY DUKE OF NEWCASTLE HIS BOOKE 1676"

There is strong evidence that William Cavendish acquired the Harley manuscript of Christine's works, including the *Livre de la cité des dames*, during the months that he and Margaret spent in Paris and the Netherlands. The manuscript came into the possession of Louis of Bruges sometime around the death of Anthony Woodville in 1483. William and Margaret lived in Paris from 1645 to 1648 and in Antwerp from 1648 to 1660. At the beginning of the Harley manuscript, along with the signatures of other owners, the phrase "Henry Duke of Newcastle his booke 1676" is written.[30] The year 1676 was when William died, and Henry his son acquired his father's estate. William's death on December 25, as well as the official use of March 24 as the beginning of the new year (until 1751), clarify that there were only three months during which Henry could have acquired the manuscript when Henry was duke, after his father's death. Henry organized and attended the funeral on January 22, officially took his seat on February 15, and was named Knight of the Garter on February 17, which did not leave a great deal of time for a trip to the Continent.[31] It seems far more likely that William acquired the manuscript in Paris or the Netherlands and refrained from putting his own name on it. William was much more interested in literature than Henry, who seemed to regard books primarily as property, as his signature and his various wills attest.[32]

Although wills frequently mention valuable manuscripts, William and Henry do not mention books unless their inheritance is in doubt.[33] William mentions no books at all in his will, although he owned several, probably because his estate was left solely to his son, who would automatically inherit all books. Henry does mention books "at Clarkowell House," but only when he is afraid they will be sold, in the drafts of his will in 1689, which assume that his estate will be in the hands of trustees until a grandson is born. In later wills, in 1691, when his heirs are definitively identified as his daughter Lady Margaret, duchess of Clare, and her husband John Hollis, the earl of Clare, books are not mentioned either.[34] Clerkenwell House would have been a logical place for Christine's manuscript, since the house was willed by William to Margaret in January 1667–8, and was a residence held by the Cavendish family from at least 1631, and rebuilt around 1667. Henry complained strongly about his father's decision to will this house and others to Henry's step-mother, Margaret.[35] His drive to possess his father's estate and to keep it unified after his own death are registered in his assertion of ownership in the Harley manuscript in 1676 and in his directive in 1689 that "the Tapestry Hangings & Beds, Brass [works] & Bookes at Clarkowell House" be brought to Bolsover Castle to be "preserved by his Trustees" and not to be used to pay debts.[36] Henry is insistent on preserving the valuables of his estate, but he also does not distinguish books from other household items. The manuscript finally became part of the Harleian collection when Henry's son-in-law the earl of Clare left the Cavendish estates to his only daughter Henrietta, who married Edward Harley, the second earl of Oxford.[37] The compilers of the *Catalogue of the Harleian Manuscripts* note that the Harley manuscript of Christine's works "was once in the collection of the Duke of Newcastle," but they also acknowledge that a mystery remains about who owned it before Henry and how the manuscript got to England.[38] I am claiming that William and Margaret Cavendish acquired the manuscript when they were on the Continent, and that they brought it to England at the Restoration.

The Harley manuscript was both valuable and expensive, since its two volumes are quite large, and include numerous beautiful illuminations.[39] William Cavendish was having financial problems throughout his time of residence in France and the Netherlands, but this did not prohibit him from a significant outlay of funds for a set of horses and for a lavish entertainment for Charles II.[40] He was trying desperately to maintain his position as counselor to the king, but there were strong signs that his influence was seriously waning. He would have felt it wise to keep up the appearance of wealth and prestige that horses, entertainments, and expensive books could offer. It is interesting that during the time of William's entertainment for the king, held on February 25, 1658, the court was in Bruges, the location of Louis' library.[41] William may have acquired the manuscript in his trips between Bruges and Antwerp.[42]

The Harley collection includes a large number of Christine's works, as well as a clear attribution of the works to Christine. The variety of Pizan's works in the collection and the remarkably self-assertive illumination representing Christine's gift of the manuscript to Queen Isabeau of Bavaria, the wife of King Charles VI of France, might have reminded William of his wife. Nevertheless, William's proficiency in French and Margaret's difficulty with the language make William the more likely reader. However William could have translated the works out loud as he read to her. Neither Margaret not William ever mention Christine's name, but few did at the time, even in France. Margaret rarely mentions the name of any woman writer. She clearly refers to, but does not name, Lady Mary Wroth; perhaps Margaret preferred to have no rivals, perhaps previous women writers were considered less as precursors and more as liabilities.[43]

FEMALE ORATIONS

Cavendish expressed a number of views that were similar to those of Christine: that the powers of understanding in men and women are equal; that, if women were sent to school, they would be as intellectually gifted as men; and that, no matter what their education, women should not be lawyers or, in Cavendish's case, preachers.[44] Whether or not Cavendish received these views from Christine, Cavendish departs from Christine in characterizing and satirizing the debate about women as the product of an academy that cannot advance the interests of women. In her *Orations,* she parodies the attempt of women to interject their own arguments into the debate when she suggests that these arguments are just as fruitless as all the exercises in rhetoric in the volume, intended to display the inadequacies of disputation itself.[45] But Cavendish does not simply satirize the game of constructing arguments for and against; she also develops her own ability to play the game, and thus obtains to some extent the training lost to her through the gender exclusion practiced by the schools.

Cavendish explicitly states that her *Orations* are a set of exercises in which she argues on both sides of the question, "my Orations for the most part are Declamations, wherein I speak *Pro* and *Con,* and Determine nothing. . . ."[46] Yet the work is also a satire of this method at arriving at nothing, so central to the academic curriculum.[47] This purpose is made explicit in the last section, "Scholastical Orations," which displays its claim that the schools have become impractical through "A Sleepy Speech to Students," praising the "Dreaming Life" rather than the contemplative and active life.[48] Finally Cavendish opens to debate by the "scholars" the subject that underlies the entire volume:

> We *study* to *Argue;* and *Argue* to *Study:* for, the chief Design of our *Study,* is only to dispute . . . but, all Disputes are more full of *Contradictions,* than *Information;* and all *Contradictions,* confound the Sense and Reason. . . . (324)

Knowledge of Christine's *Cité des dames* must have increased Cavendish's sense of the futility of considering issues of gender through the debate about women, since the Harley manuscript would have brought home how long the controversy had been going on and yet still determined nothing. Women were not yet admitted into the schools, women were still attacked for being monsters, or "Hermaphrodites," as Lord Denny put it in his consideration of Lady Mary Wroth's *Urania.*[49] After speeches by men against and for "the liberty of women," the *Female Orations* stage the entrance of women writers into a discourse shaped within the elite masculinist establishment (*Orations,* Part XL, 239–246). These *Female Orations* are unusual in that there are seven positions formulated rather than two, but they are characteristic of the *Orations* in general in that no conclusion is reached. As most teachers of the *Female Orations* have discovered, it is impossible to tell how the seven speeches relate to Cavendish's point of view. Anna Battigelli argues, "*Orations* is thus less a feminist statement than it is a cautionary warning about the disputatious nature of the human mind."[50] The speeches create the sense not only that no conclusion is in sight, but that these speeches could reproduce themselves endlessly since they are the function of disputation itself rather than a personal point of view or a call for action. As the second orator declares about the first, "she has not declared a *Remedy,* or shew'd us a way out of our *Miseries:* but, if she could, or would be our Guide, to lead us out of the *Labyrinth* Men have put us into, we should . . . adore and worship her."(240). Part of this labyrinth, according to Cavendish, is the debate about women itself.

Yet Cavendish does not simply expose the uselessness of disputation. She in fact uses the *Orations* as an opportunity to experience some aspect of the educational rituals open to men able to attend the universities. In *Sociable Letters,* her letter writer expresses a desire to possess the gift of eloquence: "in my Opinion, there is no Musick so Sweet, and Powerful as Oratory, for Sweet Words are better than a Sweet Sound, and when they are joyned together, it Ravishes the Soul" (#117; see also #27, 28). *Sociable Letters* constructs an origin for the *Orations*—very much after the fact, since the first edition of the *Orations* was published two years before the *Letters.* Nevertheless the letter writer claims that her correspondent has urged her to the task: "In your last letter you Advised me to Write a Book of Orations, but how should I Write Orations, who know no Rules in Rhetorick, nor never went to School?" (#175)

Despite their spoofing of the schools, then, the *Orations* also gave Cavendish the opportunity to learn the "Rules in Rhetorick." She did this in her 178 orations, but also, unnoticed by critics of Cavendish, in her use of the textbook *The Foundation of Rhetoric* (1563), a translation by Richard Rainholde of Aphthonius' *Progymnasmata* (late fourth century).[51] Both Rainholde and Aphthonius include a model oration on the questions "whether one should marry" (Aphthonius) and "whether it is best to marie a wife" (Rainholde).[52] The text was a site of origin for the academic controversy about women.

Rainholde's text also determines the subjects that Cavendish addresses in her section on "Several Causes Pleaded in Several Courts of Judicature." Rainholde and Cavendish provide examples of speeches on the subjects of adultery, theft, and the cause of a widow.[53] As Rainholde with Aphthonius, so Cavendish with Rainholde, the original speech is used as a starting point for a creative rewriting. Rainholde follows Aphthonius in dividing theses into "Civill . . . that doe pertain to the state of the commonwealth" and "contemplative . . . because the matter of them is comprehended in the minde."[54] Cavendish reinvents this into her division between "Orations of *Fancy,* and Orations of *Business:* as also, between Orations of *Publick Employments,* and *Private Divertisements*" ("A Prefatory Oration").

In her "Orations of *Business*," Cavendish exercises her ability to plead a case in a fictional law court, and thereby attempts to prove that she, like women in general, would "have as clear an understanding as Men, if we were bred in Schools to mature our Brains."[55] But such work would never extend beyond exercise form for Cavendish, since her confidence in her abilities combined with an equally strong sense that women should never be "Pleaders, Attorneys, Petitioners, and the like."[56] Such views are very like those of Christine de Pizan, who entered the arena of debate in manuscript but also concluded, "though God has given women great understanding . . . it would not be at all appropriate for them to go and appear so brazenly in the courts like men, for there are enough men who do so."[57] Christine's view is based on an argument from nature: "one could just as easily ask why God did not ordain the men to fulfill the offices of women, and women the offices of men. . . . to each sex [God] has given a fitting and appropriate nature and inclination to fulfill their offices. . . ."[58] This is in fact the argument of the fifth orator in Cavendish's *Female Orations:* "to have Female Bodies, and yet to act Masculine Parts, will be very Preposterous and Unnatural. In truth, we shall make our selves like the *Defects* of Nature, and be *Hermaphroditical,* neither perfect Women, nor perfect Men, but corrupt and imperfect Creatures" (243). This argument is developed in response to the fourth orator, who claims that women should in fact enter the arenas of men. These include "Courts of Judicature," but also sites that make the opinion seem excessive:

> let us Hawk, Hunt, Race; and do the like Exercises that Men have; and let us converse in Camps, Courts, and Cities; in Schools, Colledges, and Courts of Judicature; in Taverns, Brothels, and Gaming Houses; all which will make our *Strength* and *Wit* known, both to Men, and to our own selves (242)

For Cavendish, as for Christine, a woman presenting an argument in the law courts is as "brazen" as entering into "brothels." This suggests that the very wit and eloquence that Cavendish admired made the woman-orator shameful when she displayed these abilities in person in a public forum. Although Cavendish did agree that women should receive an education equal to men, she also argued that "Women are neither fit to be Judges, Tutors, nor Disputers" (#127).

Certainly Cavendish's reaction against "Petitioners" and "Preaching Sisters" (#51, #76) stems from her aristocratic status and royalist views. We can imagine that Christine's opinions may have led Cavendish to solidify these views. But it seems a peculiar and telling limit, that both Christine and Cavendish revel in developing their wit and skill at argument and eloquence, and yet find it unnatural for women to use these skills in person as speakers in a public forum.

—≈≈—

This essay is intended to suggest that women writers and the debate about women deserve further study because we know so little about manuscript transmission of their works and their knowledge of other writers. Nevertheless, it is not at all clear that we will find that the debate was "empowering." Cavendish's knowledge of Christine, and her reading of Richard Rainholde, taught her the rules of rhetoric, confirmed her belief that women should not be professional speakers, and convinced her that the debate led one to argue pro and con "and Determine nothing."

NOTES

I am especially grateful to the librarians at the manuscript departments of the British Library and Nottingham University Library. A visiting fellowship at the Institute for English Studies at the University of London allowed me to pursue this research, and I particularly thank the Director Warwick Gould for his advice on earlier versions of this essay. I also thank the participants in the Institute's seminar on the subject. I am indebted to Peter Blayney, Barbara Bowen, Susan Frye, Elizabeth Leedham-Green, Hilda Smith, Jennifer Summit, Mihoko Suzuki, Valerie Wayne, and Georgianna Ziegler for their discussions with me about aspects of the essay.

1. Margaret Hannay makes a parallel between Christine's city, early modern women writers, and contemporary scholars in "Constructing a City of Ladies," in *Forum: Studying Early Modern Women*, ed. Leeds Barroll, *Shakespeare Studies* 25 (London: Associated University Press, 1997), 76–87. She also studies quite precisely the effect of one woman on another in "'Your Vertuous and Learned Aunt': The Countess of Pembroke as a Mentor to Mary Wroth" in *Reading Mary Wroth: Representing Alternatives in Early Modern England*, eds. Naomi J. Miller, Gary Waller (Knoxville: University of Tennessee Press, 1991), 16–34.

2. Two recent works have explored the topic: Laurie A. Finke, *Women's Writing in English: Medieval England* (London: Longman 1999), 197–217; and Jennifer Summit, *Lost Property: The Woman Writer and English Literary History, 1380–1589* (Chicago: University of Chicago Press, 2000), 61–107. Neither of these works considers the significance of the Royal Manuscript 19 A.XIX of the *Cité des dames*

for the Tudor courts. Still important is P. G. C. Campbell, "Christine de Pizan in Angleterre," *Revue de Littérature Comparée* 5 (1925), 659–70. Berenice Carroll notes Christine's influence in England in "Christine de Pizan and the Origins of Peace Theory," in *Women Writers and the Early Modern British Political Tradition*, ed. Hilda L. Smith (Cambridge: Cambridge University Press, 1998), 26–28. See also Enid McLeod, *The Order of the Rose* (London: Chatto & Windus, 1976), 162–67. Neither Carroll nor McLeod consider Royal MS. 19 A.XIX of the *Cité des dames*. Charity Cannon Willard and Glenda McLeod have remarked that apart from the English translations that were published between 1478 and 1545, many of which did not refer to the author, no English writer until Horace Walpole mentions Christine (Willard, *Christine de Pizan*, New York: Persea Books, 1984, 211–23; Glenda McLeod, ed., *The Reception of Christine de Pizan*, ed. New York: Edwin Mellen Press, 1991). At a recent conference, I was told that no French woman writer in the sixteenth or seventeenth century refers to Christine either ("Attending to Early Modern Women," University of Maryland, November 1997). For references to her by scholars associated with the French court, see Earl Jeffrey Richards, "The Medieval 'femme auteur' as a Provocation to Literary History: Eighteenth-Century Readers of Christine de Pizan," in Glenda McLeod, 109–10; see also 127–32). Thanks to Georgianna Ziegler of the Folger Library for her help on this issue.

3. Sandra Gilbert and Susan Gubar, *The Madwoman in the Attic* (New Haven: Yale University Press, 1979), 50. See also Margaret Ezell's analysis of Gilbert and Gubar in *Writing Women's Literary History* (Baltimore: Johns Hopkins University Press, 1993).

4. Linda Woodbridge, *Women and the English Renaissance* (Urbana: University of Illinois Press, 1984), 5–6, 17. See also Walter J. Ong, "Latin Language as a Renaissance Puberty Rite," *Studies in Philology* 56 (1959), 103–24; and Joel Altman, *The Tudor Play of Mind* (Berkeley and Los Angeles: University of California Press, 1978).

5. R. Howard Bloch, *Medieval Misogyny and the Invention of Western Romantic Love* (Chicago: University of Chicago Press, 1991); Daniel Kempton, "Christine de Pizan's *Cité des Dames*," in *Political Rhetoric, Power, and Renaissance Women*, ed. Carole Levin and Patricia A. Sullivan (Albany: State University of New York Press, 1995), 15–37. Kempton argues that Christine's emphasis on her experience takes the *Cité des dames* beyond the conventional.

6. My colleagues Elizabeth Eames and Leslie Hill pointed out to me the significance of Christine's life experience.

7. Willard, 20–48.

8. Royal MS. 19 A.XIX of the *Cité des dames* in the British Library is noted by Campbell, and analyzed thoroughly as the most likely

source for Bryan Anslay's 1521 translation by Maureen Curnow in "*The Boke of the Cyte of Ladyes,* an English Translation of Christine de Pisan's *Le livre de la cité des dames,*" *Les Bonnes Feuilles* 3 (1974), 116–37. See also Sir George F. Warner and Julius P. Gilson, *British Museum Catalogue of Western Manuscripts in the Old Royal and Kings' Collections,* (London: Longman's, Green & Co., 1921), 2:322. Royal MS. 19 B.XVIII of the *Livre des faits d'armes* is described in Warner and Gilson as including "the title from an old cover (15th–16th cent.) on f.1." Other manuscripts by Christine in the royal libraries included *L'Épistle d'Othéa* (RM 14.E.II and 17 E.IV) and the *Livre des faits d'armes* (15 E.VI). In these, attribution to Christine is present at times, but hard to find. The libraries were located in several of the royal palaces, including Greenwich, Hampton Court, Richmond, St. James, and Westminister (James P. Carley, "John Leland and the Foundations of the Royal Library," *Bulletin of the Society for Renaissance Studies* 7 (1989),14; Sears Jayne, *Library Catalogues of the English Renaissance* (Berkeley and Los Angeles: University of California Press, 1956), 43.

9. For information on the tapestries, I am indebted to Susan Frye (see her "Staging Women's Relations to Textiles in *Othello* and *Cymbeline,*" in *Early Modern Visual Culture,* eds. Clark Hulse and Peter Erickson [Philadelphia: University of Pennsylvania Press, 2000], 233; and Susan Groag Bell ("A New Approach to the Influence of Christine de Pizan: The Lost Tapestries of 'The City of Ladies,'" in *Sur le Chemin De Longue Étude: Actes du colloque d'Orleans Juillet 1995,* ed. Bernard Ribemont [Paris: Honore Champion Editeur, 1998], 7–12]. The inventories are listed in W. G. Thomson, *A History of Tapestry from the Earlier Times until the Present Day,* second ed. (London: Hodder and Stoughton, 1930), 246–59. For the reference to James V, see Thomson, *Tapestry Weaving in England from the Earliest Times to the End of the Eighteenth Century* (New York: Charles Scribners' Sons, 1914), 44.

10. The Westminster Inventory of 1542 (BL) lists "Bocacio . . . les noble et renownes femmes." The *Catalogue of the Old Royal Library* (1790) lists "De claribus mulieribus" (BL Mic.c.488). The 1535 inventory of the library at Richmond lists "Bocace des nobles femmes," in Henri Omont, "Les Manuscrits Français des Rois D'Angleterre au Chateau de Richmond," *Études Romanes dédiées a Gaston Paris* (Paris: Émile Bouillon, Libraire-Éditeur, 1891), 7, 9. See also Warner and Gilson, which notes that Edward IV himself acquired a manuscript of "Boccaccio's Noble Men and Women . . . in French" (1:xii).

11. Royal MS. 20 B.XXI, "poems of Jean le Fevre." Maria Dowling (*Humanism in the Age of Henry VIII,* [London: Croom Helm, 1986], 199) assumes that the signature "Wyat" (ff.99b, 100) refers to Thomas.

12. On the ownership of Harley manuscript 4431, now in the British Library, see Campbell, 663; Curnow, 122; Sandra Hindman, "The Composition of the Manuscript of Christine de Pizan's Collected Works in the British Library," *The British Library Journal* 9:2 (1983), 96, and *A Catalogue of the Harleian Manuscripts in the British Museum,* (London, 1808), 3:144.

13. Warner and Gilson, 1:xi.

14. On Edward IV's interest in French manuscripts, his contribution to the beginnings of the royal libraries, and his friendship with Louis of Bruges, see T. J. Brown and Margaret Scheele, *The Old Royal Library* (London: Trustees of the British Museum, 1959), 3–4; and Warner and Gilson, 1:xi-xii. On Louis of Bruges' library, see C. Lemaire, "De bibliotheck van Lodewijk van Gruuthuse" in *vlaamse kunst op perkament* (Gruuthusemuseum, 1981), 211–12, 229; thanks to Hilda Smith for finding this essay.

15. In Warner and Gilson's description of Royal MS. 19 A.XIX, they write, "In the border of f.4 are introduced the white rose and the fetter-lock, perhaps indicating Richard, third duke of York (d. 1468), father of Edward IV. For the use of the fetter-lock (without a falcon) as his badge cf. His seal drawn in Cotton MS. Julius C.vii.f.177," 2:322. Curnow writes, "[Richard] may have acquired this manuscript during one of the periods when he was Commander of the English forces in France. His daughter, Margaret of York, was married to Charles the Bold, Duke of Burgundy, who owned three manuscripts of the *Cité des dames,*" 122–23. Carole Meale argues that the manuscript may have been acquired for Cecily Neville, duchess of York, rather than for Richard ("'Alle the bokes that I have of latyn, englisch, and frensch': Laywomen and Their Books in Late Medieval England," in *Women and Literature in Britain, 1150–1500,* ed. Carol M. Meale. second ed. (Cambridge: Cambridge University Press, 1996), 135.

16. Campbell, 667; Christine de Pisan, *The Fayt of Armes and of Chyvalrye* (Westminster, 1489), printer's note at the end of the text.

17. Dowling, 17.

18. Ibid; Meale, 143. Meale admits that Beaufort may have received the translation by Stephen Scrope, which also does not identify Christine as author.

19. On Elizabeth's ability to read French, see J. E. Neale, *Queen Elizabeth I* (New York: Doubleday Anchor Books, 1957), 14, 68.

20. On librarians and catalogues, see Brown and Scheele, 3–4; and Sears Jayne and Francis R. Johnson, in *The Lumley Library* (London: Trustees of the British Museum, 1956), 292–96.

21. See Curnow; Constance Jordan, *Renaissance Feminism* (Ithaca: Cornell University Press, 1990) 104–6; Summit (61–107). Diane Bornstein reprints the text in *Distaves and Dames: Renaissance Treatises for and about Women* (Delmar, N. Y.: Scholar's Facsimiles and Reprints,

1978). Cynthia Brown studies how sixteenth-century "English printers failed to publicize or even acknowledge Christine's authorship," in
"The Reconstruction of an Author in Print: Christine de Pizan in the
Fifteenth and Sixteenth Centuries" in *Christine de Pizan and the Categories of Difference,* ed. Marilynn Desmond (Minneapolis: University
of Minnesota Press, 1998), 215–35. Summit argues that Christine's
works printed without her name were used to formulate the ethos of
the learned secular gentleman, not the learned lady. She also effectively handles the question about whether the obscuring of Christine
as author resulted from medieval disregard for authorship or gender
bias (63–4). According to Peter Blayney, there was no conventional
number of books issued in a printing during the early sixteenth century, but, if a book sold out in ten years, it was doing fairly well (private communication). Since there was no second printing, we can
conjecture that the 1521 translation was not widely in demand.
22. Jordan, 104–6; Margaret Ferguson, comments during 1999 SAA
seminar on "Early Modern Women Writers and the Pamphlet Debate
on Gender."
23. Dowling, 223–31.
24. Thanks to Liz Stevenson for the reminder that Christine defends
women rulers.
25. *The Poems of Aemilia Lanyer,* ed. Susanne Woods (New York: Oxford
University Press, 1993, xvii, 18). Lady Susan had been married to
Reynold Grey, earl of Kent, until his death in 1573, but the earl's seat
was not in Kent, but in Wrest Park in Bedfordshire, and Lanyer
would have been four years old when the earl died. After Lady Susan
married Sir John Wingfield in 1581, they lived at times in Greenwich,
as Lady Susan's mother had. Since Greenwich was originally part of
Kent, and Lanyer would have been twelve to eighteen years old between 1581 and 1587, she probably grew up in the household in
Greenwich (*The Complete Peerage,* ed. H. A. Doubleday and Lord
Howard de Walden [London: St. Catherine Press, 1929], 7:171; Edward Hasted, *The History and Topographical Survey of the County of
Kent,* [Canterbury: Simmons, 1778], 1:488).
26. Lanyer refers to Queen Elizabeth and "vertuous ladies" in *Poems,* 8,
12. On Agrippa and Lanyer, see Esther Gilman Richey, "'To Undoe
the Booke': Cornelius Agrippa, Aemilia Lanyer and the Subversion of
Pauline Authority," *ELR* 27 (1997), 106–28.
27. See Sheila Delany, "'Mothers to think back through': Who Are They?
The Ambiguous Example of Christine de Pizan," in *Medieval Texts
and Contemporary Readers,* eds. Laurie A. Finke, Martin B. Shicht-
man (Ithaca: Cornell University Press, 1987), 177–97.
28. Cavendish, *Sociable Letters,* ed. James Fitzmaurice (New York: Garland, 1997), letter #111, p. 120. Further citation from the letters will
come from this volume, and appear in the text by letter number.

29. See Anna Battigelli, "Political Thought / Political Action: Margaret Cavendish's Hobbesian Dilemma," in *Women Writers and the Early Modern British Political Tradition*, 51–2.

30. *A Catalogue of the Harleian Manuscripts in the British Museum*, 3:144.

31 *DNB; Complete Peerage*, 9:527; "The Calendar," in *The Oxford Companion to English Literature*, ed. Margaret Drabble (Oxford: Oxford University Press, 1985), 1126–28.

32. Private communication with Hilda Smith; see also her article "'A General War amongst the Men . . . but None amongst the Women': Political Differences Between Margaret and William Cavendish," in *Politics and the Political Imagination in Later Stuart Britain* (Rochester: N. Y. University of Rochester Press, 1997), 144–6. For William's interest in literature, see also Margaret J. M. Ezell, "'To Be Your Daughter in Your Pen': The Social Functions of Literature in the Writings of Lady Elizabeth Brackley and Lady Jane Cavendish," *The Huntington Library Quarterly* 51 (1988), 281–96.

33. Public Record Office 1677–22. PROB 11–353; 11/Hall/22, 11/353/22. Dated October 4,1676, probated 24 Feb.1676/7. I am indebted to Elizabeth Leedham-Green of Cambridge University Library, who pointed out the link between books and wills.

34. Cavendish Papers, October 20, 1686 (Pw 1: 285); December 12, 1689 (Pw 1: 286) ; May 26, 1691 (Pw 1: 289), Nottingham University Library.

35. Robert Payne, March 22, 1631–2, *Historical Manuscripts Commission, Portland Papers*, 2:122. William settled Clerkenwell House on Margaret on January 15, 1667–8. Henry remarks on this as an "unkindness" shown his family in 1671 (quoted in Goulding, *Margaret (Lucas) Duchess of Newcastle*, Lincoln: Lincolnshire Chronicle Ltd., 1925, 20).

36. Cavendish Papers, December 12, 1689 (Pw 1: 286), Nottingham University Library.

37. Edward Harley, 2nd Earl of Oxford, *Complete Peerage*, 10:267.

38. *A Catalogue of the Harleian Manuscripts in the British Museum*, 3:144.

39. For a description of the manuscript and a complete list of works, see Hindman, 93–123.

40. *DNB;* Kathleen Jones, *A Glorious Fame* (London: Bloomsbury, 1988), 128.

41. Douglas Grant, *Margaret the First* (London: Hart-Davis, 1957), 174.

42. In France during this time, there were several manuscripts of Christine's works in the French king's library (Suzanne Solente, "Christine de Pisan," *Histoire littéraire de la France* [Paris: Imprimerie Nationale, 1974], 40:382–84), but no texts printed. For references to

her by scholars associated with the French court, see note 2. For the French printed texts on the debate during this period, see Ian Maclean, *Woman Triumphant* (Oxford: Clarendon Press, 1977), 64–87.

43. Mihoko Suzuki pointed out that both Christine and Cavendish write in numerous genres. Jones notes Margaret's problems with French (*A Glorious Fame*, 61). Hilda Smith commented that William could have translated for his wife, and that Cavendish did not encourage rivals. Cavendish refers to Denny's response to Wroth in *Sociable Letters*, 4.

44. *The Book of the City of Ladies*, tr. Earl Jeffrey Richards, second ed. (Persea Press, 1998), 32 [I.11], 63 [I.27], 31[I.11]. Cavendish, "Preface to the Reader," *The World's Olio; Sociable Letters*, #127, 144.

45. I agree with Anna Battigelli's views on this point developed in "Political Thought / Political Action," 51–53. For a different view, see Suzuki's forthcoming book, *Subordinate Subjects* (Ashgate).

46. *Sociable Letters*, "The Preface," 8.

47. On Cavendish as a satirist, see Suzuki, "Margaret Cavendish and the Female Satirist," *SEL* 37 (1997), 484–500.

48. *Orations of Divers Sorts Accommodated to Divers Places*, second ed. (London: A. Maxwell, 1668), 311. All citations of the *Orations* refer to this edition, and page numbers will appear in the text.

49. *Poems of Lady Mary Wroth*, ed. Josephine Roberts (Baton Rouge: Louisiana State University, 1983), 32–5.

50. Battigelli, "Political Thought / Political Action," 53.

51. Raymond E. Nadeau, "The *Progymnasmata* of *Aphthonius* in Translation," in *Speech Monographs* 19 (1952): 264–85; and Richard Rainholde, *The Foundation of Rhetorike* (New York: Scholars' Facsimiles and Reprints, 1945). See also Altman, 45–53.

52. Nadeau, 281; Rainholde, Fol. liiii-verso to lv-verso.

53. Rainholde, Fol.lix-lxii, xxxiii-xxxvii, lviii-verso; Cavendish, 86–90, 90–4, 99–102.

54. Fol.liv.

55. Cavendish, "Preface to the Reader," *The World's Olio*.

56. Quoted from *The World's Olio* in Jones, *A Glorious Fame*, 40.

57. *City of Ladies*, 30–32 (I.11).

58. Quoted from *The World's Olio* in Jones, *A Glorious Fame*, 40.

CHAPTER 2

ANNE SOUTHWELL AND THE PAMPHLET DEBATE: THE POLITICS OF GENDER, CLASS, AND MANUSCRIPT

Elizabeth Clarke

Various economies of writing operate in the early part of the seventeenth century, some involving money, others not, all of them primarily male-oriented, and therefore operating in a distinctive way for individual early modern women. "Constantia Munda," in authoring the satiric pamphlet *The Worming of a mad Dog*, shows herself to be in a unique relationship to male-dominated literary culture: that is, if the feminine pseudonym conceals a female author. There are few candidates for the identity of "Constantia Munda": she had a knowledge of Latin and possibly Greek, an extensive familiarity with the formal gender debate, and a facility in the satiric mode.[1] Anne, Lady Southwell, is probably one of the best we have, and this article begins with a consideration of her qualifications for authorship of *The Worming of a mad Dog*. Her elite education, confidence as an author, and interest in the gender debate are manifest in her manuscript poetry: but Anne Southwell also outlines in her manuscript work a previous career in "flouting," which is rhetorically configured scorn, and is

Esther Sowernam's derogatory description of Joseph Swetnam's pamphlet—in other words, exactly the kind of writing in *The Worming of a mad Dog*.[2]

It is not easy to date the start of the rhetorical activity of Anne Southwell, who was born in 1573, with confidence. Folger MS. V.b.198 is headed "The workes of the Lady Ann Sothwell: Decemb:2nd 1626" and although a number of verse epistles and elegies can be dated to the late 1620s and early 1630s, some of the poetry appears of an earlier date.[3] However, evidence of an embryonic literary practice is recorded in a 1614 volume that is particularly useful in a consideration of the gender pamphlets: it covered some of the same ground and was at least as popular as Joseph Swetnam's *Arraignment of Lewd, idle, froward, and unconstant women* over a similar period of time. There were nine impressions of *A Wife, now the Widdow of Sir Thomas Overbury* before 1616 and another ten after that. It is one of the publications that capitalized on the murder of Sir Thomas Overbury and the subsequent trial and conviction of Frances Howard for the crime. Critics have speculated that the gender pamphlet war had some connection with this event and with other Jacobean scandals involving women, but the Overbury volume has an explicit link, and some of Anne Southwell's writing is in it. As well as a reprinting of Overbury's famous poem "The Wife" and his "Characters," it contains what appears to be a printed record of one or more "Newes" games, with contributions by some of the most brilliant young wits of the day, including Thomas Overbury himself, John Donne, Sir Thomas Roe, Cecily Bulstrode, and, Louise Schleiner suggests, another woman, Anne Southwell.[4] This attribution is based on the initials A. S. subscribed to two of the "Newes" pieces in the first edition: the other "Lady Southwell" in the volume may be Elizabeth Southwell rather than Anne. However, her authorship of the "Newes" pieces is made somewhat more likely by the fact that Anne Southwell was involved in marriage negotiations for the daughter of Lord and Lady Somerset.[5] Such a close association with Robert Carr and Frances Howard makes her involvement with Overbury, Carr's secretary, in the period before 1609, when the "Newes" games must have been played, much more plausible. What these contributions demonstrate is full participation in a specific rhetorical economy: the terms of the game seem to privilege rhetorical skill in a particular and limited context. The results demonstrate possession of the rhetorical capital of sententiae and maxim, the stuff of grammar school commonplace books, and the ability to recast it into a series of witty remarks that have at least a tangential relevance to the subject set for the game: "Newes from the Court," for example, or "Newes from Sea." The prevalence of misogynist maxims—even Anne Southwell includes "That Man, Woman, and the Divell, are the three degrees of comparison"—is probably explained not by any formal rule but by the huge proportion of misogynist maxims in circulation.[6]

The commodification of misogyny into tokens of rhetorical skill that are available for deployment by women is demonstrated vividly in two sites of textual exchange: the manuscript miscellany, which circulates rhetorical commonplaces within a textually constructed scholarly community, and the printed commonplace book, which by the early sixteenth century was explicitly offering to a wider audience a version of the personal repository of rhetorical *copia* that was the product of an elitist education. Nicholas Ling's 1597 printed commonplace book *Politeuphuia: Wits Common wealth*, which went into ten editions by 1620, offers five pages of assorted apothems under the title "Woman." Of these, all but two are misogynist, but there is little to choose between the last misogynist maxim and the first apparently nonmisogynist saying, in terms of the implications for real women:

> A woman in her wit, is pregnable, in her smile, deceauable, in her frowne, reuengeable, in her death, acceptable. A faire, beautiful, and chast woman, is the perfect workmanship of God, the true glory of Angels, the rare miracle of earth, and the wonder of the world.[7]

Newly enfranchised would-be wits (such as Joseph Swetnam, perhaps) were offered a rather unbalanced diet, at least in this particular commonplace. As Ann Moss asks of such printed collections, "were their intended readers being led toward the verbal sophistication and rhetorical empowerment claimed for the Latin commonplace-book, or was 'popular' culture merely being given a certain veneer, and proverbial wisdom being set fast in a new format?"[8]

Bodleian MS Don. c.54 is a verbally sophisticated manuscript miscellany kept by the Welsh judge Richard Roberts in the 1620s, and its terms of rhetorical commodification are rather more complex. The manuscript is deliberately re-creative of the masculine environment of the Inns of Court in an earlier, more glittering age: a poem on folio 21, "Convivium Philosophicum," celebrates the joint talents of a bevy of wits, including John Donne, Lionel Cranfield, Henry Neville, John Hoskins, Richard Marten, Henry Goodyer, Inigo Jones, and Thomas Coryat. Other poems by John Donne are transcribed, as is "a libel" on Robert Carr's marriage to Frances Howard,

and Overbury's "The Wife." As in the 1614 printed volume, Overbury's "The Wife," apparently a celebration of a woman's potential
for good, functions ironically in the explicit context of the author's
murder by a woman: the poem puts in place a series of structures to
restrain women to the path of virtue, whilst the context suggests the
difficulty of the whole endeavour and allows more emphasis to passages on women's learning as "hazardous" and injunctions to "barre
the meanes" of lust in a wife.[9] One of the dedicatory poems in *A
Wife, now the Widdow* even suggests that it was for writing the poem
that Overbury was killed.[10] That the poem should be read misogynistically is suggested by a couplet transcribed on the first page of the
manuscript, "Discription of weomens qualities":

> Litle and softe, long and loud
> fare and foolish fowle and proud (f.2^r)

and is apparently confirmed by the closing witticism, translated thus,
which is included, in its Latin form, in *Politeuphuia:*

> There is no woman good at all, or if some good be had
> I knowe not how the thinge is good, and yet the woman bad.
>   (f.25^v)

However, some of the pieces in between offer a kind of balance, suggesting that misogyny is not the only currency in which the manuscript is dealing: wit is also exercised around idealist commonplaces
about women, demonstrating rhetorical display as the more important commodity. This is one of two such double-edged verbal exercises, the English version following a Latin acrostic, "Upon the word
uxor by doctor Barlowe now Bishop of Lincolne":

> The w. is double woe
> The i. nought els but iealousie
> The f. is favoringe flatteringe fraude
> The e. what els but miserie
> Thus w with i with f with e
> Makes nothinge els but miserie
>
> The w. is double wealthe
> The i. is ioy and iolitie
> The f. is frendship fast and firme
> The e. ease with equalitie
>   Thus w with i with f with e

Makes ioiefull frends, bringes weales felicitie
Wherefore God grant that guift to mee
That I a married man may be[11]

Although women-hatred within this medium is not consistent or necessarily self-conscious, there is of course a fundamental misogyny implicit in the use of the category "Woman" as a site for male verbal display. Exercises such as the one quoted above pivot on a knife-edge, and although this particular epigram decides in favor of marriage, there is more than a little sense of arbitrariness about such a conclusion. Moreover, the tendency of the formal defence to collapse into its opposite, as in the various appropriations of "The Wife," indicates an inherent instability. Barnabe Rich's "defense," *The Excellencie of good women* (1613), consistently threatens to deconstruct itself in this way. Such "defenses" have a strong link with the mock encomium, which was itself a form of paradox, a discourse beloved of the Inns of Court.[12] A misogynist extract in Edward Pudsey's commonplace book from a revel held at the Middle Temple around 1610 is entitled "out of yᵉ defenc of womens inconstancye" and illustrates a delight in paradoxical argument in that milieu: the complete piece was printed as "A Defence of Womens Inconstancy" in the 1633 edition of Donne's works, among the *Paradoxes*.[13] More definitively attributed to Donne is the paradox entitled "That it is possible to find some vertue in some women," which ends "to confirm this opinion the World yields not one Example."[14] All this means that discourses around the commonplace "Woman" are particularly difficult to read: they are inflected by a distinct textual and cultural history. In particular, the reader must be alert to irony in the presentation of discourses apparently in defence of women—misogyny, on the other hand, is not subject to this kind of undermining.

Men and, it seems, some women, wishing to establish a reputation for wit at various levels, find plenty of stock in the apothems about women circulating in the period. The "Conceited Newes," which gives all the appearance of being assembled from various maxims in the players' memories (or commonplace books—it is not clear whether performance was impromptu or in written correspondence, or both), were themselves broken down again by would-be authors searching for marketable sentences. William Parkhurst, Henry Wotton's secretary from 1604 to 1610, transcribed selected passages, many of them misogynist, from the "Conceited Newes" into his own commonplace book.[15] The printed volume *A Wife, now the Widdow* shows Anne Southwell at ease in this kind of literary stock market:

she is in possession of a wealth of rhetorical phrases that she can disburse in marketable form, including misogynist commonplaces. She is operating successfully in different arenas: the private game, at which she obviously performed well (she is the only player with two pieces in the volume), and the more public arena of print, which provided the material for another manuscript commonplace book (probably through consumption of the published version, although Evelyn Simpson posits a manuscript correspondence between Donne and Wotton).[16] Each of these markets is delineated and enabled by class divisions. The game is obviously played at an elite level, with a few select players, access to which is part of the appeal to the buyers, who thus feel they can deal in the same currency (the title page offers "private *passages of Wit, betweene sundrie Gentlemen*").[17] Henry Wotton's secretary, in particular, was packaging the "Newes" games for his own use. All of this is the more interesting as the volume has been posited by Linda Woodbridge as influenced by the gender debate. Overbury's "Wife," as she points out, contains arguments from the gender debate, and his "Characters" begins with a standard defence and attack, pairing "The good Woman" and "A very Woman."[18] It is clearly participating in the market in stereotyped representations of women identified by Diane Purkiss, and demonstrates exactly what Ann Moss has designated as the main discursive effect of commonplace culture: "a model of ready response and repartee, a mode of improvisation within a set of norms."[19]

Jean Klene has shown some of the verbal parallels between the contributions of "A. S." to the Newes game and Anne Southwell's manuscript verse as part of her project to establish the identification of "A. S." with Anne Southwell. Interesting and suggestive on a different level are the similarities between some of the arguments in "The Wife" and Anne Southwell's poetry. Anne Southwell returns to the gender controversy throughout her manuscript and in various different genres. At one end of the rhetorical spectrum is this short piece, another metaphorical "kick" from a downtrodden woman:

> All.maried.men.desire.to.haue good wifes:
> but.few.giue good example.by thir liues
> They are owr head they wodd haue vs thir heles.
> this makes the good wife kick the good man reles.
> When god brought Eue to Adam for a bride
> the text sayes she was taene from out mans side
> A simbole of that side, whose sacred bloud.
> flowed for his spowse, the Churches sauing good.

This is a misterie, perhaps too deepe.
for blockish Adam that was falen a sleepe[20]

This poem reworks a commonplace of Jewish Midrash, the significance of woman being taken from man's side, employed sometimes misogynistically, as in John Donne's dour sermon for the marriage of Francis Nethersole and Lucy Goodyer in 1619: "She was not taken out of the *foot*, to be troden upon, nor out of the *head*, to be overseer of him: but out of *his side*, where she weakens him enough, and therefore should do all she can, to be a Helper."[21] Rachel Speght and Esther Sowernam use this commonplace to suggest equality between man and woman.[22] Anne Southwell is not so commonplace, nor so prosaic: she draws on the typological interpretation, the wounding of Christ's side to bring forth the mystical bride, the Church. She obviously draws confidence from the female gender of the Bride, as in a version of the above lines included in a formal defence of Eve that begins:

S[r], giue mee leaue to plead my Grandams cause.
and prooue her Charter from Iehouaes Lawes.[23]

Much of Anne Southwell's shorter verse participates in the literary practice of commonplace: her short poem "Envy" owes much to the list of negative maxims under that heading. However, what Anne Southwell clearly considered to be her most important work is her stanzas on the Decalogue. The poems exist in two rather different versions, one in the Folger manuscript and one in British Library MS Lansdowne 740, a manuscript collection that also includes an important group of Donne's poems. Anne Southwell's section appears to be a draft of a presentation manuscript to the king, either James I or Charles I.[24] In this sense her work is hardly "private," but her repudiation of printed publication is explicit, and not limited to the woman writer. It is the participation of the author in a cash economy that is seen as the degrading aspect of print:

Who writes for pence, be<e> he<e> soe turpified
& lett those nine Chima'raes bee his nurse.
to teach him crawle the Heliconian hill
& in Pernassus dipp his iuorye quill.[25]

Within this aristocratic contempt for printed publication, Anne Southwell is aware of particular problems for the woman writer. Her most far-reaching contributions to the gender debate are contained in verses on the Fourth Commandment. She insists, as does Overbury, that women do have souls, in defiance of traditional misogynist argument. Even the "shell" conceit here is also used in "The Wife":

> Are you denyed soules then, you shelles of men,
> are they but hatched in you & flye away. (155)

Although the principles of wit and repartee are clearly operating, she is careful to point out the serious consequences for women of this error:

> twill bee to late when you in hell shall grone
> to curse those so^{u}les that taught you, you had none. (158)

It is in this theological context that Anne Southwell engages with the particular problems of the woman writer, which she sees as caused by the negative reaction of men. To avoid unfair criticism, the female author has to engage in doubtful textual strategies:

> then must you frame a pittifull epistle
> to pray him bee a rose was borne a thistle. (156)

This may be a playful glance at her own dedicatory epistle in this manuscript, probably addressed to James I, the Scottish thistle trying to be an English rose. The following stanza defends the woman prophet, and it is tempting to posit that she has in mind Eleanor Davies, whose husband was attorney general for Ireland and whose family Anne Southwell seems to have known: if so, the Lady Eleanor must have had a reputation as a prophet before the vision of 1625 that is the originating prophetic impulse claimed throughout her printed works. The defence most closely related to her own writing career, however, is of the "sanguin woman" (157). Despite the superiority of the sanguine disposition in a man, "a sanguin woman is of all accurst." She cannot help making jokes, but it is at a high price: "shee must bee merry though her neck were burst." Misogynist judgment condemns the merry woman as less than virtuous: "it cannot bee / goodnes & mirth should hold a simpathy." Henry Peacham's 1612 emblem gives some sense of why sanguinity is judged according to gender:

> The Aierie *Sanguine* . . .
> By nature is benigne, and gentlie meeke,

To Musicke, and all merriment a frend:
As seemeth by his flowers, and girlondes gay,
Wherewith he dightes him all the merry May.

So far the sanguine humor seems positive for women and for men.
The second stanza offers no problem for the sanguine man, but one
could imagine why sanguine women are suspect:

And by him browzing of the climbing vine,
The lustfull *goates* seene, which may import,
His pronenes both to women, and to wine,
Bold, bounteous, frend vnto the learned sort.[26]

The association here of learning, wit, drunkenness, and lechery, characteristic of sanguinity, is fatal to a woman's reputation.

Anne Southwell's verses on the third precept in the same manuscript indicate that she is speaking from experience in witty, learned
discourse. She is talking about her own practice of "flouting," which
is satirical, witty writing, the offspring of "a sanguin witt." This un-
broken colt led her into trouble:

when first I backed this iade hee dashed at princes
& almost broke my neck from of his back. (138)

This is a tantalizing glimpse of an Anne Southwell who dared to
make fun of royalty, but there is nothing in either of the surviving
manuscripts that comes close to "flouting." This is no surprise, however, as she has given up this kind of writing: "flouting" is fit only for
"shallow wits" at court who play games, perhaps the "Newes" games
of her own past. Cecily Bulstrode's fate in Jonson's poem "An Epigram on the Court Pucell" vividly demonstrates the truth of Southwell's observation that the conjunction of "goodnes & mirth" was
not allowed for in a woman. In contradistinction to the "wild hott
proud snorting Dromedarye" that is wit, Southwell characterizes her
present writing as "a sluggish asse," perhaps the moralistic stanzas of
the Decalogue poetry. However, this has to be part of a *humilis*
topos. The section of the fourth precept that deals specifically with
women writers offers a higher vision of her poetic function. Although
some "amorous Idiotts" use poetry as "the packhorse of theyr passion," Southwell employs it in the service of a higher love:

To speak in verse, yf sweet & smoothly carryed
to true proportions loue is euer maryed. (152)

What follows is a love song in the tradition and language of the biblical Song of Songs. In some ways this use of an authorized, feminized subject position is an obvious move for a woman poet to make, and Aemilia Lanyer had made it in *Salve Deus Rex Judaeorum:* but any woman daring to exploit the female-gendered poetic voice of the biblical text did so in defiance of Protestant interpreters of the Song of Songs, who deliberately degendered the voice of the Bride so that they could apply it to the Church of Christ as a whole, or even more anachronistically, to the individual male Christian. Henry Finch, himself an Inns of Court man, wrote a 1615 commentary that ruthlessly appropriated the text for "The Christian man": his gloss on the phrase "thou hast ravished my heart, my sister, my spouse" is "For he doth behold us as the brethren of Christ."[27] Anne Southwell clearly gains much confidence from the female gendering of the Bride, both as poetic voice in the Song of Songs and as the Church who is the Spouse of Christ. This is why she insists on the privacy of her writing: it is enclosed in manuscript, and composed by the intimate inspiration of God. It thereby escapes the mercenary economies in which worldly rhetoric is implicated:

for mee, I write but to my self & mee
what gods good grace doth in my soule imprint
I bought it not for pelf, none buyes of thee
nor will I lett it at soe base a rent
        as wealth or fame, wch is but drosse & vapor
        & scarce deserues the blotting of a paper. (151)

Printed publication is taboo for this kind of writing. Her friend, the curate of Acton, Roger Cox, who preached her funeral sermon and who himself wrote poetry, understood exactly her construction of herself as a poet. He places her, the spiritual virgin who is also the Bride of Christ, within the enclosed Garden of the Song of Songs, where only the inspiring breath of the Holy Spirit can penetrate: "Awake, O north wind, and come, thou south; blow upon my garden, that its spices may flow out."[28] His play on her name figures successful female poetic composition as *copia* bestowed by gift:

The South winde blew vpon a springing Well:
Whose waters flowed & the Sweete streames did swell. (Folger
    MS f.73^r, *The Southwell-Sibthorpe Commonplace Book* 113)

Southwell's construction of herself as the Bride has sequestered off her writing: manuscript is the walled garden, the privacy of which is the condition for inspiration to flow.

That Anne Southwell was not overscrupulous in confining herself to manuscript and being chary of her reputation is shown by
one male reader's response to the printed text of Rachel Speght's
A Mouzell for Melastomus. The Beinecke Library copy is annotated
in a way that shows the woman's body elided with her text.[29] Her
declarations of chastity are met with disbelief, specifically because
she has engaged in publication: he notes that she is "by reason of
[her] publique booke now not soe good as common." He represents her praise of marriage as an overflow of sexual desire into her
writing: the publication of her text is self-advertisement to men.
There is a distinct tone of sexual titillation in the comments. The
commendatory poems provoke two grossly sexual rewritings: "If
he that for his Countrie / dothe expose" is glossed "Doth shee
fight for her Cunt- / rie." "But that she beares the triumph quite
away" becomes "Thy mistris beares [your] prick and prize away."
The volume is a graphic illustration of the sexualization of
women's printed texts in this period.

The satiric prose of "Constantia Munda," with its invocation of
bodily functions and familiarity with the indecent works of Juvenal
and Martial, is already sexualized. The allusions of both Munda and
Sowernam to suspect Latin writers are extremely transgressive in a
woman's text. Also foreign to Anne Southwell's careful self-
presentation are the transgressive terms in which Esther Sowernam
constructs herself. Her prefatory narrative of the evening table talk
invokes the nonserious discourse of the paradox, often used as material for amusing dinnertime conversation.[30] An equal number of
men and women are present, but no husband: a gentleman visiting
her (apparently alone) brings her a copy of the Swetnam book. Her
letter to the apprentices of the City of London, a group with ambivalent social and moral status, suggests that she knows them
rather better than a woman of good reputation should and under-
lines her own denotation of herself—"neither maid, wife, or
widow"—in the same formulation as Swetnam's prostitute. Moreover, she explicitly leaves the spiritual seclusion of the Garden to
display the spiritual, rhetorical (and possibly sexual) secrets she has
learned there: "I haue entred into the Garden of *Paradice,* and
there haue gathered the choysest flowers which that Garden may afford, and these I offer to you" (A4[r]). Rachel Speght calls her a self-
conceited creature, with some cause: she employs the kind of
rhetorical style, larded with Latin tags, that is characterized by
Overbury as typical of "An Innes of Court man."[31] "She" allows
herself the "libertie" to leave religiously orthodox writing behind

after the first section of her pamphlet and adopt risky arguments in praise of self-display, including makeup, which was universally condemned in this period (36–7).

These discourses seem to me heavily coded as misogynist impersonation. Rachel Speght thinks that both "Esther Sowernam" and "Constantia Munda" are real women, but she is not a participator in the rhetorical economy within which they are writing, as Linda Woodbridge makes clear, casting implicit suspicion on the other two "women-authored" treatises: "Hers really is what earlier defenses pretended to be—a response to an attack in print."[32] "Constantia Munda" characterizes *A Mouzell for Melastomus* perfectly: "tis a doubt whether she hath shown more modesty or gravity" (15). Neither attribute characterizes her own writing. The first sentence shows her as learning nothing from her mother "Prudentia," launching into the virulent attack accompanied by the explicit bodily imagery that is typical of her style throughout the pamphlet. One of the jokes is that she is better at male-dominated, commonplace wit than her male but distinctly lower-class adversary. "She" organizes less commonplace English and Latin examples into an effective denunciation of his treatise. Classical authors are trawled for positive opinions about women (29). The ladylike distaste of Swetnam's use of Juvenal, "that Pagan Poet . . . whose filthy reprehension opened the doores of unbridled luxurie, and gave a president of all admired wickednesse, and brutish sensualitie, to succeeding ages" is somewhat undermined by her obvious familiarity with that poet's work (9–10). Swetnam is compared to the biblical "railer" of the commonplace books, Rabshekeh. Strangely, one of his problems seems to be gender transgresson: he is worse than a "masculine scold," i.e., a man engaging in a scurrilous discourse more typical of a woman (26). However, *The Worming of a mad Dog* is on the whole a coherent and fluent diatribe reinforced by examples from commonplace culture. By contrast, "Constantia Munda" accuses Swetnam of the abuse of commonplaces:

> you . . . stretch your shallow inuentions on the triuiall subiect of euery shackragge that can but set penne to paper: so in the handling of your base discourse, you lay open your imperfections, *arripiendo maledicta ex titulo*, by heaping together the scraps, fragments, and reuersions of divers english phrases, by scraping together the glaunders and offals of abusive termes, and the refuse of idle headed Authors, and making a mingle-mangle gallimauphrie of them. Lord! How you have cudgeld your braines in gleaning multitudes of similies as twere in the field of many writers, and thrasht them together in the floure of your owne deuizor: and all to make a poore confused misceline. (21)

It is difficult to see in this diatribe anything but the contempt of a master of commonplace culture for an incompetent imitator of it.

Even *A Mouzell for Melastomus* was widely considered to be by a man, as Rachel Speght herself complains.[33] I wonder whether anyone inside the seventeenth-century context I have sketched ever thought that "Esther Sowernam" or "Constantia Munda" were women writers. If they had been women, their elitist education would have brought them into a different marketplace, one where female "honor" was the chief commodity. Both treatises, however, show an explicit disregard for the currency of female honor in the early seventeenth century. I suspect that, to participants in Renaissance literary culture, both would have looked like rhetorical *jeux d'ésprit* by male authors, versions of the mock encomium. Set in the context of the author's dubious self-construction, Sowernam's defence of women collapses into its opposite: "Constantia Munda's" discourse, if read as female-authored, tends to confirm the stereotype of the railing, sexually explicit woman. "Railing" is discouraged in both sexes, as we have seen, but it is women who are usually punished for it: in Arthur Golding's translation of Ovid's *Metamorphoses,* the Theban women, the daughters of Buippye and Niobe, are all transformed for that crime (no men are guilty of the same lapse of taste).[34] In the seventeenth century, "railing" was increasingly how transgressive women talked to men. "Peters trouble" in John Heath's epigram of that name is a railing wife; Samuel Rowlands sees "railing" as the prelude to physical husband abuse; and Humphrey Mill associates railing only with prostitutes.[35] Rachel Speght's hostile annotator accuses her several times of the same transgression, despite the relative restraint of her intervention in the debate.

By contrast, Anne Southwell is painfully aware of the double standard for men's and women's writing in her attempt to acquire capital in the difficult marketplace of elitist poetic composition.[36] Erica Longfellow has suggested that her second marriage, in 1626, to a younger man who was her social inferior, highlighted an anxiety about status: this may account for the contempt for printed publication expressed in the manuscript, as well as the careful quest for a mode of rhetoric that could not be construed as incompatible with virtue.[37] That this was not a personal neurosis may be seen from the correspondence of a family that Jane Stevenson and Peter Davidson suggest might have contained "Constantia Munda" amongst its womenfolk, the Ishams of Lamport.[38] A letter of 1642 from Justinian Isham to his four well-educated daughters lists his idea of preferred reading for them—St. Augustine, Daniel Featley, Thomas à

Kempis and Richard Sibbes, pious authors to a man. These works constituted the favorite volumes of their mother, "a Religious & Discreet Woman." Amongst the qualities he lists for them to aspire to, in the tradition of the most repressive conduct books, are "Modestie," "Obedience," and "Silence."[39] This last was obviously a relative silence: he also holds up to them as a role model the wife of Lord Edward Montagu of Boughton. Ann Montagu, née Crouch, was a poet, of sorts. Her moral advice to her children is framed in verse simply to make it more palatable, an "excuse" for poetry widely used by women and men in the seventeenth century, from George Herbert's "Church-porch" onward, and which explicitly distances the author from the self-display that is the point of commonplace culture. This stanza ends 160 moralizing verses:

> I willing was to put these noates
> in verse to please your minde
> & reade them ought practise them much
> in them trew joy yowle finde.[40]

This, the kind of writing practice implicitly approved of by the Isham patriarch, illustrates vividly the limits of the rhetorical horizons of many potential woman writers.

There may be another, less negative reason, however, for real women such as Anne Southwell and Rachel Speght to abandon the discourse of the commonplace so prevalent in *The Worming of a mad Dog*. It is difficult to say anything new in a rhetoric made up of recycled verbal units: commonplace culture is entrenchedly conservative. This, I think, was why "Constantia Munda" wrote a pro-woman treatise: it was an intellectual challenge. As I have argued, the readership of *The Worming of a mad Dog* would enjoy the spectacle of a so-called female author confirming the misogynist stereotypes of women's discourse. At the same time, the assumption that the author was male would allow admiration of his command of argument and example. This is the limit of masculine invention: to rewrite misogyny in the paradox, the mock encomium, or, as I have suggested, male impersonation of female voices. Anne Southwell and Rachel Speght, by contrast, employ a rhetoric self-consciously purged of verbal display to argue a consistent position: although their intended readership is clearly very different, both writers want to change seventeenth-century attitudes toward women rather than embellish existing opinion with wit.[41] Excluded from misogynist culture, these women are the forerunners of the radical authors who were to promote change, in the serious discourses of pamphlet, prophecy, and holy poetry, amongst the increasingly literate populace of a revolutionary seventeenth century.

NOTES

1. *Early Modern Women Poets: An Anthology,* eds. Jane Stevenson and Peter Davidson (Oxford: Oxford University Press, 2001), prints the poem from her pamphlet (197), suggests Lady Tanfield or Bathsua Makin as possible authors, and makes this comment on the identity of "Constantia Munda": "there were certainly other educated gentlewomen born c. 1590–1600 who could have written such a work, not all of whom are known to us: for example, the earls of Huntingdon, the Audleys, the Herberts, and the Ishams of Lamport in Northamptonshire were all gentry or noble families with a strong commitment to the education of daughters." This paper argues that there were other limitations on women's publication of verse besides lack of education.
2. *Esther hath hanged Haman,* 2. All references to the anti-Swetnam pamphlets in this paper are taken from *Female Replies to Swetnam the Woman-Hater,* ed. Charles Butler (Bristol: Thoemmes Press, 1995).
3. Jean Klene concludes that the version of the Decalogue in the Folger manuscript was written before the death of James I. *The Southwell-Sibthorpe Commonplace Book: Folger MS. V. b.198,* ed. Jean Klene (Tempe, Ariz.: MRTS, 1997), xxxii.
4. Louise Schleiner, *Tudor and Stuart Women Writers* (Bloomington: Indiana University Press, 1994), 114.
5. Sarah Ross, *"The compleate Character of Female perfection": Female Honour and Lady Anne Southwell's Religious Verse,* unpublished paper given at "Women, Text and History," Oxford graduate seminar (November 1998), 8.
6. *The "Conceited Newes" of Sir Thomas Overbury and His Friends, a facsimile reproduction of the ninth impression of 1616 of Sir Thomas Overbury His Wife,* ed. James E. Savage (Gainesville, Florida: Scholars' Facsimiles and Reprints, 1968), 226.
7. Nicholas Ling, *Politeuphuia: Wits Common wealth* (London, 1597), f. 26ᵛ.
8. Ann Moss, *Printed Commonplace Books and the Structuring of Renaissance Thought* (Oxford: Clarendon Press, 1996), 208.
9. Savage, *"Conceited Newes,"* 55.
10. Ibid., 11.
11. Bodleian MS Don. c.54, f.22ᵛ.
12. John Donne, *Paradoxes and Problems,* ed. Helen Peters (Oxford: Clarendon Press, 1980), xx.
13. Bodleian MS Eng. Poet. d.3, f.87.

14. *Paradoxes and Problems,* 21.

15. See Peter Beal, *Index of English Literary Manuscripts, 1450–1625,* part 2 (London: Mansell, 1980), 562.

16. Evelyn Simpson, "John Donne and Sir Thomas Overbury's 'Characters,'" *MLR* 18 (1923), 410–415.

17. Savage, *"Conceited Newes,"* 223.

18. Linda Woodbridge, *Women and the English Renaissance: Literature and the Nature of Womankind, 1540–1620* (Urbana: University of Illinois Press, 1984), 118.

19. Diane Purkiss, "Material Girls: The Seventeenth-Century Woman Debate," in *Women, Texts and Histories 1575–1760,* eds. Clare Brant and Diane Purkiss (London: Routledge, 1992), 69–101. Moss, *Printed Commonplace Books,* 208.

20. Folger MS V.b.198, f.16^r

21. Arnold Williams, *The Common Expositor: An Account of the Commentaries on Genesis, 1527–1633* (Chapel Hill: University of North Carolina Press, 1948), 91; *The Sermons of John Donne,* eds. George R. Potter and Evelyn M. Simpson (Berkeley and Los Angeles: University of California Press, 1953), 2:344.

22. *A Mouzell for Melastomus,* 10; *Esther hath hanged Haman,* 6.

23. f.26^v (actually, f.26^r). This and all future citations taken from Klene, *The Southwell-Sibthorpe Commonplace Book.* This particular leaf has been tipped into the manuscript the wrong way round, thus making nonsense of the Defense of Eve. Jean Klene has not noticed the mistake, and has printed the poem with the second half first. I owe this insight to Jonathan Gibson, A.H.R.B. Research Fellow on the Perdita Project at Nottingham Trent University.

24. Jean Klene believes this treatise was rewritten for Charles I, on the basis of lines excised from the Folger version (*The Southwell-Sibthorpe Commonplace Book,* xxxii). However, lines added to the Folger version include a reference to "Demonologye" (139), which I take to be a compliment to James I.

25. *The Southwell-Sibthorpe Commonplace Book,* 151.

26. Henry Peacham, *Minerva Britanna* (London, 1612), 127.

27. Henry Finch, *Observations on the Song of Solomon* (London, 1615), 96.

28. *Song of Songs,* 4:16: see also 4:12–16.

29. I owe this discussion to F. W. van Heertum, in her *Critical Edition of Joseph Swetnam's The Araignment of Lewd, Idle, Froward, and Unconstant Women* (The Cicero Press: Nijmegen, 1981), 87–8.

30. *Paradoxes and Problems,* xxxi.

31. Savage, *"Conceited Newes,"* 145.

32. Woodbridge, *Women and the English Renaissance,* 89–90.

33. *Mortalities Memorandum* (London, 1621), sig. A2^v.

34. *The xv Bookes of P. Ovidius Naso, entytuled Metamorphosis,* tr. Arthur Golding (London, 1587), 51b, 67, 70.

35. John Heath, *The House of Correction* (London, 1619), 36b; Samuel Rowlands, *Good Newes and Bad Newes* (London, 1622), sig. C3; Humphrey Mill, *The Second part of the Nights–Search* (London, 1646), 82, 117, 149, 161.
36. *The Southwell-Sibthorpe Commonplace Book,* 156.
37. Erica Longfellow, *"Bee wise as serpents, innocent as Doues": Lady Anne Southwell's indictment of Adam,* unpublished paper, given at English Faculty Graduate Renaissance Seminar, Oxford, 1999.
38. Stevenson and Davidson, *Early Modern Women Poets,* 197.
39. Northamptonshire Record Office, MS IC 3415.
40. Northamptonshire Record Office, Montagu of Boughton Correspondence, 3:247.
41. Ann Rosalind Jones argues for the superiority of the medium of prose for consistent argument, a benefit that she sees as extending to all three female-voiced pamphlet writers: "From Polemical Prose to the Red Bull: The Swetnam Controversy in Women-Voiced Pamphlets and the Public Theater" in *The Project of Prose in Early Modern Europe and the New World,* eds. Elizabeth Fowler and Roland Greene (Cambridge: Cambridge University Press, 1997), 122–137.

PART II

PRINT, PEDAGOGY,
AND THE QUESTION OF CLASS

CHAPTER 3

MUZZLING THE COMPETITION: RACHEL SPEGHT AND THE ECONOMICS OF PRINT

Lisa J. Schnell

In an important essay that is now over a decade old, Jean Howard gestures toward the subversive possibilities that print held for women in the early modern period:

> If every cultural site is a site of social struggle, attention to the specifics of that struggle may reveal the lapses and contradictions of power that produce social change. Thus, even if, as has been argued, the invention of printing and the admittedly slow increase in women's literacy in the early modern period in part simply increased the ways in which women could be controlled and interpellated as good subjects of a patriarchal order (witness the outpouring of books on housewifery and female piety after the 1580s as documented by Suzanne Hull), nonetheless skills in reading and writing allowed some women access to some authorities (such as scripture) and to some technologies (such as print), which allowed them to begin to rewrite their inscriptions within patriarchy.[1]

Howard is chiefly concerned in her essay with the ideological import of the fiction of cross-dressing in the all-male bastion of the

Renaissance stage. But the powerful statement she makes here
about female textual production is a concise articulation of one of
the primary assumptions that has governed the critical discussion of
early modern women's writing.

Howard's Gramscian invocation of resistance counters the potentially static Althusserian model of the interpellated ideological subject. It also summons a dialectical model of history that has become
a powerful and useful critical model for many feminists: men inter-
pellate; women resist. She is careful to use qualifiers like "some" in
describing the women who resisted their interpellations by the patriarchal forces around them, but there exists nonetheless a certain totalizing tendency in the way Howard understands the early modern
woman in print. Diane Purkiss refers to the "logocentric cycle" that
is set up in certain reading strategies "whereby a female signature
prompts a reading strategy designed to uncover female consciousness
in texts, and this consciousness in turn is held to manifest the presence of a female author."[2] As Purkiss is right to insist, this strategy is
troubling not only because it "elides the literary and textual aspects"
of female textual production, but because it is politically risky, rein-
scribing "singular notions of women's essential character or voice,
writing the female as something immediately visible or identifiable."[3]
And certainly, until only very recently, the study of early modern
women writers has been marked by the overwhelming tendency to
see women authors—and indeed, sometimes even just female signatures—as a largely undifferentiated category.[4]

Nowhere is this more true than in the enormously popular seventeenth-century debate on gender, which came to a head in the years
approaching 1620 with the 1615 appearance of a particularly scurrilous pamphlet and the several replies that followed close on its
heels. Joseph Swetnam's *The Arraignment of Lewd, idle, froward and
unconstant Women* occasioned at least three published responses
from writers who claimed to be women: Rachel Speght's *A Mouzell
for Melastomus,* Esther Sowernam's *Esther hath hanged Haman,* and
Constantia Munda's *The Worming of A mad Dog,* all published in
1617. Taking their cue largely, I think, from Gilbert and Gubar's
powerful (and powerfully entrenched) model of the subversive potential of print, many of the feminist critics who have written about
the 1617 pamphlets base their arguments on the assumption, as Jean
Howard does in the passage with which I began, that the courageous
entrance into the technology of print allows women to "begin to
rewrite their inscriptions within patriarchy."[5] What Howard and others fail to take into consideration is the fact that print was not only a

technology but also a growing *economy* in the period. And this was particularly true of the seventeenth-century controversy over gender, a middle-class controversy fueled (or created) by canny booksellers who recognized a market when they saw one. In the essay that follows, I want to look particularly at the fate of Rachel Speght, the one writer in the controversy who was inarguably a woman. Viewing Speght's pamphlet *A Mouzell for Melastomus* and the response to it by the pseudonymous Ester Sowernam in the context of a fledgling literary economy affords an entrance to a version of early modern women's literary history that looks quite different from Howard's.

The Business of Woman Hating

The seventeenth-century debate on gender, as Katherine Henderson and Barbara McManus point out, was a product of the burgeoning middle class, and particularly the tastes and interests of the middle-class male:

> Alongside the age-old picture of the woman as dangerous sexual temptress these pamphlets place the portraits of the scolding, domineering shrew and the vain spendthrift ruinously draining her husband's finances. These are not new images of women, for they appear as early as Hesiod, but they are given special prominence in the Renaissance attacks, presumably because of their particular appeal to the bourgeois audience of these pamphlets.[6]

In the massive *Middle-Class Culture in Elizabethan England,* Louis Wright widens this picture:

> A serious undercurrent of intelligent thinking upon woman's status in a new commercial society is evident even in some of the more jocular treatises. Nor was this vital social problem, which became the theme of an increasing number of writers eager to please a public interested in every phase of the relations of men and women, the sole concern of middle-class men of letters. . . . But it is clear that the taste and opinions of the commercial elements in society had an important influence upon the development of new social ideas as well as upon the literature in which these ideas were reflected.[7]

Despite the somewhat reductive formulation of literature as a mirror of society, Wright reminds us, as does the passage from Henderson and McManus, that middle-class society was a highly *commercial* society in the early seventeenth century and that the place of women in that economy was the subject of considerable anxiety. As Diane Purkiss succinctly puts it, "woman is less an object of interest in herself than a site of conflict between classes and discourses."[8] Her prodigality is an issue because, as Purkiss points out, "she can spend money but cannot produce it."[9] She is also a pleasure—a sexual pleasure—who can be exchanged for money or gifts. And yet the pleasure that she produces is more or less the same regardless of her price or the status of the consumer. And that makes her a commodity without real measure, and with a highly unstable value, an obvious locus of anxiety in the male-defined economies of early modern England.

A common seventeenth-century proverb, explained by Swetnam in the first chapter of his 1615 *Arraignment,* perfectly illustrates this particular male anxiety:

> Jone is as good as my lady; according to the Country-mans Proverbe, who gave a great summe of money to lye with a Lady, and going homewards, he made a grievous mone for his money, and one being on the other side the hedge, heard him say, that his Jone at home was as good as the lady.[10]

And yet despite the specificity of this economic anxiety, one senses in Swetnam a more generalized threat:

> For women have a thousand wayes to intise thee, and ten thousand waies to deceive thee, and all such fooles as are suitors unto them, some they keepe in hand with promises, and some they feede with flattery, and some they delay with dalliances, and some they please with kisses: they lay out the foldes of their hare to entangle men into their love, betwixt their breasts is the vale of destructions, & in their beds there is hell, sorrow & repentance. Eagles eat not men till they are dead but women devour them alive.[11]

The danger clearly seems to be that male sexual pleasure is also male vulnerability. One of the reasons that pamphlets such as Swetnam's often conflate female speech with female sexual entrapment seems to lie in the perceived threat that women would speak aloud of the male vulnerability they were privy to as objects of male pleasure, a vulnerability, once revealed, that might topple the myth of unassailability on which an exclusively masculine economy was based.

And yet while Swetnam's pamphlet brilliantly radiates its masculine anxiety in these spectacular displays of misogyny, the overall tone of the *Arraignment* differs substantively from the harshly moralistic cadence adopted by its puritanical cousins; it is clearly one of the "jocular treatises" to which Wright refers. It is hard to imagine, for instance, any of the Protestant conduct manuals containing Swetnam's scatological anecdote involving Socrates, whose response to being hit over the head with a chamber pot by his wife is, "ha ha . . . I thought after all this thunder there would come raine."[12] Or the anecdote involving Annynious, in which the joke is shared even by the shrewish wife, for whom laughter—entertainment—functions as a kind of cure for her ill-temperedness:

> There is an history maketh mention of one named Annynious, who invited a friend of his to go home with him to supper, but when he came home he found his wife chiding and brawling with her maydens, whereat his guest was very much discontented. Annynious turning to him, said; good Lord how impacient are thou? I have suffred her these twenty yeares, and canst not thou abide her two houres? By which meanes he caused his wife to leave chiding, and laughed out the matter.[13]

Such anecdotes are clearly meant to entertain, and Swetnam seems to have this in mind from the very beginning, when he introduces the pamphlet as itself a form of prodigal entertainment, a "Bearbaiting of women."[14]

Behaving in many ways like Beaumont and Fletcher's *Knight of the Burning Pestle*, which was performed only a few years before Swetnam composed his *Arraignment,* the entertainment trope in Swetnam's pamphlet functions at once rhetorically inside the text and pragmatically within an economy *outside* of the text. *Knight of the Burning Pestle* famously lampoons the new bourgeois in England in the characters of the boorish grocer and his outspoken and vulgar wife. The two memorably "buy" *The Merchant's Daughter,* the play they have ostensibly come to see, for their apprentice Rafe, who becomes the valiant and nearly eloquent Knight of the Burning Pestle in the hilarious rewrite that is directed by the grocer and his wife from the audience. The multivalent entertainment trope of the play brilliantly explores the nature of theatrical illusion inside the play, but it also gestures to a world outside the play in its portrayal of the vulgar bourgeois worldview of the (only too believable) grocer and his wife, a worldview that is beginning, more and more, to exploit entertainment as something that can be bought and sold in the new merchant economy.

Like Beaumont and Fletcher, Swetnam and his bookseller both understand the purchasing power of the new merchant classes and

see into their anxieties. Misogyny sells, particularly when it is also en-
tertaining. Significantly, though, entertainment in this instance
comes in the form of print, not a play. And that marks Swetnam's *Arraignment* and the appearance of the several responses that it occasions as a more significant literary event than we may have yet
recognized. Typically, we put the appearance of *print* entertainment
for the middle classes—avid reading for pleasure—somewhere in the
second half of the seventeenth century in England. And we usually
refer to those earliest forms of middle-class print entertainment as
precursors to the novel.

It would be an enormous taxonomic stretch to refer to any single
one of the pamphlets in the Swetnam controversy as a precursor to
the novel.[15] And yet, there is much to be gained by putting the controversy in the light of recent studies of the origins of the English
novel, particularly those by Lennard Davis (*Factual Fictions: The Origins of the English Novel*) and William Warner (*Licensing Entertainment: The Elevation of Novel Reading in Britain, 1684 - 1750*). Davis
argues for a discursive theory of the rise of the novel that involves
what he calls an "ensemble" of written texts, an ensemble in which
he includes ballads, newspapers, and letters, but also nonnarrative
printed material such as parliamentary statutes, advertisements, and
printer's records. "In opening the field in this way," claims Davis, "it
is possible to trace a discourse which may be considerably wider, with
different limits and rules than our modern conceptions of fiction and
the novel allow us to apply to the eighteenth century."[16] The aim of
Davis' book is to "understand the system of order that exists among
texts, as well as between texts and society."[17] Warner takes us closer
to understanding the way in which Swetnam's *Arraignment* and, in
fact, the entire controversy, with its aims of entertainment, might
participate in the rise of novel reading when he "redefines the literary history of the novel so that it becomes a subset of the cultural history of print entertainments."[18] Certainly the controversy, as an early
example of printed popular entertainment, contributes to the *conditions* of novel reading in England (part of the relationship of text to
society that Davis talks about) by assisting in the establishment of an
avid reading public, a middle class willing to pay to be entertained by
small books issued in serial form.[19]

But if Swetnam (and, I will argue, his pseudonymous respondent
Sowernam) seems particularly aware of the entertainment value of
the controversy,[20] Speght, the only one of the eight major contributors to the Swetnam and cross-dressing controversies of 1615–1620
to publish under her own name[21] and, of all eight writers, perhaps

the only woman, seems thoroughly ignorant of her participation in a market-driven entertainment economy. The question of what happens to her, a real woman with earnest aims in a patently artificial environment, thoroughly disturbs the feminist positivism inherent both in the majority of critical pieces on the controversy and in the more general approach to early modern women in print. A paradise of women this controversy most emphatically was not.

A Muzzle for a "Minister's Daughter"

In his edition of the pamphlets that make up the Swetnam controversy, Simon Shepherd tells the story—as best as he can reconstruct it—of the publication of Esther Sowernam's pamphlet, *Esther hath hanged Haman*. Arguing for his hypothesis that the pseudonymous Sowernam is indeed a woman, Shepherd claims that the only place we can see unassailable evidence of male involvement with the pamphlet is in the history of its publication:

> The 1616 and 1617 reprints of Swetnam's work were printed by Thomas Snodham to be distributed by Thomas Archer. It was Snodham who, early in 1617, printed Sowernam's pamphlet, but for a different distributor (Snodham possibly venturing on his own?). It could be that he arranged for Sowernam to answer Swetnam: she tells us that a gentleman brought her a copy of Swetnam's work at the start of the Michaelmas Term (9 October). Certainly someone seems to have rushed her pamphlet out before she was quite ready for it, since she tells us in the preface to the second part that she is planning a third part, which never appears. . . . It is easy to see the reason for Snodham's haste: on 14 November 1616 it was revealed that the original distributor, Archer, already had his hands on an answer to Swetnam (Speght's pamphlet).[22]

Constantia Munda, another pseudonymous respondent to Swetnam later in the same year that Speght wrote *A Mouzell*, may also have been associated closely with a printer. As Shepherd tells us, "Munda's printer was Purslowe, one of the 1615 printers of Swetnam, for Thomas Archer. Purslowe printed Munda for a different distributor. The pamphlet seems a rushed job: the syntax and structure are a mess, and there is no paragraphing."[23] As for Speght, Barbara Lewalski fills in that side of this picture when she speculates that, most likely, the young woman was, herself, "solicited by Archer to write this rejoinder in an effort to reawaken the controversy two years later and sell more books."[24]

Despite the fact that neither Shepherd nor Lewalski extend their discussion of these facts much beyond the telling of them, they seem to me to be enormously significant details in a critical understanding of the controversy as a whole and of Speght's particular position inside it. First of all, it is clear that a few printers and one bookseller in particular—Thomas Archer—manufactured and choreographed the entire Swetnam controversy. Secondly, the publishing history makes it clear that there was a market behind the controversy that was driven by popular taste, not by high standards of literary excellence. Speght, perhaps known in certain circles as a learned young woman with literary aspirations, seems to have quite unwittingly been adopted by the profit-minded Archer, who may have slightly misjudged his author. Certainly Speght's *Mouzell* seems in its earliest pages to advertise a wide gulf between the author's pious naiveté and the interests of a much more entertainment-minded reading public.

A Mouzell for Melastomus is unclouded by complicated justifications and equivocations. Unvexed by irony, written in an unabashedly plain style, the pamphlet is the work of an idealistic young woman, an intelligent eighteen year old urgently defending her sex not with radical feminist ideas but with a carefully argued Protestant polemic. Well read but not, perhaps, particularly well educated in the ways of the world, Speght's naiveté is best evinced by the dedicatory epistle, in which she addresses women of considerably higher rank than herself and appeals both to a sense of female solidarity and to her assumption that her addressees will protect her from the scurrilousness of people like Swetnam:

This my briefe Apologie (Right Honourable and Worshipfull) did I enterprise, not as thinking my selfe more fit then others to undertake such a taske, but as one, who not perceiving any of our Sex to enter the Lists of encountring with this our grand enemy among men, I being out of all feare, because armed with the truth, which though often blamed, yet can never be shamed, and the Word of Gods Spirit, together with the example of virtues Pupils for a Buckler, did no whit dread to combate with our said malevolent adversarie. And if in so doing I shall bee censured by the judicious to have the victorie, and shall have given content unto the wronged, I have both hit the marke whereat I aymed, and obtained that prize which I desired. But if *Zoilus* shall adjudge me presumptuous in Dedicating this my *Chirograph* unto the personages of so high rank; both because of my insufficiency to literature and tendernesse in yeares: I thus Apologize for my selfe; that seeing the *Bayter of Women* hath opened his mouth against noble as well as ignoble; against the rich as well as the poore; therefore meete it is that they should be joynt spectators of this encounter. And with-all in regard of my imperfection both in learning and age, I need so much the more to impetrate patronage from some of power to sheild mee from the biting wrongs of *Momus,* who oftentimes setteth a rankling tooth into the sides of truth.[25]

The earnestly self-assured tone of the epistle, the slightly ostentatious display of learning, the careful mimicry of the well-established trope of the humility topos, the ambitious expectations of audience—all these things point to a well-meaning, literarily determined young woman who, for all her learning, may not have had the tools to recognize irony.

And indeed, the three pseudonymous poems "In praise of the Author and her Worke" that follow Speght's own epistles, poems almost certainly solicited by the bookseller Archer, would seem to flout the young woman's relative unworldliness. The first poem, by 'Philalethes,' compares Speght to the biblical David, for "with the fruit of her industrious toyle, / To this Goliah [*sic*] she hath given the foyle" (10). All of which might be read without irony until the third and final stanza, when, with the kind of equivocation often associated with epigrammatic verse, the author writes:

> Admire her much I may, both for her age,
> And this her Mouzell for a blacke-mouth'd wight,
> But praise her, and her worke, to that desert,
> Which unto them belongs of equall right
> I cannot; onely this I say, and end,
> Shee is unto her Sex a faithfull friend. (10)

Similarly, 'Favour B.' in his encomiastic verse:

> Her wit and learning in this present Worke,
> More praise doth merit, then my quill can write:
> Her magnanimitie deserves applaud,
> In ventring with a fierie foe to fight:
> And now in fine, what shall I further say?
> But that she beares the triumph quite away. (11)

Aside from their equivocal claims that Speght's skill surpasses their powers of description, both Philalethes and Favour B. seem most concerned to point out Speght's age and status: the first writer compares the "young encombatant" to "little David" (10); the latter refers to her as "a Virgin young, and of such tender age, / . . . Shee having not as yet seene twenty yeares" (11). Speght—and by extension her book—is being cannily marketed in these poems as a kind of spectacle, an entertainment: come see the little virgin take on the big bad misogynist!

Indeed, the persona we encounter in the carefully organized tract that follows lives up to her billing. Enthusiastic and eager to demonstrate her learning, she writes about things she could not possibly know about first hand, but on which she is only too willing to declaim:

> Marriage is a merri-age, and this worlds Paradise, where there is mutuall love. Our blessed Saviour vouchsafed to honour a marriage with the first miracle that he wrought, unto which miracle matrimoniall estate may not unfitly bee resembled: For as Christ turned water into wine, a farre more excellent liquor; which, as the Psalmist saith, *Makes glad the heart of man;* so the single man is by marriage changed from a Bachelour to a Husband, a farre more excellent title: from a solitairie life unto a joyfull union and conjunction, with such a creature as God hath made meete for man, for whom none was meete till she was made.(22)

Speght's strategy, as Purkiss incisively points out, and as this passage illustrates, "is to negotiate a position for woman to speak, write and defend herself from within the discourses of morality which insisted on her silence, to oppose Swetnam by abducting authority from the very discourse he disrupts."[26] Unfortunately, the context in which she writes—particularly the market-driven context—did not appreciate such strategies except to flout them. And indeed, once we get to the pamphlet by Sowernam, we discover that Speght has—quite literally—been set up as a kind of sacrificial virgin in the controversy, her earnest and ingenuous ambition only grist for the mill that was Thomas Archer's book trade.

Sowernam's response to Speght's pamphlet was virtually immediate.[27] There is no telling who this writer was, or even if she was a woman.[28]But debate about the sex of the author of the Sowernam pamphlet obscures what seems to me to be the real set of corrections that are being offered by this writer to Speght. We have only to look at Sowernam's dedicatory epistle to be struck by the enormous difference between this tract and Speght's. Like Speght, Sowernam dedicates her pamphlet to "all right Honorable, Noble and Worthy Ladies, Gentlewoman,"[29] but that's where the resemblance ends:

> Right Honorable and all other of our Sex, upon my repair to London this last Michaelmas Term; being at supper amongst friends, where the

number of each sex were equal, as nothing is more usual for table talk there fell out a discourse concerning women, some defending, others objecting against our Sex. Upon which occasion, there happened a mention of a Pamphlet entitled *The Arraignment of Women,* which I was desirous to see. The next day a Gentleman brought me the book, which when I had superficially run over, I found the discourse as far off from performing what the Title promised as I found it scandalous and blasphemous. (218–9)

If this writer is impersonating a woman, that woman is most notably *not* from the same class as Speght: the implication is of a country-house, legal affairs in London ("Michaelmas Term" referring to the Inns of Court), the dinner party and the sophisticated table talk, a gentleman courier. Indeed, when the writer acknowledges Speght some ten lines later, she is not referred to by name, but only as a "Minister's daughter." And then, stripping away the equivocations of the poems that introduce Speght's work, she says:

Upon this news [of Speght's pamphlet] I stayed my pen, being as glad to be eased of my intended labor as I did expect some fitting performance of what was undertaken. At last the Maiden's Book was brought me, which when I had likewise run over, I did observe that whereas the Maid doth many times excuse her tenderness of years, I found it to be true in the slenderness of her answer. . . . So that whereas I expected to be eased of what I began, I do now find myself double charged, as well to make reply to the one, as to add supply to the other. (219)

In the pamphlet itself, we are struck both by Sowernam's unstinting refusal to capitulate to a Protestant morality and by the tremendous difference in tone from Speght's pamphlet. First, there is a colossal display of learning: on the first page, and in a segment of no more than ten lines of prose, Sowernam quotes from or alludes to St. Jerome, St. Chrysostom, Julian the Apostata, "Lucian the Atheist," and Homer, all of which seems deliberately aimed at putting Speght in her place. Furthermore, where Speght is earnest and ingenuous, Sowernam is detached, witty, experimental in form, including in her tract a parody of a formal indictment of Swetnam (a display, perhaps, of her worldly expertise in legal affairs). The pamphlet is simply a lot more fun to read than Speght's. And clearly that is precisely the point. For while the argument is immensely learned, it seems clear that Sowernam's stake in this matter is that of someone involved, as Linda Woodbridge has said, not in a serious defense of women, but in a "sophisticated literary sport."[30]

Speght stumbles onto this playing field in a clerical collar, and she suffers no small degree of humiliation at the hands of (perhaps a great impersonator of) a woman who is dressed much more appropriately for the game. Furthermore, whether or not Esther Sowernam was really a woman, the upper-middle-class posturing of the writer raises the question of whether the aristocratic and high-ranking bourgeois female audience to which Speght directed her pamphlet would ever have been interested in a "regular" middle-class woman's call for sexual equality. Although it would be wrong to generalize absolutely, it would by and large seem true that women of the aspiring ruling class had no interest in fighting for anything like "rights" if it would mean the loss of privilege. Then, as now—and surely we *do* recognize this from within our own time and place—it is chiefly middle-class women who take up the battle for women's rights. Yet—and surely we also recognize this—the everywhere-implied charge of humorlessness that is launched at the earnest, and I think admirable, Speght from somewhere in the upper and urbane reaches of the social atmosphere has the overall effect of canceling her challenge to patriarchal power, which is also the power of the aspiring ruling class and, in this case, the power of a successful middle-class entertainment economy.[31]

"I FEELE MY SELFE NOT VERY WELL"

Four years after the Swetnam controversy, Speght writes and publishes *Mortalities Memorandum*. Notably, Thomas Archer's name is not on the title page; she had found a new bookseller, Jacob Bloome, for her new volume. Also, she dedicates the book to her godmother, Mary Moundford, who, though well placed socially as the wife of a prominent court physician, might have been slightly more predisposed to the young woman's literary endeavors. Still, Speght makes it clear that she has hardly forgotten her flogging at the hands of her critics, particularly those who claimed that her clergyman father had written *A Mouzell for Melastomus*:

> Having bin toucht with the censures of the other, by occasion of my *mouzeling Melastomus*, I am now, as by a strong motive induced (for my rights sake) to produce and divulge this ofspring of my indevour, to prove them further futurely who have formerly deprived me of my due, imposing my abortive upon the father of me, but not of it. Their varietie of verdicts have verified the adagie *quot homines, tot sententiae*, and made my experience confirme that apothegme which doth affirme Censure to be inevitable to a publique act.[32]

And though she claims here to have gamely taken the censure in stride, she squeezes a few sour grapes into the opening words of her epistle to the reader: *"Readers too common, and plentifull be; / For Readers they are that can read a,b,c. / And utter their verdict on what they doe view, / Though none of the* Muses *they yet ever knew"* ("To the Reader" 1–4). Speght's use of the word "common" would seem to demonstrate that she is fully aware of the class-inflected attacks on her and, notably, that she is not above slinging some of the same mud. In this case, however, she equates class with literary ability, claiming, by implication, that she is fully acquainted with the muses in a way that Sowernam and Munda are not. Again, it seems, Speght has missed the point: the controversy was never about who was the "better" writer, but who could most entertain, who could sell the most books. Speght's invocation of class overlooks the crucial middle-class economy of the book trade. Class, nonetheless, remains a prominent issue for Speght in the self-described "sequel" she writes to her ill-fated pamphlet of 1617. And her exploration of it in *Mortalities Memorandum*, while it continues to demonstrate the collision of Speght's class sensibility with the considerably more sophisticated sensibilities of her censurers, also demonstrates without distortion why reading the gender controversy of the seventeenth century as an early modern example of feminist unanimity bears so little fruit.

In many ways a richer, more interesting volume than the earlier pamphlet, *Mortalities Memorandum* is made up of two long poems. The first is an autobiographical allegory entitled "The Dreame," in which the speaker, Speght, seeks life-giving Knowledge in a garden with the help of several female companions. Speght's dreamscape is "most pleasant to the eye" (21) but otherwise indescribable: "Where stranger-like on every-thing I gaz'd, / But wanting wisedome was as one amaz'd" (23–4). Her surroundings are not beyond description; they are beyond *her* description. The allegorical earth, unfamiliar and inhospitable, forces silence on Speght. The wisdom she "wants" for speech thus becomes the quest of the poem, and a host of female allegorical figures are made responsible for directing the dreamer on her quest.

The sympathetic character Thought is the first to approach the dumbfounded Speght. Responding to Thought's inquiry as to her state, Speght replies that she suffers from a grief called Ignorance. Her intent, she tells Thought, has always been "to seeke the golden meane" (55) but in spite of her vision, she involuntarily falls "into extremes" (57). She asks to be relieved from the responsibility for these errors of judgment. Beneath her careful response to Thought is her frustration, even indignation, with a system that imprisons her in a kind of paradox of objectification: through her ignorant eyes, the world is so completely objectified—"I know not what is bad or good" (54)—that she is forced to revert to the most extreme form of subjectification—"I measure all mens feet by mine owne shooe" (65), a metrical allusion to her sense of literary isolation.

Thought counsels the dreamer to seek Knowledge in Erudition's garden, an Eden whose natural sustenance will cure the ailments of the disconsolate dreamer. Suddenly, however, the eavesdropper Disswasion bursts upon the scene with his own brand of advice:

> Disswasion hearing her assigne my helpe,
> (And seeing that consent I did detect)
> Did many remoraes to me propose,
> As dulnesse, and my memories defect;
> The difficultie of attaining lore,
> My time, and sex, with many others more. (104–9)

The dreamer's instinctive reaction to Disswasion's diatribe is to "re-coyle and yeeld" (112), a response with which Speght was no doubt sadly familiar. What is significant, however, is the response of the female community around her. Thought is suddenly joined by an entire company of female companions who all take arms against the enemy Disswasion: "No, quoth Industrie, be assured this, / Her friends shall make thee of thy purpose misse" (120–21). Truth initiates the most sustained response to the interloper's objections, first summoning Paul—"Both man and woman of three parts consist, / Which Paul doth bodie, soule, and spirit call" (127–8)—and then invoking the standard model for the defense of women by providing examples of significant women from history who were recognized for their intellectual power: Mary ("she the better part did love" [139]); Cleobina, Demophila, and Telesilla, ancient poetesses; Cornelia, an eloquent Roman writer; Hypatia, an astronomer; Aspatia, a rhetorician. The last exemplary woman Truth names is the artist Areta:

> Areta did devote her selfe to art:
> And by consent (which shewes she was no foole)
> She did succeed her father in this schoole. (149–51)

The particular canniness that Areta exhibits is an ability to work within the dominant—male—ideology toward her own ends, something we have seen Speght attempt to do in the *Mouzell*. The continuation of Truth's lecture, now directed to Speght, in fact manifests yet another example of that strategy. The speaker narrates, "Thus having sayd, she turn'd her speech to mee, / That in my purpose I might *constant* bee" (156–7, emphasis mine). The word "constant" is repeated three times in the next four stanzas; yet, it is removed from its popular usage as the masculinist definition of eros—a woman's constancy to her man—and is instead transformed into an intellectual virtue that leads directly into a utopian garden of unrestrained intellectual pleasure. As the dreamer wanders with another female companion, Desire, through the garden, she is schooled on the female intelligence that governs the place:

> True Knowledge is the window of the soule,
> Through which her objects she doth speculate;
> It is the mother of faith, hope, and love;
> Without it who can vertue estimate? (217–20)

The dreamer willingly obeys the counsel of Desire, "To covet Knowledge daily more and more" (232), and she does so "till some occurrence called [her] away" (234). However, on her way back to that "place" from whence she came, the dreamer is forced to travel through an inhospitable landscape, home to all the real-life oppressors of her literary fate, who we find covered with only the sheerest allegorical veil. In this hostile environment she has a skirmish with a "full fed Beast" [Swetnam] (242), encounters "a selfe-conceited Creature" who "past her censure on my weake exployt" [Esther Sowernam] (249–50), and meets "the childe of Prudence" [Constantia, daughter of Prudentia Munda] (256). And then, suddenly, a monster with whom neither we nor she are familiar appears, a "fierce insatiable foe" (268) who, "without respect of age, sex, or degree . . . did devoure and could not daunted be" (270–71). He is, she realizes, Death, and at the very moment of recognition he throws a "perceiving [pearcing] dart" at her mother (281). This, in turn, causes her "so to weepe" that she awakes—and finds that her "dreame was true" (282, 284).

The incident serves as a segue to Speght's meditation about death in the eponymous poem that follows the "Dreame" in the volume. As such, it points to the many ways in which death functions as subject matter for Speght in this, her last published writing. Barbara Lewalski, noting, as many others do, that the long poem on death is "replete with religious commonplaces" and undistinguished in prosody, nonetheless acknowledges its interest as a cultural artifact:

"[Speght's] experience with the market-driven *querelle* controversy may have prompted her to recognize the large middle-class market for books on piety, devotion, and self-analysis as an opportunity for a would-be professional woman writer."[33] Purkiss goes one step further and suggests that behind the volume lies "immediate imperatives such as literary competition and the defence of reputation."[34] Referring to the last section of the "Dreame," Purkiss asserts that by "stigmatising her competitors . . . Speght makes apparent the economic stakes in the production of responses to Swetnam; the debate was a game with two sides, and the female signatories jostle for position, explaining away their own apparent superfluity by criticizing each other."[35]

Certainly, wound around the seemingly inviolate edifice of scripture in *Mortalities Memorandum,* are the reminders of what has come before:

> If poverty be our appointed lot,
> Our griefe is great, reliefe and comfort small,
> We must endure oppression, suffer wrong,
> The weake in wrestling goeth to the wall:
> If we be bit, we cannot bite againe,
> If rich men strike, we must their blow sustaine.
>
> If we be eminent in place of note,
> Then stand we as a marke for envies dart,
> Conjecture censures our defect of worth,
> Inquirie doth anatomize each part,
> And if our reputation be but small,
> Contempt and scorne doth us and ours befall.(71)

We recognize this immediately as self-referential, an oblique description of Speght's own situation as a pious and fair-minded middle-class woman with literary ambitions. Her struggle, as "The Dreame" illuminates, is against the "inquirie" that "doth anatomize each part," the dismantling of her vision of a united female community, regardless of degree, by her critics. The impossibility on earth of ever discovering that integrated community is abundantly expressed in *Mortalities Memorandum* in the trope of the diseased body:

> The bodie is in danger (every part)
> Of hurt, disease, and losse of sense, and lym,
> Auditus unto deafnesse subject is,
> Visus of blindnesse, or of being dym,

Gustus of savours, bitter, tart, and sowre,
Olfactus unto loathsome stinks each houre. (69–70)

"The Dreame" is the unsuccessful attempt to construct a coherent intellectual self from the disparate pieces of the body Speght writes of here; *Mortalities Memorandum* is its sequel. And as such, it elegizes the failed earthly utopia by turning to a heavenly utopia that, within the confines of this poem, cannot possibly fail:

What is this world, if ballanced with heaven;
Earths glorie fades, but heavenly joyes indure,
This life is full of sicknesse, want, and woe;
But life through Christ hath no disease to cure.
In heaven there is no maladie or paine,
But melodie, true comfort to maintaine.(66)

The playful linguistic transformation of "maladie" into "melodie" in the last two lines of the stanza suggests a fantasy of heaven as a place where literary skill will determine one's individual reality.

Speght constructs the walls of her own Jerusalem, a place where neither age, sex, nor degree counts for anything, with the various constituents of this last literary exercise. And for Speght, this takes the form of literary equality: the ultimate triumph of death is its capacity to make every person's story end the same way:

The greatest Monarch of earths Monarchie,
Whom God with worldly honours highly blest,
Deaths Beesome from this life hath swept away,
Their stories Epilogue is *Mortuus est.*
For Death to all men dissolution brings,
Yea, the Catastrophe it is of Kings.(79)

And yet, the volume is not just the next round in a literary catfight. For in order for Speght to claim victory against her earlier censurers— the victory of a social vision as much as a desire for literary achievement—she has to take herself out with them. And she seems poignantly aware of that throughout the volume, but particularly in the episode involving the death of her mother. Whether she awakes from her dream to find her real mother dead or to find, as I think is more likely and in keeping with the general allegorical tone of the poem, that Knowledge, the "mother of faith, hope, and love" (57) from Erudition's garden, is dead, it is clear that that death also signals the dissolution of Speght's own identity. *Mortalities Memorandum* is

the attempt by Speght to write a sequel to both the Swetnam controversy and the final terrifying vision of the "Dreame" that will negate
both the censoriousness of her critics and the rapaciousness of Death
in the "Dreame" by claiming victory through a Christian understanding of salvation. But it is an ambivalent victory for the literarily ambitious Speght. For in order for Speght to rise above the pettiness of the
Swetnam controversy to embrace the revolutionary social power of
Death, she must also, paradoxically, accept its silence. This is finally
where Speght's elaborate apology leads her: the final gesture in her attempt to reclaim the social vision she embraced in 1617 is to censure
herself, to determine and then to impose the terms of her own isolation. She is never heard from again—the critics seem surprised, but
they shouldn't be. She has been conquered by a new economy that
has crushed her own literary idealism, and she has written her own literary obituary.

NOTES

1. Jean Howard, "Crossdressing, the Theatre, and Gender Struggle in
   Early Modern England," *Shakespeare Quarterly* 39 (winter 1988),
   427–8.
2. Diane Purkiss, "Material Girls: The Seventeenth-Century Woman
   Debate," in *Women, Texts and Histories 1575–1760,* eds. Clare Brant
   and Diane Purkiss (London: Routledge, 1992), 71.
3. Purkiss, 71.
4. Examples abound of pseudonymous texts to which are affixed the
   caricatures of female signatures: Jane Anger, Ester Sowernam, Constantia Munda, Joan Hit-him-home, Mary Tattlewell. Purkiss' argument is supported by the inclusion of all the above in one of the most
   influential anthologies of early modern women's writing, a collection
   whose title alone goes directly to the heart of her critique: Betty
   Travitsky's *The Paradise of Women* (New York: Columbia University
   Press, 1989). But beyond the title of the collection, the short blurbs
   on the pseudonymous writers in particular reveal the unexamined logocentric assumptions of which Purkiss is justly critical. In the case of
   Jane Anger, for instance, an early entrant into the early modern debate on gender, Travitsky confidently asserts, "The individual who
   wrote under this pseudonym apparently is the earliest woman to have
   written a feminist pamphlet in England" (103). Purkiss, on the other
   hand, suggests that "[t]he names do not clearly illustrate female
   agency; rather, they illustrate the taking-up of the position of a disorderly woman for the purpose of signifying disorder of some kind,
   domestic or political" ("Material Girls," 85).

5. Purkiss catalogues the responses of feminist critics to these texts, responses that enthusiastically assume the female—and feminist—authorship of all three of the 1617 pamphlets. See Purkiss, 70.

6. Katherine Usher Henderson and Barbara F. McManus, eds., *Half Humankind: Contexts and Texts of the Controversy about Women in England, 1540–1640* (Urbana and Chicago: University of Illinois Press, 1985), 24–5.

7. Louis Wright, *Middle-Class Culture in Elizabethan England* (Ithaca: Cornell University Press, 1935), 507.

8. Purkiss, 74.

9. Ibid.

10. Joseph Swetnam, *The Arraignment of Lewd, idle, forward, and unconstant women* (London, 1615), 9. See Purkiss, 76–7, for an extended discussion of this point.

11. Swetnam, 15–16.

12. Swetnam, 39.

13. Ibid.

14. Swetnam, sig. A3V. See Purkiss, 75–8, for an extended discussion of the rhetorical significance of the entertainment trope in the *Arraignment*.

15. In fact, when viewed as a whole, the pamphlets together actually bear some resemblance to the popular print entertainment that develops in the latter half of the seventeenth century: they are issued in what amounts to serial form; sexual innuendo and intrigue figure highly; there is realistic conflict between characters. In fact, there is even a semi-detectable plot involving Rachel Speght, the young naïf—virtue personified—who is dismissed by her more worldly respondents and the narrative as a whole but who resurfaces in the narrative's final installment to get the last word.

16. Lennard J. Davis, *Factual Fictions: The Origins of the English Novel* (New York: Columbia University Press, 1983), 7.

17. Davis, 8.

18. William Warner, *Licensing Entertainment: The Elevation of Novel Reading in Britain, 1684–1750* (Berkeley, Los Angeles, and London: University of California Press, 1998), xi.

19. Surprisingly, Louis Wright is the only critic I have found to acknowledge the controversy's participation in the rise of the novel: "Not the least important of the influences of the literary controversies about woman was the stirring of the public interest in still more discussion of the subject and the creation of an atmosphere favorable to the development of the drama and the novel of domestic relations" (*Middle-Class Culture*, 507).

20. Besides the self-consciousness of the bear-baiting metaphor in the introduction to the *Arraignment*, it seems equally significant that he never revisited the controversy he initiated and, almost too good to

be true if metaphors are what we're after, that his next book was a manual on fencing, *The Schoole of the Noble and Worthy Science of Defence* (1617).

21. Swetnam actually signs the epistle that introduces the *Arraignment* with the pseudonym Thomas Tell-troth.

22. Simon Shepherd, ed., *The Women's Sharp Revenge: Five Women's Pamphlets from the Renaissance* (New York: St. Martin's Press, 1985), 86.

23. Shepherd, 126.

24. *The Polemics and Poems of Rachel Speght,* ed. Barbara Lewalski (New York and Oxford: Oxford University Press, 1996), xv.

25. Lewalski, 5. All subsequent quotations from *A Mouzell for Melastomus* are from this volume.

26. Purkiss, 93.

27. According to Shepherd, Archer announced that he had in hand an answer to Swetnam's pamphlet (Speght's) on November 14, 1616. Thomas Snodham, the printer and possibly distributor of the Sowernam pamphlet, takes it to press early in January 1617.

28. Lewalski thinks it likely that both of the pseudonymous answers to Speght that appeared in 1617—Sowernam's *Esther hath hanged Haman* and Constantia Munda's *Worming of a mad Dog*—were written by men representing themselves as women (Lewalski, xv), while Shepherd clings fast to the probability that the writers are women, citing as his most compelling piece of evidence the fact that Speght refers to Sowernam as a "she" in *Mortalities Memorandum.* According to Shepherd, "given [Speght's] annoyance at being criticised it would probably have been convenient to have revealed that the 'self-conceited creature' was a man. News travelled easily and quickly in London" (86). Henderson and McManus (*Half Humankind*) seem simply to assume, like Betty Travitsky in *The Paradise of Women,* that both Sowernam and Munda are female, referring to both of them throughout their volume with uninflected female pronouns. Ironically, although Speght is arguably the only woman writer in the controversy as Henderson and McManus frame it—a hundred years from *The Schoolhouse of women* (1541) to *The women's sharpe revenge* (1640)—Speght is entirely omitted from the anthology.

29. Henderson and McManus, 218. All subsequent quotations from *Esther hath hanged Haman* are from this volume.

30. Linda Woodbridge, *Women and the English Renaissance: Literature and the Nature of Womankind, 1540–1620* (Urbana and Chicago: University of Illinois Press, 1986), 98.

31. "Constantia Munda" was the other respondent to the Swetnam controversy. Her pamphlet, *The Worming of a mad Dog,* is not without interest, but as the main clash appears to have been between Speght

and Sowernam, I have chosen, in the interests of space, to limit my discussion to the latter two.

32. Lewalski, 45. All subsequent quotations from *Mortalities Memorandum* will be from this volume and will be indicated by line number.

33. Lewalski, xxvii–xxviii.

34. Purkiss, 92.

35. Ibid.

CHAPTER 4

WOMEN'S POPULAR CULTURE?
TEACHING THE SWETNAM
CONTROVERSY

Melinda J. Gough

This essay suggests a method of teaching the seventeenth-century
gender debates that expands our definition of literature by early
modern women. My case study involves a course unit on the Swetnam controversy, taught first to undergraduates and subsequently in
a graduate seminar. In both courses, students read works by male authors such as Shakespeare, Sidney, and Jonson together with
women's writings of the period, ending with the Swetnam controversy's anonymous and pseudonymous works. The successes and pitfalls of teaching early modern women writers together with their
more canonical male counterparts have begun to be explored in
leading scholarly journals (the winter 1996 volume of *Shakespeare
Quarterly*) and at a number of conferences, namely the 1996 MLA
special session "Teaching Judith Shakespeare" and the 1997 Shakespeare Association of America seminar by the same name. The majority of this work considers how to teach the bard alongside
aristocratic women writers. Such pedagogical approaches may help
to de-center Shakespeare's authority. But they also run the risk of
merely recanonizing elite authors and genres in ways that sidestep

the more radical implications of a cultural studies approach to the early modern period. Teaching Renaissance pamphlet debates on women together with anonymously authored popular drama can provide a useful corrective to this tendency, one that allows us to refine rather than delimit understandings of early modern women as consumers, authors, and subjects of popular culture.

I am likely not the first to teach the Swetnam controversy in a course on Shakespeare and women writers. To date, however, there has been little public attempt to theorize the teaching of such texts in conjunction with one another. This theoretical gap exists in part because the anonymous or pseudonymous authorship of many texts in the pamphlet controversy complicates received notions of gendered authorship central to gynocritical archaeological projects. After all, the female authorship of texts such as the *Urania* and *The Tragedy of Mariam* has been the central consideration for justifying their inclusion on Renaissance syllabi. Yet as Diane Purkiss has pointed out, the search for a tradition of women's writings at times has resulted in a tautological cycle "whereby a female signature prompts a reading strategy designed to uncover female consciousness in texts, and this consciousness in turn is held to manifest the presence of a female author."[1] Such an approach, Purkiss notes, is not only logically suspect; it is also politically dangerous insofar as it threatens to reinscribe essentializing notions of woman's character or voice. As a feminist teacher of the early modern period, I encourage my students to challenge such universalizing notions of gender on ideological and historical grounds. I have found that including texts from the seventeenth-century woman debates in a course on male and female writers engages students in such a critique while avoiding the resilencing of women that post-structuralist methodologies might seem to imply. Studying the Swetnam controversy while viewing authorship itself as an intertextual and collaborative phenomenon can expand our notions of early modern women's agency. Attending to not only literary and social contexts but also the material conditions and practices of the playhouse allows students and scholars alike to concretely challenge received notions about the anonymity and silence of nonelite women in particular.

The two courses this case study discusses were offered at Oklahoma State University in the Department of English. Because the department has no established upper-division course number devoted to special topics in Renaissance literature, I offered the undergraduate course within the familiar rubric of "the Shakespeare course" and advertised it widely under the title "Shakespeare and

Shakespeare's Sisters." This course was organized loosely around types of rebellious women represented in the literature of the period: "Shrews and Scolds" (*Taming of the Shrew*); "Virgins and Amazons" (*Midsummer Night's Dream*); "Cruel Beloveds and Cross-Dressers" (*As You Like It,* Shakespeare's *Sonnets,* Wroth's *Love's Victory, Hic Mulier,* and *Haec Vir*); "Witches" (*Macbeth* and *The Witch of Edmonton*); and "Learned Women: Patrons, Translators, and Playwrights" (*Antony and Cleopatra,* Sidney's *Tragedie of Antonie,* Cary's *Tragedy of Mariam,* and Jonson's *Volpone*—the latter's Lady Politic Would-Be as a satire of the self-styled learned woman). In our final unit, entitled "The Debate about Women," students recognized many of these same female types in two pamphlets—Joseph Swetnam's *Arraignment of Lewd, idle, froward, and unconstant women* (1615) and Esther Sowernam's *Esther hath hanged Haman* (1617)—as well as the anonymous play *Swetnam the Woman-hater Arraigned by Women* (published 1620). The second course, "Gender and Authorship in the Early Modern Period," was an advanced special topics graduate seminar, the scope of which allowed for greater diversity of texts by women, including Wroth's sonnet sequence, Margaret Cavendish's play *The Convent of Pleasure,* and Rachel Speght's pamphlet *A Mouzell for Melastomus* (1617). Requiring students to read secondary criticism, the course also encompassed more explicit theorizing on the relationship between authorship and female agency (see Appendix).

The first reason to read the pamphlet controversies in such courses stems from a pedagogical difficulty aptly articulated by Nancy Gutierrez: when students read the bard and early modern women authors side by side, they may well continue to privilege William over his "sisters" on the basis of aesthetic criteria.[2] Indeed, while feminist academics often choose particular texts—to edit, interpret, and teach—on the basis of intellectual and political considerations, students coming to these same texts, especially for the first time, often experience them on a largely aesthetic level, taking pleasure (or not) in ways that may be learned but are generally experienced as intuitive and hence universal. Students often experience unfamiliar closet dramas by women, for example, as boring or difficult. To discourage such reactions, I used a number of strategies. For example, I avoided placing male and female authors in pairs, which implicitly encourages competition; instead I grouped them in triangles. Equally importantly, I further "evened the playing field" by including popular literary genres among the works by women. My working definition of the "popular" considered target audience but also availability: early

modern popular culture thus included any text or performance "produced by and offered for the enjoyment or edification of the largest
combinations of groupings possible within that society," but also any
text or performance "familiar because it was cheap enough to buy or
to gain admission to see, or was free to be heard and seen, or even
performed oneself."[3]

Finding such popular works by women, however, proved easier said
than done. Looking to scholarship on Renaissance women's writing,
I found little discussion of nonelite women, "nonelite" defined as the
95 percent of the population neither noble nor gentle.[4] Likewise, historical studies of early modern popular culture have tended to follow
the lead of Peter Burke, who confessed that he had "too little to say
about women, for lack of evidence."[5] Gynocritical scholars of the
English Renaissance, too, seemed to have concluded that a search
such as mine could only be fruitless. According to Barbara Kiefer
Lewalski, for example, "the only texts we have through which to explore how Jacobean women read and began to write themselves and
their culture are by women of position, education, and privilege."[6] I
suspected nonetheless that studying the reception and performance of
popular genres could prove more useful to an understanding of early
modern women than pronouncements such as Lewalski's and Burke's
might suggest. This belief stemmed in part from my involvement as a
coleader for two workshops on early modern women's popular culture at the 1997 Attending to Early Modern Women conference and
the 1999 Berkshires Conference on the History of Women. Drawing
on research regarding nonelite women as consumers and performers
of popular materials such as ballads, jigs, and jests, these workshops
asked in what sense poor female ballad sellers, illiterate fishwives and
alewives, and female alehouse customers might be considered "authors" as well as consumers. We looked for answers in the oral genre
that Joy Wiltenburg has termed "street literature": pamphlets and
broadsides containing "songs, jokes, news, and stories," all of which
"reached a far wider audience than more sedate volumes . . . [since
m]any who were unable or unwilling to buy or read the texts heard
them sung or spoken in taverns, fairs, and streets."[7] If writing is no
longer deemed the sole measure of literacy, new understandings of
women's cultural agency might also be implied by recent research on
women and theatrical production, including records that challenge
notions of women's exclusion from Renaissance popular and courtly
performance as well as playhouse audiences.[8]

Including such questions and popular materials in our course
readings involved numerous subdecisions. First, I chose Frances

Dolan's edition of *The Taming of the Shrew* as one of our texts because it reproduces a number of shrew-taming ballads and orally circulated tales, offering a cogent and compelling argument for reading the play as part of this larger popular discourse about wife beating and taming in the period. Startled at being asked to imagine a continuum between Shakespeare's play and such "low brow" forms, students found their assumptions about the bard's genius suddenly subject to question. In the graduate seminar, students theorized this experience when asked to categorize Dolan's critical and editorial methodologies: for example, noting that her edition lacks the traditional introductory biographical sketch of Shakespeare, graduate students voiced the recognition that Dolan in effect substitutes "early modern culture" for the author's life as privileged context through which readers should interpret the play. Having read Foucault's "What is an Author?" graduate students mused on the "author-function" and its particular resonance for understanding Shakespeare's cultural authority in relation to popular discourses available to and about women. Such questions aptly set the stage for our subsequent discussions about early modern women authors and the pseudonymous and anonymous pamphlets of the Swetnam controversy.

Another choice of reading material—*The Witch of Edmonton*—required undergraduate students to read popular drama with roots in or analogues to popular printed forms. This play paired nicely with *Macbeth* for a discussion of witchcraft, but also allowed us to foreground questions of collaborative authorship and intertextuality. To address such issues I brought to students' attention the trial literature on which Dekker, Ford, and Rowley drew in writing this play. "To what extent can the real Elizabeth Sawyer, the witch whose words are 'recorded' in these trial pamphlets and quoted in the play, be said to be one of the 'authors' of this collaboratively written text?" I asked. As Marion Wynne-Davies has argued, although "the word 'author' has come to mean the setting forth of written statements with a concurrent claim to the sole ownership of that text," this definition is not universal but itself has a history: until the seventeenth and eighteenth centuries, a looser sense of literary property allowed the term "author" to connote more widely "the initiator or instigator of a work, someone who gave existence to something in any number of ways," such that Queens Anna of Denmark and Henrietta Maria were referred to by various foreign ambassadors as "authoresses" of masques they patronized and in which they performed. For Wynne-Davies, the masque considered as a collective cultural construct offers a discourse that "opens up 'authorship' to women."[9] But popular pamphlets and drama may also serve this function, including not only elite but also poor women among the ranks of cultural agents. Attending to Mother Sawyer's status as the initial, living speaker of words repeated in both trial transcripts and a popular play enabled my students to imagine not only powerful queens but even an illiterate, poverty-stricken woman as an "initiator or instigator" of dramatic and textual forms and hence as a kind of "author" in her own right.

My third important decision when forming our reading lists was to teach *The Tragedie of Antonie* in a manner meant to introduce students to historically specific notions of authorship relevant to this "closet drama" but also useful for later discussions of the woman debate. In this section of the course, students read Sidney's translation of Garnier's play together with Shakespeare's *Antony and Cleopatra*. Comparing Enobarbus' famous description of Cleopatra's barge with Shakespeare's source for this passage in North's Plutarch solidified students' new understanding that Shakespeare's authorial talent could not be equated with originality per se. When we turned to Sidney, contextualizing her work in light of Renaissance theories of translation and imitation, our discussions centered around a set of related questions: what is the status of a translation in relation to the "original" work, especially in this period? was translation gendered at this time, and if so, how? and finally, could translation be considered women's writing, and if so, in what ways might it give women a "voice"?

A handout based on Reina Green's discussions of women and translation in the early modern period addressed these questions on several levels, beginning with a brief outline of relevant facts.[10] For example, approximately one-third of the works published by Renaissance Englishwomen in this period were translations; although John Florio calls translation "defective" and "femall," his own most influential work was a translation of Montaigne; translation, moreover, was considered essential to male education in the period, and the majority of Renaissance translations were by men. Translation was not considered work worthy of women only, then; so too the view of translation (and of literary imitation more generally) as a second-class form of writing stemmed more from a Romantic concept of the author than from actual early modern views. Given these facts, choosing what text to translate or imitate could be as important an act of political agency for a woman as was her choice to write at all. So although we might initially reject as proto-feminist Renaissance women's translations of religious work insofar as religious doctrine of the period tended to support traditional gender hierarchies, in historical context such translations could have been seen as especially daring politically if the works translated espoused prohibited doctrines: while feminist critics make much of Cary's *Tragedy of Mariam* as the first original drama in English by a woman, for example, Cary's decision to translate and publish the *Reply of the Most Illustrious Cardinall of Perron* (1630) might have been more bold an act than was her choice to write a play.

Armed with such ideas about imitation and translation as vehicles for literary and political agency, we then turned to Sidney's *Tragedie of Antonie*. Familiar with the plot after having read Shakespeare on the same subject, students at both undergraduate and graduate levels nonetheless found Sidney's verse and syntax exceptionally difficult. To overcome this problem, the undergraduates responsible for leading a class session on Sidney's play devised small-group exercises aimed to help their peers better understand the literal level of Antony and Cleopatra's long speeches, moving from such basics to an appreciation of Sidney's thematic content and formal innovations. To this end, the student presenters chose what they found to be particularly difficult scenes from Sidney's play and "translated" them into modern English on handouts from which we read aloud in class. Reading such student-authored "translations" made studying Sidney fun: class members quickly noted the increased pacing accomplished by shifts from lengthy speeches to short, rhymed interchanges between characters. As a result, they returned to Sidney's text able to appreciate this closet drama on its own terms rather than judging it negatively by comparison with more familiar, popular dramatic genres. Further, these undergraduate adaptations of Sidney proved useful tools in my graduate seminar two years later. Having read Shakespeare together with North's Plutarch, graduate students read aloud the undergraduate translations of Sidney; I then asked whether they would consider the undergraduate students to be in any sense "authors" of those passages, and the answer was a resounding "yes." In light of these exercises and discussions, students were more willing to consider Sidney's translation as art and Shakespeare's writing as intertextually informed. They thus broadened their previous notions of singular authorship while simultaneously coming to appreciate the contributions of women translators.

After laying the groundwork by thus questioning the authority and originality of the single author, we turned to the Swetnam controversy. When I first decided to include this unit in my undergraduate course, I had assumed that both the pamphlets and the play were authored by women. My belief was based on statements by the editors of *Half Humankind,* who argue strongly for female authorship of the pamphlets; additionally, the appearance of *Swetnam the Woman-hater* on the list of works available through the Brown Women Writers' Project led me to believe that the database compilers must have had some evidence for its female authorship.[11] A further survey of secondary materials on the seventeenth-century pamphlet debates made me reconsider such assumptions. While critics and editors such as Ann Rosalind Jones, Betty Travitsky, Elaine Beilin, and Simon Shepherd seemed to take women's authorship largely for granted, despite the occasional footnote to the contrary, someone like Anthony Low, in a 1997 review article of recent Renaissance nondramatic criticism, could assert the male authorship of such pamphlets with equal aplomb, claiming that Speght's tract "was the first and only woman's contribution to the famous quarrel."[12] If neither the popular nature nor the female authorship of such texts could be taken for granted, I wondered, how would I teach this material? And how would I justify having included it on our syllabus?

One clear reason to teach the unit lay precisely in its potential for disrupting assumptions about the relationship between an author's gender and the meanings of his or her text. Absence of knowledge of the author's gender in turn opened up for consideration collaboration between an all-male acting company and its female patrons. In the case of *Swetnam the Woman-hater,* these patrons included women both royal (Queen Anna, the titular patron of the company performing this play) and base (paying female spectators at the Red Bull, the theatre where it was performed).

To address this issue of collaboration between the acting company and its women spectators, I placed the unit on the Swetnam controversy immediately following a class period devoted exclusively to the broader topic of women in the theatre. For this session, students read the documents on women and theatrical affairs in the *Renaissance Drama by Women* anthology.[13] Assembling evidence representing women as spectators, performers, employees, patrons, and owners of theatres, the editors of this anthology usefully discuss the genuine influence that women from all socioeconomic groupings had on the English Renaissance theatre as paying customers and even shareholders in acting companies. With such questions in mind, students were well prepared to read the play *Swetnam the Woman-hater Arraigned by Women* with an eye to the central role it imagines for female spectators.[14]

Each course devoted two weeks to the Swetnam controversy. Students began by dividing into small groups for a formal debate, one side arguing Swetnam's position and the other Sowernam's.[15] Having to argue a thesis out loud helped students envision more strongly a sense of audience and purpose for their own argumentative essays. Moreover, the activity of debating generally tends to make students more actively engaged in the material under consideration, and these debates were no exception. Students became highly animated during their "performances" of Swetnam and Sowernam, gleefully imitating the pamphlets' most witty rejoinders, jests, and arguments and making them their own (much the same way that students had adapted Mary Sidney's verse to their own). They thus gained a better grasp of the pamphlets than would have been possible had I merely rehearsed for them an outline of the arguments under consideration. In post-debate discussions, for example, students reflected on the way in which the discursive disorder of Swetnam's pamphlet makes Sowernam's more structured response appear reasoned and logical. Graduate students gained an even better appreciation for Sowernam's rhetoric by comparing her pamphlet to Speght's. Asked to contrast the personae and arguments of these two tracts, they expressed admiration for Speght's ability to assert her own authority as both *writer* (signing the pamphlet with her own proper name) and nuanced *reader* capable of interpreting Swetnam but also scripture. If Sowernam's "voice" appears cool and collected by contrast with Swetnam's, they noted, Speght's seems even more so when contrasted with both.

Familiar with the female-voiced pamphlets that respond to Swetnam's attack on women, students then turned to the play that gives dramatic voice to this debate. *Swetnam the Woman-hater* begins with Atticus, King of Sicily, grieving the death of his eldest son. His second son, Prince Lorenzo, is missing and presumed dead. Atticus forbids his daughter Leonida to see the man she loves, Lisandro, Prince of Naples. Yet Leonida and Lisandro do meet and are caught. A public disputation is held to decide the relative guilt of men and women in love, a debate whose outcome will determine which of the two lovers will be killed and which merely banished. Meanwhile, Lorenzo, the lost prince of Sicily, has returned to spy out treachery in the kingdom. Hearing of his sister's plight, Lorenzo disguises himself as the Amazon Atlanta and volunteers to speak for women in the formal dispute. Lorenzo/Atlanta's opponent in the debate is none other than Swetnam himself. Driven out of Bristol and London by mobs of angry women, Swetnam has come to Sicily under the alias "Misogynos" and soon struts his stuff as the Advocate for men and against women in the formal dispute.

Asked to compare the pamphlets with the on-stage debate between Swetnam/"Misogynos" and Lorenzo/Atlanta, students found
marked resemblances. A more heated discussion ensued when we discussed the play's decision to give responsibility for women's defense
to a male character impersonating a woman. One female undergraduate suggested that having a man take up the female cause legiti-
mated that cause. Others, male and female, pointed out that because
Lorenzo/Atlanta loses the debate, the play implies that had a real
woman argued the case, she might have been more effective. One
writes:

> As a man, Lorenzo/Atlanta is debating Swetnam, also a man. This
> means that Swetnam did not defeat a woman in his debate. The pos-
> sibility here is that had a woman been debating Swetnam, she might
> have won. Lorenzo, not being female, did not have the same view-
> point that a woman would in the same situation. The best he could
> do . . . was to try to gather as many references as he could to justify a
> female situation in Leonida's defense.[16]

This student essay does not specify the basis—essential or cultural—for
Lorenzo's limited viewpoint with respect to the woman debate.
Nonetheless, it makes claims for a specific female knowledge and thus a
specifically gynocentric epistemological and rhetorical power. One
graduate student final exam makes a similar assertion, but more sophis-
ticatedly inflects identity politics with notions of social construction:

> What is interesting about Lorenzo's cross-dressing is the degree to
> which it is successful. His ability to so flawlessly . . . perform the female
> gender goes unquestioned throughout the play, and it is in this, per-
> haps, that we can find a way around the play's apparent ideological
> dilemma: while the play may seem to suggest that women cannot de-
> fend themselves, the failure of a cross-dressing man to defend women
> adequately can be read as an indication that the defense of women is
> something only women are capable of doing properly.[17]

The overwhelming student reaction to the onstage debate, however,
was outrage: male and female students alike sensed that the play had
betrayed the expectations raised by its title. To them, the fact that
within the fiction the defense of women is taken up by a man seems
condescendingly to imply women's inability to defend themselves. By
giving the starring role in the defense of women to a male character,
the play may offer only a backhanded compliment to women, undermining their defense by insinuating women's incapacity themselves

to articulate it. Students further inferred from Lorenzo/Atlanta's role a new possibility about the pamphlets themselves: by giving the defense of women to a man disguised as a woman, might the play suggest that the pamphlets with female signatures, too, could only have been penned by men? This reading seems to support Elizabeth Harvey's assertion that "[v]entriloquizations of women in the Renaissance achieved the power they did partly because so few women actually spoke and wrote, but representations of women's speech that were current in literary and popular accounts, as well as in ventriloquizations, fostered a vision that tended to reinforce women's silence or marginalize their voices when they did speak or write." If having a cross-dressed man defending women seems such a betrayal, I asked, what does this imply about playwrights such as Shakespeare, male authors who in a sense could be said to "cross-dress" along with the male actors insofar as the only women's voices in their plays are male, ventriloquized via female characters like Kate and Rosalind? Undergraduate students in particular reacted to this question with stunned silence, as if contemplating an analogy between Lorenzo and their beloved Shakespeare was too much to bear. For the first time, it seemed everyone in the room had realized that studying women writers was not equivalent to studying women characters in works by male writers, that attending to women's writings could be a valuable act in and of its own right.

In the graduate course, this realization was underscored when students considered Ann Rosalind Jones's claim that in translating prose to drama, *Swetnam the Woman-hater* silences what in the pamphlets had been extended, rhetorically adept passages offering valuable "proof of women's ability to reason and argue."[18] Extending such insights, graduate students were struck by the way in which the play has women defeat Swetnam not verbally so much as physically:

> Since the conflict has not been resolved by legal and so-called rational argument [after the formal disputation], the play turns to violence. The violence of Leonida's execution is intended, in part, to quiet her and the women's claims that she has been misjudged and treated unfairly. The action [her death] is not a settling of the argument but an attempt to teach women to be silent, chaste, and obedient. The violence once begun spreads to Misogynos who plans to use Atlanta for sport, then discard her, another woman used as a target for his aggression. Undeceived by Misogynos' claims to love her, Atlanta fights back, physically striking and pummeling Misogynos until he surrenders. Then she turns him over to a group of revenge-hungry women who physically torment him and when the play ends he is in a muzzle,

finally quieted not by superior arguments but by superior strength (emphasis mine).

Though women may be vindicated, the play does not offer women an *articulate* voice to the same extent that the female-voiced pamphlets do.

Yet from a different perspective the shift from words to action, prose to theatre, may not entirely disempower women.[19] This anonymous play, refusing to announce its author's gender, dramatizes in particularly vivid form how a focus on women's writing per se may prove a limited strategy for assessing a given text's contribution to early modern women's cultural agency. An alternative approach would be to consider the play in light of performance and reception conditions.

This topic formed the basis of our final session on the Swetnam controversy. Discussion focused on the play's prologue and epilogue, both of which make direct appeals to women spectators in the audience of the Red Bull playhouse.[20] Discussing the prologue in light of our readings on women and the theatre, students produced thoughtful close readings. On the one hand, the prologue makes explicit the play's reliance on women spectators: Loretta announces that "The Women are All Welcome" and asks those female audience members to "Lend but your kind assistance." On the other hand, the prologue acknowledges the demand for misogynist humor, to which the play, like Swetnam's pamphlet, panders: "the men will laugh, I know, to see us railed at and abused." The epilogue treats with similar ambivalence the play's dependence on female spectators for its success. The stage directions for the epilogue read, "Enter Swetnam muzzled, hal'd in by Women." The scene thus recalls not only Speght's metaphor of muzzling but also the mob of women within the play who literalize that metaphor as part of their arraignment of "Misogynos." Swetnam complains, "Is't not enough, / I haue withstood a tryall? beene arraign'd? / Indured the torture of sharp-pointed Needles? / but I must stand, / To haue another Iurie passe on me?" Loretta insists on the necessity of this final jury, i.e., the women in the audience, for "It was a general wrong; therefore must haue / A generall tryall, and a Iudgement too." According to Hilda Smith,

If a woman faces a particular problem it is the feminist's first inclination to place this problem into the context of women's defined sexual role. She (and feminists are overwhelmingly female) will more quickly than a nonfeminist pose the question 'why' about any difficulty which befalls an individual woman. . . . If a feminist learns of the restrictions placed upon an individual woman her immediate response is to place this instance within her understanding of the general pattern of women's existence. And it is this chain of thought, above all else, which stamps an individual as a feminist.[21]

Loretta, by this definition, may be considered a proto-feminist character, insofar as she insists that the wrong done to Leonida by Atticus and then Swetnam/Misogynos is not merely an insult to her personhood that she alone can forgive but instead constitutes an attack on Leonida's entire sex. Indeed, the play concludes with Swetnam's appeal to not only Leonida but also her collective sisterhood, the women in the Red Bull audience:

> I now repent,
> And thus to you (kind Iudges) I appeale.
> . . . .
> And here for-euer I put off this shape,
> And with it all my spleene and malice too,
> And vow to let no time or act escape,
> In which my seruice may be shewne to you.
> And this my hand, which did my shame commence,
> Shall with my Sword be vs'd in your defence.

Swetnam, like the male actor who plays him, quite literally gets the last word. That word, however, includes concessions designed to flatter women spectators. The epilogue thus registers the small but real power of audience demand, that of the female audience in particular. Indeed, the play may have been designed especially to appeal to the tastes of nonelite women spectators, including the noisy "oyster wives" and "fish wives" known to frequent the Red Bull, just as contemporary works of prose fiction drew on the pamphlet controversy in an appeal to a more literate female readership. If the middle-class Rachel Speght asserted in print her right to read and judge, these less literate women at the Red Bull playhouse likewise asserted their right to see, hear, and judge. That power, in turn, is registered in performance but also in the printed script alluded to in the epilogue's last lines. The shift from prose to playhouse may have limited women's voices in one sense, but in another it may also have expanded the occasions available to women for exercising influence over popular cultural forms.

Direct appeals to women spectators like that of this epilogue make perfect sense given what theatre historians have to tell us about the financial arrangements of Queen Anna's servants, the acting company that performed this play. According to G. E. Bentley, the land on which the Red Bull theatre was built had been leased to Aaron Holland by one Anne Bedingfield, executrix for her late husband Christopher.[22] Moreover, in 1612, several years before *Swetnam the Woman-hater* was produced, a woman—Susan Baskerville—inherited the shares her husband, the clown Thomas Greene, had owned in this acting company; as Cerasano and Wynne-Davies note, Mrs. Baskerville eventually achieved near complete financial control over the company, a power that was already quite pronounced by 1618 - 19, the period during which *Swetnam the Woman-hater* was likely performed.[23] In very concrete terms, then, not only noble women like Queen Anna but also women investors of the middling sort—namely Susan Baskerville—enjoyed influence, including direct financial influence, over this theatre and its male actors.

Contemporary depictions of Red Bull audiences, indeed, attest to the power of even the poorest female spectators. For example, Dekker's prologue to *If This Be Not a Good Play, the Devil is in It*, dedicated to the Queen's Men at the Red Bull, complains: "A play whose Rud[e]ness, Indians would abhore, . . . fill[s] a house with fishwives, Rare, they all Roare. / It is not Praise is sought for [now] but Pence, / Tho dropd, from Greasie-apron Audience."[24] Like the prologue and epilogue to *Swetnam the Woman-hater*, these lines suggest a Red Bull playwright's reluctant alliance with the lower-class women who patronized him through their "pence." In light of such evidence about women in the playhouse, my students determined that although the *Swetnam* epilogue asks women in the audience to take mercy on a (reformed) misogynist character—a somewhat suspect request—it does imply that these women, by asserting their right to look and judge, maintained a measure of autonomy and agency, one to which the all-male acting companies needed to make at least tongue-in-cheek concessions in order to achieve an imaginatively successful comic ending and mount a commercially successful play.

The Swetnam controversy stuck with my students: more than one-third of the final papers by undergraduates discussed the pamphlets and play; the unit also dominated exam essays in both courses. Debunking myths of unified authorship did not destroy student interest in women writers; on the contrary, all students wrote about women's writings even though they were not required to do so. And when asked to compare works by male, female, and anonymous authors in terms of gender roles, students offered complex, non-essentialist interpretations. For example, one undergraduate wrote:

Scanfardo, referring to the goodness in some women, tells "Misogynos," "Methinks you are too general; some, no doubt /As many men,
are bad: condemn not all for some" (I.ii. 360–1). So too the reader
must also be aware of the stereotypes placed on both male and female
authors. Readers often rely on a gender-indicating name to determine
the way in which they expect the author to write.

Such students owe a significant debt to feminist scholars engaged in
uncovering early modern women's voices. Without the archaeological projects such scholars have engaged in, our courses simply would
not have been possible. Passages like this one, however, confirm that
in significant ways our students have much to teach us as well.

APPENDIX

GRADUATE SEMINAR SYLLABUS

GENDER AND AUTHORSHIP
IN EARLY MODERN ENGLAND

FALL 1999

Shakespeare in Love celebrates women's literary and theatrical agency. In
doing so, however, the film arguably privileges notions of the single, unified
author; of literary creativity as the expression of authentic emotion and experience; and of gender identity as natural rather than constructed. What difference did gender really make in the production and consumption of early
modern English literature? Was there actually a Renaissance for women, and
for women writers in particular? To address such questions we will read
poems and plays by men and by women, some popular pamphlets and dramas penned with pseudonymous and anonymous signatures, contemporary
documents on women and theatre, and a number of critical essays.

We will begin with *The Taming of the Shrew,* a play that either enforces or
calls into question the prevailing paradigm of the Renaissance woman as
chaste, silent, and obedient. We will then consider this paradigm in works
by Shakespeare and his contemporaries both male and female: Elizabeth
Cary's *Tragedy of Mariam;* sonnet sequences by Philip Sidney and Mary

Wroth; three comedies (*A Midsummer Night's Dream*, Wroth's *Love's Victory*, and Margaret Cavendish's *The Convent of Pleasure*); and two "translations" (Shakespeare's *Antony and Cleopatra* and Mary Sidney's *Tragedie of Antonie*).

Much critical analysis of gender in such works has assumed that all women were de facto excluded from the stage during this period and that nonelite women in particular faced a more extreme silencing. Indeed, all of the female-authored plays on our reading list were written by aristocratic women for private performance, not for the professional stage. Yet recent archival and theoretical work indicates that women actively shaped popular literary and theatrical materials in concrete ways. Turning to a selection of contemporary documents on women and theatre, we will therefore attend to nonelite women in an attempt to consider "why the all-male stage wasn't." This section of the course will begin with popular debates about women, including pamphlets penned with male and female signatures and an anonymous play—*Swetnam the Woman-hater Arraigned by Women*—which draws on those pamphlets and calls on nonelite women spectators to defeat the play's misogynist character. This defeat is only accomplished, however, in alliance with Atlanta the Amazon (really the prince Lorenzo in disguise). What does it mean that not only a boy actor but also a male character in drag is required to vanquish the misogynist? To answer this question and explore its implications for our assessment of female agency in the period, we will consider "cross-dressing and the difference it makes" in *Swetnam the Woman-hater* and *The Roaring Girl*, comparing these Renaissance performances with those of Gwyneth Paltrow and Joseph Fiennes in the recent film *Shakespeare in Love*.

All of the women authors and characters studied this term may be considered Shakespeare's contemporaries or "sisters." So we will end, appropriately, with Shakespeare's fictional sister Judith in Virginia Woolf's *A Room of One's Own*. Given the variety of real and imagined early modern women in our readings, what strengths and weaknesses can we now discern in Woolf's myth? in the gynocritical projects it has inspired?

COURSE GOALS:

- to read and discuss a range of sixteenth- and seventeenth-century English works, dramatic and nondramatic, elite and popular
- to actively engage with several influential strands of criticism in Renaissance studies, particularly debates about gender and the literary canon
- to develop and exercise skills in presenting ideas orally and in leading class discussion
- to gain expertise as scholars by developing skills as readers, critical thinkers, and persuasive writers of argument
- to write a term paper that is potentially publishable

TEXTS:

Cavendish, Margaret, *The Convent of Pleasure and Other Plays* (Johns Hopkins)
Cerasano and Wynne-Davies, eds., *Renaissance Drama by Women* (Routledge)
Shakespeare, *Taming of the Shrew: Texts and Contexts* (Bedford Critical Edition)
A Midsummer Night's Dream (Folger Shakespeare Library Edition)
Antony and Cleopatra (Arden Edition)
Evans, ed., *Elizabethan Sonnets* (Everyman)
Henderson and McManus, *Half Humankind* (Illinois)
Woolf, *A Room of One's Own* (Harcourt Brace)

READINGS AND ASSIGNMENTS:

Weeks 1 and 2	Introduction; Shakespeare, *The Taming of the Shrew;* Dolan, chapters 3 and 4. *Recommended:* Foucault, "What is an Author?"
Week 3	Cary, *The Tragedy of Mariam. Recommended:* "The Lady Falkland Her Life" (in Ferguson and Weller, eds., *The Tragedy of Mariam*)
Week 4	Sidney, *Astrophil and Stella. Recommended:* Jones and Stallybrass, "The Politics of *Astrophil and Stella*"
Week 5	Wroth, *Pamphilia to Amphilanthus. Recommended:* Masten, "'Shall I turne blabb?': Circulation, Gender, and Subjectivity in Mary Wroth's Sonnets"
Week 6	Shakespeare, *A Midsummer Night's Dream;* Montrose, "'Shaping Fantasies': Figures of Gender and Power in Elizabethan Culture"
Week 7	Wroth, *Love's Victory. Recommended:* Lewalski, "Mary Wroth's *Love's Victory* and Pastoral Tragicomedy," and Miller, excerpt from *Changing the Subject*
Week 8	Cavendish, *The Convent of Pleasure*
Week 9	Shakespeare, *Antony and Cleopatra;* Plutarch, excerpt from "Life of Marcus Antonius"
Week 10	Mary Sidney, *Tragedie of Antonie*
Week 11	Swetnam, Sowernam, Speght. *Recommended:* "Part I: The Contexts" (*Half Humankind*)
Week 12*	*Swetnam the Woman-hater;* Gough, "Contextual Materials for *SWH*" (*Renaissance Women On-Line*). *Recommended:* Purkiss, "Material Girls: The Seventeenth-Century Woman Debate"; Harvey, *Ventriloquized Voices,* introduction and chapter 1
Week 13	"Documents: Women and Theater"; Howard, "The Materiality of Ideology"; Thompson, "Women/'women' and the stage"
Week 14	*Shakespeare in Love;* Dekker and Middleton, *The Roaring Girl*
Week 15	*The Roaring Girl;* Woolf, *A Room of One's Own*

NOTES

1. Diane Purkiss, "Material Girls: The Seventeenth-Century Woman Debate," in *Women, Texts and Histories 1575–1760,* ed. Clare Brant and Diane Purkiss (London: Routledge, 1992), 69–101, esp. 71. See also Elizabeth D. Harvey, *Ventriloquized Voices: Feminist Theory and English Renaissance Texts* (London: Routledge, 1992), esp. 15–53.

2. Nancy Gutierrez, "Why William and Judith Both Need Their Own Rooms," *Shakespeare Quarterly* 47.4 (winter 1996), 424–32.

3. This formulation combines David Mayer's definition of popular drama (as cited in Alexander Leggatt, *Jacobean Public Theatre* [London: Routledge, 1991], 28) with Pamela Allen Brown's definition of the popular in *Better a Shrew than a Sheep: Gender and Jest in Early Modern England* (Ph.D. dissertation, Columbia University, 1998), 6.

4. Nonelite persons included artisans, day laborers, and retailers; rural smallholders; and citizens and burgesses. See Andrew Gurr, *Playgoing in Shakespeare's London* (Cambridge: Cambridge University Press, 1987), 50–80.

5. Peter Burke, *Popular Culture in Early Modern Europe* (New York: Harper Torchbooks, 1978). Tim Harris summarizes this tendency in "Problematising Popular Culture," in *Popular Culture in England, c. 1500–1850,* ed. Harris (New York: St. Martin's Press, 1995), 4. For additional work addressing this gap, see the essays by Martin Ingram and Bernard Capp in *Popular Culture in Seventeenth Century England,* ed. Barry Reay (London: Croom Helm, 1985), and Susan Amussen, "The Gendering of Popular Culture in Early Modern England," in Harris, *Popular Culture in England,* 49. For a justification of women's history as a discipline, based on the assertion that history should not be equated with understandings of the elite alone, see Hilda Smith, "Feminism and the Methodology of Women's History," in *Liberating Women's History: Theoretical and Critical Essays,* ed. Berenice A. Carroll (Urbana: University of Illinois Press, 1976), 368–84.

6. Barbara Kiefer Lewalski, *Writing Women in Jacobean England* (Cambridge, Mass.: Harvard University Press, 1993), 4.

7. Joy Wiltenburg, *Disorderly Women and Female Power in the Street Literature of Early Modern Germany and England* (Charlottesville: University Press of Virginia, 1992), 29–30. On women as ballad audiences and buyers, see Wiltenburg, 25–31, 38–9, and Jonathan Barry, "Literature and Literacy in Popular Culture: Reading and Writing in Historical Perspective," in Harris, *Popular Culture in England,* 66–94, esp. 82. On women singing and selling ballads, see Hyder Rollins, "The Black-Letter Broadside Ballad," *PMLA* 27 (1919), 277, 308, 319–23, and Wiltenburg, 27. On the ballad genre more generally, see Natascha Wurzbach, *The Rise of the English Street*

Ballad, 1550–1650 (Cambridge: Cambridge University Press, 1990). On nonelite women represented in ballads, see also Diane Dugaw, *Warrior Women and Popular Balladry, 1650–1850* (Cambridge: Cambridge University Press, 1989). For women performing in popular games, festive dances, and jigs, see Charles Read Baskervill, *The Elizabethan Jig and Related Song Drama* (Chicago: University of Chicago Press, 1929), esp. 11, 13, 19, 33, and 110. On women and jest, see Brown, who notes that such popular texts and performances would be either affordable to most women or available to all through reading aloud or oral repetition from memory (6–7). Ballads cost a penny; so did spaces in the pits of public theatres. Jests and ballads circulated in alehouses, where a quart of ale or beer cost twopence. Pamphlets or chapbooks cost anywhere from three- to four-pence for shorter texts and up to shillings or pounds for longer ones.

8. David Cressy, in *Literacy and the Social Order: Reading and Writing in Tudor and Stuart England* (Cambridge: Cambridge University Press, 1980) estimates a less than 10 percent literacy rate for Englishwomen from 1580 to 1700, with up to 20 percent for women in London. Yet, as Margaret Spufford has noted, such statistics, because based on signing ability, elide crucial differences between reading and writing training and thus likely underestimate female reading ability (*Small Books and Pleasant Histories: Popular Fiction and its Readership in Seventeenth-Century England* [1981; rprt. Athens: University of Georgia Press, 1982], esp. xvii–xviii, 34–7). See also Barry; Keith Thomas, "The Meaning of Literacy in Early Modern England," *The Written Word: Literacy in Translation* (Oxford: Clarendon Press, 1986), 97–131; and Margaret Ferguson, "Attending to Literacy," in *Attending to Women in Early Modern England,* ed. Betty Travitsky and Adele Seeff (Newark: University of Delaware Press, 1994), 265–79. On women playgoers, see Alfred Harbage, *Shakespeare's Audience* (New York: Columbia University Press, 1941), 74–9; Gurr, esp. 6–9, 19–20, 28–30, 61–4; Richard Levin, "Women in the Renaissance Theatre Audience," *Shakespeare Quarterly* 40 (1989), 165–74; Jean E. Howard, *The Stage and Social Struggle in Early Modern England* (London: Routledge, 1994), 73–92; and Kathleen McCluskie, *Renaissance Dramatists* (Atlantic Highlands, N. J.: Humanities Press International, 1989), 87–99. Ann Jennalie Cook, in *The Privileged Playgoers of Shakespeare's London* (Princeton: Princeton University Press, 1981), argues that "playgoing was much above the reach of the poorer sort" (271). But cf. Martin Butler, *Theatre and Crisis, 1632–1642* (Cambridge: Cambridge University Press, 1984). Recent studies that defy the notion of an "all-male stage" in early modern England include James Stokes, "Women and Mimesis in Medieval and Renaissance Somerset (and Beyond)," *Comparative Drama* 27.2 (1993), 176–96, and Ann Thompson, "Women/'women' and the stage," *Women and Literature*

in Britain, 1500–1700, ed. Helen Wilcox (Cambridge: Cambridge University Press, 1996), esp. 103–6. For women as performers of jigs and ballads, see n. 7 above; for paintings and carvings of women dancers, minstrels, musicians, tumblers, and jugglers, see Clifford Davidson, *Illustrations of the Stage and Acting in England to 1580* (Kalamazoo, Mich.: Medieval Institute Publications, 1991).

9. Marion Wynne-Davies, "The Queen's Masque: Renaissance Women and the Seventeenth-Century Court Masque," in *Gloriana's Face: Women, Public and Private, in the English Renaissance,* ed. S. P. Cerasano and Marion Wynne-Davies (New York: Harvester Wheatsheaf, 1992), esp. 79–80.

10. Reina Green, "Translation," *Renaissance Women Online* (http://textbase.wwp.brown.edu/c/s.dll/dynaweb-wwp/nph-dweb/dynaweb/wwptextbase/gcm.essays/@Generic_Book-TextView/609;hf+0).

11. *Half Humankind: Contexts and Texts of the Controversy about Women in England, 1540–1640,* ed. Katherine Usher Henderson and Barbara F. McManus (Urbana: University of Illinois Press, 1985). More recently, McManus has offered an alternative model for teaching the gender pamphlets that encourages students to identify the range of subject positions available in this discursive context and then to specify the gendering of those subject positions ("Whose Voice Is It, Anyway? Teaching Early Women Writers," paper delivered at "Attending to Early Modern Women: Crossing Boundaries," College Park, Maryland, November 8, 1997).

12. Ann Rosalind Jones, "Counterattacks on 'the Bayter of Women': Three Pamphleteers of the Early Seventeenth Century," in *The Renaissance Englishwoman in Print: Counterbalancing the Canon,* ed. Anne M. Haselkorn and Betty S. Travitsky (Amherst: University of Massachusetts Press, 1990), 45–62; Travitsky, "The Lady Doth Protest: Protest in the Popular Writings of the Renaissance Englishwoman," *English Literary Renaissance* 14.1 (winter 1984), 255–83; Travitsky, "The Possibilities of Prose," in *Women and Literature in Britain, 1500–1700,* ed. Helen Wilcox (Cambridge: Cambridge University Press, 1996), 234–66; Elaine V. Beilin, *Redeeming Eve: Women Writers of the English Renaissance* (Princeton: Princeton University Press, 1987), esp. 247–85; Simon Shepherd, *The Women's Sharp Revenge: Five Women's Pamphlets from the Renaissance* (New York: St. Martin's Press, 1985); Anthony Low, "Recent Studies in the English Renaissance," *Studies in English Literature* 37 (1997), 197. Susan Gushee O'Malley acknowledges the pseudonymous nature of Sowernam's signature in her *Defences of Women: Jane Anger, Rachel Speght, Ester Sowernam and Constantia Munda,* vol. 4 of *The Early Modern Englishwoman: A Facsimile Library of Essential Works.* See also Megan Matchinske, "Legislating Middle-Class Morality in

the Marriage Market: Ester Sowernam's *Esther hath hang'd Haman*,"
ELR 24.1 (winter 1994), 154–83; Constance Jordan, "Gender and
Justice in *Swetnam the Woman-Hater*," *Renaissance Drama* 19
(1989), 149–69; and especially Valerie Wayne, "The Dearth of the
Author: Anonymity's Allies and *Swetnam the Woman-hater*," in
*Maids and Mistresses, Cousins and Queens: Women's Alliances in Early
Modern England*, ed. Susan Frye and Karen Robertson (New York:
Oxford University Press, 1999), 221–40.

13. S. P. Cerasano and Marion Wynne-Davies, eds., *Renaissance Drama
    by Women: Texts and Documents* (London and New York: Routledge,
    1996).

14. On female playgoers' influence on the drama of the period, see also
    Linda Woodbridge, *Women and the English Renaissance: Literature
    and the Nature of Womankind, 1540–1620* (Urbana: University of
    Illinois Press, 1984), esp. 252; Theodore Leinwand, *The City Staged:
    Jacobean Comedy, 1603–1613* (Madison: University of Wisconsin
    Press, 1986), esp. 137–39; McLuskie, 28–99; and Levin, 165–74.

15. Each group chose three points central to the argument of their as-
    signed pamphlet and then paraphrased those points as vividly and
    persuasively as possible.

16. For a related assessment, see Coryll Crandall, "The Cultural Implica-
    tions of the Swetnam Anti-Feminist Controversy in the 17th Cen-
    tury," *Journal of Popular Culture* 2.1 (summer 1968), 136–47, esp.
    142.

17. This student goes on to argue that cross-dressing in *Swetnam the
    Woman-hater*, the *Roaring Girl*, and *Shakespeare in Love* implies the
    performative as opposed to essential nature of gender difference, but
    also that Lorenzo's failure to defend women through his cross-dress-
    ing, contrasted with Moll and Viola's relative success in their male
    disguises, suggests women's greater ability to perform both male and
    female roles.

18. Ann Rosalind Jones, "From Polemical Prose to the Red Bull: the
    Swetnam Controversy in Women-Voiced Pamphlets and the Public
    Theater," in *The Project of Prose in Early Modern Europe and the New
    World*, ed. Elizabeth Fowler and Roland Greene (Cambridge: Cam-
    bridge University Press, 1997).

19. Jones herself seems split on this question. Cf. her "Revenge Comedy:
    Writing, Law, and the unishing Heroine in *Twelfth Night, The Merry
    Wives of Windsor*, and *Swetnam the Woman-Hater*," in *Shakespearean
    Power and Punishment*, ed. Gillian Murray Kendall (Madison, N.J. :
    Fairleigh Dickinson University Press, 1998), 23–38.

20. See also Roxana Stuart, "Dueling en Travestie: Cross-Dressed
    Swordfighters in Three Jacobean Comedies," *Theatre Studies* 38
    (1993), 29–43.

21. Smith, 370–71.

22. Gerald Eades Bentley, *The Jacobean and Caroline Stage,* vol. 3 (Oxford: Clarendon Press, n.d.), 158–60.
23. *Renaissance Drama by Women,* 159.
24. Quoted in Gurr, 225; on rowdy audiences at the Red Bull, see also 64, 65, 78, 95, 132–3, and 185. Dekker is one of the proposed authors for *Swetnam the Woman-hater Arraigned by Women.*

PART III

WOMEN'S SUBJECTIVITY IN
MALE-AUTHORED TEXTS

CHAPTER 5

THE BROADSIDE BALLAD
AND THE WOMAN'S VOICE

Sandra Clark

Despite a common view that the appeal of early modern street literature was to a predominantly male audience,[1] there is ample evidence that the broadside ballad had a particular appeal for women. Any account of its reception history would notice the many references in the period to the popularity of ballad singing with young women. It is claimed that, in the eighteenth century, most professional ballad singers were women,[2] but in the seventeenth century, though a woman pedlar sometimes helped a male partner to sell ballads, there were only a few women actually known to have sung publicly before the Restoration.[3] The traditional, or folk ballad, was commonly transmitted through women's singing;[4] there are many references in the seventeenth century to women in domestic situations singing ballads of all kinds, and there is a strong tradition of female transmission from early times up to the nineteenth century.[5] The histories of the traditional and the broadside ballad are closely interconnected,[6] and it would be misleading to regard them as completely separate genres, even if their origins might appear to be antithetical. Singing, like story telling, was very much a woman's act in the early modern period, and the ballad, though produced as a printed object available to be read, was sold to an audience by a singer and circulated as much by singing as by reading.

But ballads can be said to be more directly expressive of the woman's voice through textual means. Increasingly in the course of the seventeenth century, ballads were addressed to particular groups, or target audiences, rather than, as earlier, being formulated toward a collective audience.[7] Many seventeenth-century ballads are specifically addressed to women, especially where the subject (marriage, relations between the sexes, gossip, confessions of criminal women) has gender-related interest; and many are written from a woman's perspective, often with first-person delivery, though this need not mean, of course, that such a speaker represents women's interests. But it is also worth remembering that a "woman's voice" need not be directly presented, but can be mediated through a gender-neutral perspective that shows sympathy to women. There is no evidence to refute the general assumption that the writers of the ballads were all male; certainly the names of the known writers are men's, though a very high proportion of all known ballads (including those nonextant) are anonymous. The ballads were delivered mostly by male singers, but this was an age when male presentation of female roles onstage was an accepted convention, and an element of virtuosity in the transvestite performer expected. It is sometimes assumed that only one singer delivered the ballad, but many dialogue ballads seem to call for a second performer, and it is tempting to wonder if this second performer might not sometimes, as in the case of William Nynges' wife, have been a woman.[8] Traveling ballad-mongers, who sold broadsides along with other wares, may not necessarily have been skilled singers, of course;[9] but nonetheless, the dramatic and performative aspect of the street ballad separates it generically from other printed materials, and constitutes an important part of its unique role, situated as it was on the boundaries between the oral and the written, and between commercial transaction and free circulation. It was also the cheapest, most accessible, and most widely available form of print, produced in enormous quantities from the mid-sixteenth century onward.[10] Like many cultural productions of the "small" tradition,[11] it was consumed at all levels of society. Because it was delivered to its first audiences in public spaces such as marketplaces, alehouses, and playhouse entrances, the ballad was equally available to women and to men listeners. The presentation had to be such as to attract a wide audience, and no doubt the skills of the presenter may, at least initially, have counted for as much as those of the writer and the appeal of the material. The opportunity for an audience to contribute to the performance, by joining in with the refrain, increased the ballad's appeal and enhanced its role as a vehicle of communal feeling.

The street-ballad genre has been interestingly related to the pamphlet debate on gender by Diane Purkiss in "Material Girls: the Seventeenth-Century Woman Debate."[12] She makes a fascinating and plausible case for its importance as one of the generic origins of Swetnam's pamphlet, and a source for the formation of his speaking position. But in her (very proper) concern to forge links between Swetnam's discourses of misogyny and those in the ballads, I believe she underrepresents the range of positions on gender roles in the ballads, as well as making no allowance for the kinds of factors I have been discussing. Recent social historians of the early modern period have drawn on ballad materials to correct what they regard as an overemphasis by historians on patriarchal oppression as the prime constituent of early modern gender relations.[13] And there are in fact connections which can be made between these ballads and the Swetnam debate, where analogies for the kinds of proto-feminist position taken by Sowernam and Speght can be easily found in the ballads, as will, I hope, emerge in my later discussion. For instance, the Joan Sharp poem which concludes *Esther hath hanged Haman* takes the view that men's hypocritical and self-interested attitudes toward women's sexuality condition women's behavior:

> If you ask how it happens some women prove naught:
> By men turned to serpents they are over-wrought.
> What the serpent began, men follow that still:
> They tempt what they may to make women do ill.
> . . .
> It proves a bad nature in men doth remain,
> To make women lewd their purses they strain.
> For a woman that's honest they care not a whit:
> They'll say she is honest because she lacks wit.
> They'll call women whores, but their stakes they might save—
> There can be no whore but there must be a knave.[14]

The conclusion is that neither sex is blameless but that the sexual misdemeanors of which Swetnam and his fellow misogynists accuse women are largely the result of cultural conditioning whereby women's interests and values are constructed and determined by those of men. Speght in *A Muzzle for Melastomus* also takes a position of compromise, acknowledging the need for both spouses to make adjustments if the marriage is to succeed as a partnership. She writes that "as yoke-fellows they are to sustain part of each other's cares, griefs and calamities"; the husband, as "the stronger vessel" should bear "a greater burden" than the wife, but even so he should not regard his status as head of the household in too absolute a sense:

> Thus if men would remember the duties they are to perform in being heads, some would not stand a tip-toe as they do, thinking themselves lords and rulers, and account every omission of performing whatsoever they command - whether lawful or not - to be matter of great disparagement and indignity done them. Whereas they should consider that women are enjoined to submit themselves unto their husbands no otherways than as to the Lord (Shepherd, p. 72).

The majority of writers who discuss gender relations in popular literature tend to class ballads with pamphlets and domestic drama as primarily concerned with the enforcement of male social and sexual control over women as right and preeminently natural. Probably this is the initial impression to be gained from any broad consideration of the content of ballads. But I would like to suggest that this impression can be nuanced, and that in content as well as form there is not only good evidence of an alternative voice, but also, as in the medieval and Tudor antecedents of the street ballad described by F. L. Utley in *The Crooked Rib*,[15] the potential for satire at the expense of male values. I am not sure that I would go as far here as F. O. Waage, who has identified a "strong tendency in all social ballads to vindicate covertly their women,"[16] but for all ballads about shrews, scolds, and cuckoldry, with titles like "The Cruell Shrow," "The Cucking of a Scold," "The Cuckolds Lamentation," "The Essex Man cozened by a Whore," and "My Wife will be my Master," it is possible to cite an equally extensive selection differently inflected: "The Married Womans Case," "The Patient Wife betrayed," "The Carefull Wife's Good Counsel," "The Married Wives Complaint," "A Womans Work is Never Done."[17] Martin Parker and others wrote paired ballads, setting out antithetical views on the same subject, for example, "The Married Womans Case" and "The Married Mans Case" (lost), "A Fairing for Maids" and "A Fairing for Young-Men," "Keep a Good Tongue in Your Heads" and "Hold Your Hands, Honest Men," "The Wiving Age" and "The Cunning Age." It is evident that there was a demand for ballads that appealed distinctively to women, with an appeal capable of being heightened in performance.[18]

To illustrate the nature of the ballads' appeal for women, and the textual strategies by which it was organized, I might have chosen from several groups of ballads, particularly those concerned with witty maids, or with women's gossip; but in order to make a link with the pamphlet debate, I have restricted my discussion to ballads on marriage. The ballads share many of the positive views of marriage expressed in the Swetnam response pamphlets, but they differ substantially on some aspects. Generally, their overall view of marriage is much less idealized and more negative, and the textual and performative strategies enable a plurality of perspectives unavailable to the pamphleteers. The ballads constitute an interesting forum for debating marriage; the range of viewpoints is wider than might be allowed by those who think the genre dominated by the interests of the patriarchy, and the dramatic potential of the ballads' presentation in the public forum creates the chance for comic performers to challenge or subvert their texts as well as to express them directly. Tessa Watt notes a libel investigation in 1584 which records an apparently standardized ballad with individual names of local people inserted.[19] Not all ballads are comic, and the presenter has many roles, some of them didactic. Especially in ballads with terms like "counsel," "lesson," or "warning" in their titles, s/he may be an authoritative figure, instructing the audience. Many ballads afford no opportunities for irony or satire in delivery, but instead aim to inculcate moral values and offer guidance on conduct in the manner of the marriage manuals, or the pamphlets of Speght or Sowernam. For example, in "The Marryed Man's Lesson, Or A Disswasion from Jealousie" (*RB* 3:231–3), the presenter gathers his audience to offer them counsel: "You men who are marri'd, come hearken to me." His subject is happy marriage, and he advocates an open, tolerant attitude and an acceptance of human weakness as the prime factors in creating it:

> A wife that's indifferent—betweene good and ill—
> Is shee that in huswifery shewes her good will,—
> Yet sometimes her voyce shee too much elevates;
> Is that the occasion for which her hee hates?
> A soveraigne remedy for this disease
> Is to hold thy tongue; [then] let her say what shee please:
> Judge! is not this better th[a]n to fight and [to] scratch?
> For silence will soonest a shrew overmatch.

The last verse is addressed to both sexes:

> Now, lastly to both men and women I speake . . .
> Bee loving and tractable each unto other,
> And what is amisse let affection still smother.

"The Carefull Wifes Good Counsel" (*RB* 3:478–80), as its title suggests, is another ballad of advice, largely delivered in the wife's voice. She is characterized in the title and through her refrain, "Save something for a rainy day." She urges her spendthrift husband to consider that the companions with whom he spends his time in preference to her will desert him when his money runs out: "The hostess she will flout at thee" and "Your jovial boon-companions, too / Will likewise take their leave of you." In the last three stanzas, the husband responds, and accepts his wife's advice, picking up her refrain: "Thy words have so prevail'd on me; / No longer will I run astray, / But think upon a rainy day." Thrifty husbandry is a traditional attribute of a good wife, and the ability to redeem a wastrel husband is proverbial.[20]

"A Fairing for Maids" (*RB* 8:676–78) takes a different line; it consists of the advice of a woman offered as a present to women contemplating marriage.[21] In a simple proverbial style, the presenter makes caveats about hasty marriage and fortune-seeking husbands. Marriage is viewed as a risky undertaking for a woman; the refrain goes, "For when you are bound, then you needs must obey." The single life is praised, in terms that challenge the notion that the early modern unmarried woman's identity was constructed through patriarchal constraint. Marriage is seen as a condition that a woman (and in the equivalent ballads, a man) is free to choose or reject. Even if this did not correspond with the economic reality of most women's lives, it was clearly a vision of a life that many imagined living:

> Whilst you are single, there's none to curb you:
> Go to bed quietly and take your ease.
> Early or late there's none to disturb you
> Walk abroad where you [will], and when you please.

Marriage is acceptable if the woman is lucky enough to find "a constant youth," but this may not be easy. In such "counsel" ballads, the text does not lend itself to irony. They may well have been used for entertainment on communal occasions, such as weddings, where social values of the community at large were celebrated and confirmed.[22]

Many marriage ballads take the form of a dialogue, which has origins in the medieval *debat* and the jig, where an element of dialectic between the viewpoints is inbuilt. Sometimes the debate is resolved by the capitulation of one party to the views of the other, as in "A Pleasant New Ballad" (*PG* 36) or "Robin and Kate; or, A bad husband converted by a good wife" (*RB* 2:413–18). In the first part of "A Pleasant New Ballad,"[23] the wife abuses the husband for his in-

adequacies, and he attempts to mollify her; in the second, the roles
are reversed. Each partner assumes an equally extreme position, the
wife as Lady Pride, the husband as a despotic patriarch:

> [*Wife*] Nay, thou art not worthy to carry my Fan,
> I will be supplied by a propperer man:
> And wee'l haue our Coach & horse to ride at pleasure
> And thou shalt ride by on foot, and wait our leisure.
>
> [*Husband*] Dame Ile make you know that I am your head,
> And you shall be ready at board, or in bed,
> To giue me content, or else be sure of this,
> Both gowne and lace, horse and Coach all you shall misse.

In the end the wife gives in and they are reconciled. The husband
gets the last verse: "Why that's a good Wench, now come kisse & be
friends / Put out all the Candles Ile make thee amends." In "Robin
and Kate" the partners are less antagonistic; Robin wants to live as a
prodigal and a free man, enjoying the pleasures of male company in
the alehouse, while Kate begs him to stay at home with her and not
waste their money. She is characterized as loving and affectionate,
never losing her temper or showing impatience: "I prethee, my joy,
doe not take at the worst / The words that I speake in the heat of affection." She insists that she has no desire to overrule or control him,
as he accuses her of doing: "Alas! my deare Luif, thou mistakest me
much, / I do not command thee, that's not my intention, / For my
humble duty unto thee is such / that one word of anger to thee Ile
not mention." Finally, he is persuaded and agrees to stay at home:
"Now all my delight in thy bosom shall dwell." Undeniably, the tone
and linguistic structures of this ballad create possibilities for irony. A
male singer could easily subvert Kate's protestations in his delivery,
using her voice to express a theatrical notion of 'woman' as a role,
and thus endorsing misogyny.[24] But equally, the verses could be sung
so as to support the viewpoint they express; and a reader, or non-
professional performer, would be more likely to interpret the ballad
in this way. A debate structure is implicit in "The Woman to the
Plow, And the Man to the Hen-Roost" (*RB* 7:185–9), in which the
presenter addresses himself to both sexes ("Both Men and Women,
listen well . . .") and narrates an account of a couple who exchange
domestic chores. Each fails in the other's tasks.[25] The man's inepti-
tude is no less than the woman's, and there is no implication that her
household duties are the easier:

> Nothing that he in hand did take
> Did come to good; once he did bake,
> And burnt the bread as black as a stock;
> Another time he went to rock
> The cradle, and threw the child i'th'floor,
> And broke his nose, and hurt it sore.

The solution is a return to the status quo, given as a recipe for conjugal contentment:

> Take heed of this, you Husband-men,
> Let Wives alone to grope the hen,
> And meddle you with the horse and ox,
> And keep your lambs safe from the fox.
> So shall you live Contented lives
> And take sweet pleasure in your Wives.

Such poems as this[26] show ballad writers as concerned to address women's interests as men's, and to reinforce the values of marriage as a working partnership. That husbands and wives have different perspectives, but of equal emotional weight, is acknowledged in pairs of ballads, linked by content, format, and sometimes tune, like "Hold your Hands, Honest Men" (*RB* 3:243–4) and "Keep a Good Tongue in Your head" (*RB* 3:237–42), or "The Cuckold's Complaint" (*RB* 7:431) and "The Scolding Wife's Vindication" (*RB* 7:194–7). Wurzbach notes that the answer ballad was a "common literary procedure" in the seventeenth century, and also an advertising technique. A ballad that had proved itself popular would be followed by another designed to imitate or reply to it, and the sales of both would be boosted. She suggests that the procedure constitutes "a kind of discussion forum."[27] In "Keep a Good Tongue in Your head," the husband describes the wife's many virtues; she is beautiful and fecund, a good needle-woman and weaver, controls her servants efficiently, and is witty on appropriate occasions: "With eloquence she will dispute; / Few women can her confute." But, as the refrain insists, "she cannot hold her tongue." In "Hold your Hands, Honest Men," the wife extols her husband, who is tall, handsome, active, athletic, learned, and well traveled, but likewise has a single defect:

> I have as compleat a man
> As any poor woman can;
> He makes my heart to leap

His company to keepe
It comforts me now and than:
There's few exercises
That man enterprises
But he well understands;
Yet, like a dart,
He wounds my heart;
I, for my part,
Must bear the smart;
For he cannot rule his hands.

The short lines, regular rhyme scheme, and emphatic refrain help to create a light mood, and in both ballads there is scope for comic delivery through the characterization of the first-person narrator, and for possible irony in the account of the spouse's virtues; but at face value they problematize the issue of marital violence, whether verbal or physical, and present it for reflection. Neither poem singly offers a solution to the problem it describes; but taken together as companion poems, they may imply the possibility of a solution in compromise.

"The Cuckolds Complaint, or, The Turbulent Wife's Severe Cruelty" (*RB* 7:431), presented by the husband, is in two parts; the first stresses how the wife's unreasonable behavior obliges the husband to take over the most intimate of her domestic duties:

I am forced to wash her Smock, and the Child's s[odd]en
    clouts also;
Though I sit up till Twelve a clock: a Curse of a cruel Shrow!

But the second, with changed refrain, "The world is turn'd upside down," describes his previous life as a reveler and man of means, and his regret that he has lost it. A skilled performer could exploit the disjunction between the two parts to mock or satirize the narrator's complaint; in the light of part two, the complaint of part one stems from something other than female disorderliness. "The Scolding Wife's Vindication" again locates the cause for the wife's behavior in the husband and takes as its theme the idea that the husband's sexual inertia drives the wife to excessive behavior. The refrain consists of variations on the line "he nothing at all would do." She describes the frustrations of her condition: she is "a Buxome Dame" in her "blooming Prime," which she fears will pass without fruition; she has made strenuous efforts to arouse her husband with amorous activity and aphrodisiac foods ("I feasted him e'ery day, / With Lamb-stones, and Cock-broths too . . . / I fed him with Jelly of Chicks, /

And curious Egg-Caudles too"), but notwithstanding, "He lyes like a lump of Clay." Perhaps there is some implicit irony at the expense of the sexually demanding woman, but taken directly, this ballad invites sympathy for the woman's situation, and offers a female perspective on cuckoldry, one of the commonest topics in marital ballads.[28]

Predictably, most cuckoldry ballads are presented by a male narrator or offered from a male viewpoint. The list of titles is large.[29] Many treat masculine failure in the sexual arena mockingly; the cuckold is an absurd, comic figure who has failed as a man. The best that can be said for him is that his situation is universal, and not worth lamenting. In "A Catalogue of Contented Cuckolds; Or, A Loving society of Confessing Brethren of the Forked Order" (RB 3:481–3), a series of tradesmen—brewer, baker, cook, tailor, turner, and so forth—meeting in a tavern in turn describe their situations to the refrain "yet I swear by this glass of sparkling wine / I will now be contented, and never repine." However, in "My Wife will be my Master" (RB 7:188–9), set to a tune with the suggestive title "A taylor is no man," the husband, who presents the ballad, is intimidated and effeminate; his inability to cope with a masterful wife, who spends her time like a man, drinking in taverns, makes him a figure of fun:

> And when I am with her in bed, she doth not use me well, Sir;
> She'l wring my nose, and pull my ears, a pitiful tale to tell, Sir.
> And when I am with her in bed, not meaning to molest her,
> She'l kick me out at her beds-feet, and so become my Master.

He admits to his own helplessness:

> But if I were a lusty man, and able for to baste her,
> The would I surely use a means, that she should not be my
> master.

In "Rock the Cradle, John" (RB 7:162–4) and "The Taylor's Lamentation" (RB 7:474), the cuckolded husbands are responsible for their own predicaments; but the docile husband in "Rock the Cradle, John," an unusually accomplished ballad, by Martin Parker, which has exceptional rhythmic and narrative complexity, is treated in an equivocal tone, which balances sympathy for a man who makes the best of a bad job with mockery of his effeminate doting. When his wife gives birth to another man's child a month after their wedding, the midwife jeers at the husband's efforts to claim the child for himself; but the semidramatic mode of this ballad, which offsets direct speech from three characters against a cynical narrative commentary, allows for the possibility of the husband's response to his situation being treated with some respect:

> "See here the boy is like the Dad, which well may make your
>   heart ful glad,
> Cheer up your selfe and be not sad, for that which here is
>   done:
> His ruby lips doe plaine disclose, his cherry cheekes and dad's
>   owne nose."
> "For twenty pound I will not lose," quoth he, "my little
>   sonne."
> So well content this foole was found, he leapt for ioy above
>   the ground.
> "Old sorrow shall," quoth he, "be drown'd, since new are
>   fresh begun,
>   Rocke the Cradle, Iog the cradle, thus Ile haue it knowne,
>   I loue to rock the Cradle, the children be mine owne."

Disregarding its performative mode, ballad material such as this has been read from a clearly masculinist perspective as functioning to discourage female deviance and "reaffirm the notion of woman as a sexual being."[30] But delivered to a mixed audience in a public arena, its effect could be quite different, even empowering women.

Unlike the domestic handbooks, the marriage ballads present marriage as a condition that is not necessarily beneficial to either sex. Those that depict the disadvantages it holds for women may be read from a twentieth-century standpoint as exposing the oppressive nature of early modern patriarchal society, but it is important to recognize that in most of them this is done in a mode of female self-revelation, a mode that, in dramatic delivery, could make a strong appeal to women in the audience with similar experience. In the dialogue ballad "The Cunning Age, OR A re-married Woman, repenting her marriage" (*PG* 42), a type of gossips' song and an answer by John Cart to Martin Parker's "The Wiving Age," a remarried woman, a widow, and a young wife debate marriage.[31] The remarried woman regrets her action and wishes she had remained a widow:

> I marry'd a Boy, that now holds me in scorne,
> He comes among Whoores both euening and morne,
> While I sit at home like a creature forlorne.

The widow determines to take warning from this: "With no Skip-iacke boy a match I will make; / Two 'Sutors I haue, but I both will forsake." At one point the two join together[32] to address the young wife, who regrets her recent marriage, having been cheated by her husband; the unanimity of the speakers stresses their message:

> Oh woe is me, Cousin, that euer 'twas done,
> A beggarly slaue my affection hath wonne;
> He brag'd of his riches, whereof he had none,
> But fiue little Children, foure Girles, and a Sonne.

The penultimate stanza adopts a new textual stratagem, referring to the actual speech situation of the performance. The narrator, here the widow, points out that married women have been treated misogynistically by the ballad community, and speaks out on their behalf:

> Nay more, to abash vs, the Poets o'th'times
> Doe blazon vs forth in their Ballads and Rimes,
> With bitter inuectiue satyricall lines,
> As though we had done some notorious crimes.
> >   O this is a scandalous Age,
> >   O this is a scandalous Age.

> I would I the Poet could get in my clutches,
> He were better write ballads against ye Arch-dutches;
> There is one mad ballad that sorely vs touches,
> The hetroclite Singer, that goes vpon Crutches,
> >   Doth roare out the Wiuing Age,
> >   Doth roare out the Wiuing Age.[33]

Such self-reference, not uncommon in the ballad genre as a whole, though unusual in dramatic (as opposed to narrative or discursive) ballads, functions primarily as an advertising technique, staking a claim for ballads in the marketplace of print; but in this instance it also creates a speaking position for the women it represents, defining a voice for them even if its force is mitigated by the comic mode. The disadvantages of marriage for women are acknowledged, both im-plicitly and explicitly, in ballads that depict widowhood as a powerful and economically privileged position, or celebrate the freedom of the single life.[34] Again, the mood is predominantly comic or at least satir-ical, but in "The Married Womans Case" (*PB* 2, 74), addressed to "You Maidens all, that are willing to wed," the tone in which the woman narrator describes the miseries of her marriage to a man with venereal disease is without humor or satire:

> A woman that to a whore-monger is wed
> is in a most desperate case:
> She scarce dares performe her duty in bed,
> with one of condition so base:
> For sometimes hee's bitten with *Turnbull*-street Fleas,
> The Pox, or some other infectious disease;
> And yet, to her perill, his mind she must please.

In "A Woman's Work is never done" (*RB* 3:301–6), presented as a "song for Maids to sing," in which the detailed first-person account of an exhausting daily routine attributes to the woman a considerable degree of self-consciousness,[35] the tone and content are deliberately mundane, with no elements of irony, humor, word play, or verbal wit, even in the refrain line (variations on "I'm sure a woman's work is never done"). The woman gives a detailed and strongly realistic account of her daily routine, listing her tasks: she must rise early, make the fire, prepare breakfast, send the children to school, make her husband's dinner, keep the fire going, and so on. At night she gets neither peace nor pleasure:

> Then if my husband turns me to the wall,
> Then my sucking childe will cry and brawl;
> Six or seven times for the brest 'twill cry,
> And then, I pray you judge, what rest take I.
> And if at any time asleep I be,
> Perchance my husband wakes, and then wakes me;
> Then he does that to me which I cannot shun,
> Yet I could wish that work were oftener done.

The refrain line at this point is the one significant variation. In the last verse she addresses herself to "all you merry girles that hear this ditty" and urges the advantages of the single life: "you see that maids live more merrier lives / Then do the best of married wives." Except for the pleasure of successful dramatic impersonation by the singer, the appeal of this ballad seems restrictedly female. It elaborates on a specifically female condition, described without satire or celebration. The ballad bemoaning the married woman's lot from personal experience is not uncommon. In "The married wives Complaint of her unkind husband" (*Douce* 2, 151b) and "The Married wives complaint, OR, The Hasty Bride repents her bargain" (*Douce* 2, 144b), the wives tell similar stories of wastrel husbands, domestic violence, marriage portions squandered in the alehouse. Each praises the single life. The wife in "The Married wives Complaint of her unkind Husband" recalls earlier happy times "milking the Cows and making Hay":

> When I did lead a single life
> I had my pleasure euery day,
> I neuer knew what belong'd to strife
> But now I am bound I must obey.

Her counterpart in "The Married wives complaint, OR, The Hasty Bride Repents her bargain" voices a similar complaint against men:

> Trust not a Man Maids if you be wife
> though neuer so well you do know him
> And euery Damsell I will advize
> no farther then she can throw him.

These ballads are explicitly addressed as advice to the unmarried ("all young Maids that are to wed"), but their appeal is to all women concerned with the state of matrimony. The viewpoint is gender specific: marriage is likely to bring women more pain than pleasure, and it is not economically advantageous. Such ballads illustrate an extreme of the range of tone and attitude of which the genre was capable.

Ballads circulated freely, in larger numbers than any other form of print, and more often than not unlicensed by authority.[36] Their capacity to express and explore communal values was unique in the period; and it is worth remembering that these are the social values of the nonelite, which were characteristically secular, pragmatic, and mundane. Ballads were commonly addressed to target audiences, which frequently included women, and, probably more than any other contemporary genre, they were capable of addressing interests peculiar to nonelite women. What Wurzbach calls the "receptive impression"[37] created on an audience by a ballad singer was distinctively different from the appeal of any other form of literature, and the directness of this appeal to women, as one target group, is worth consideration.

Abbreviations:

Douce   Francis Douce Collection of ballads in the Bodleian Library, Oxford.
Euing   *The Euing Collection of English Broadside Ballads,* John Holloway, ed. (Glasgow: University of Glasgow Publications, 1971).

PB   *The Pepys Ballads,* 5 vols., facsimile edition (Cambridge: Derek Brewer, 1987).
PG   *A Pepysian Garland,* H. E. Rollins, ed. (Cambridge: Cambridge University Press: 1922).
RB   *The Roxburghe Ballads,* 9 vols., W. Chappell and J. W. Ebsworth, eds. (London, Hertford:Ballad Society, 1869–99).

NOTES

1. See for example, Joy Wiltenburg, *Disorderly Women and Female Power in the Street Literature of Early Modern England* (Charlottesville and London: University Press of Virginia, 1992), esp. ch. 3, although she does note in her comparative study that "the female voice of many English ballads represents a recognition of women's subjective experience which goes far beyond the views offered in German literature," 50. J. Sharpe, "Plebeian Marriage in Stuart England: Some Evidence from Popular Literature," *Transactions of the Royal Historical Society,* 5th ser. XXXVI (1986), 72, and by implication, Natascha Wurzbach, *The Rise of the English Street Ballad, 1550–1650* (Cambridge: Cambridge University Press, 1990), 26, take this view.

2. H. E. Rollins, "The Black-Letter Broadside Ballad," *PMLA* 34 (1919): 321.

3. See *REED,* Norwich, 115. *REED,* Somerset, pp. 495–6, mentions the involvement of women in street entertainments and in the spreading of libellous ballads, though none are mentioned by name. Diane Dugaw, *Warrior Women and Popular Balladry, 1650–1850* (Chicago and London: The University of Chicago Press, 1996), 23, gives an illustration of a woman ballad singer from the 1680s.

4. Evidence for this is to be found abundantly in F. J. Child, ed., *English and Scottish Popular Ballads,* 5 vols. (1882–1898). There are numerous contemporary anecdotes about women singing ballads, for example, Isaac Walton, *The Compleat Angler* (1653), ch. 4, and Dorothy Osborne, in E. A. Parry, ed., *Letters from Dorothy Osborne to Sir William Temple (1652–4),* London, n.d.), 84–5. See also Margaret Spufford, *Small Books and Pleasant Histories. Popular Fiction and Its Readership in Seventeenth-Century England* (London: Methuen and Co., 1981), 11–15.

5. See the introduction to J. W. Ebsworth, ed., *The Bagford Ballads. Illustrating The Last Years of the Stuarts,* 2 vols. (Hertford: printed for the Ballad Society, 1897).

6. See the introduction to Vivian de Sola Pinto, ed., *The Common Muse: An Anthology of Popular British Ballad Poetry from the 15th to the 20th Century* (London, Chatto & Windus, 1957) and A. B. Friedman, *The Ballad Revival: Studies in the Influence of Popular on Sophisticated Poetry* (Chicago and London: University of Chicago Press, 1961), 45.

7. Wurzbach, 54–9.

8. Wurzbach assumes a single performer (106), but C. R. Baskervill, *The Elizabethan Jig and Related Song Drama* (Chicago: University of Chicago Press, 1929) often implies that the broadside, like the stage jig, might have been delivered by two or more performers.

9. Tessa Watt, "Publisher, Pedlar, Pot-Poet: The Changing Character of the Broadside Trade, 1550–1640," in *Spreading the Word. The Distribution Networks of Print, 1550–1850,* eds. Robin Myers and Michael Harris (Winchester: St Paul's Bibliographies, 1990), makes this point, as do many of the contemporary commentators on ballad singers recorded in the appendix to Wurzbach.

10. See Tessa Watt, *Cheap Print and Popular Piety, 1550–1640* (Cambridge: Cambridge University Press, 1991), 11–12.

11. The phrase comes from Peter Burke, *Popular Culture in Early Modern Europe* (New York, 1978). De Sola Pinto, in the introduction to *The Common Muse,* also makes this point.

12. Diane Purkiss, "Material Girls: The Seventeenth-Century Woman Debate," in *Women, Texts and Histories 1575–1760,* eds. Clare Brant and Diane Purkiss (London: Routledge, 1992).

13. J. Sharpe, "Plebeian Marriage"; and Elizabeth Foyster, "A Laughing Matter? Marital Discord and Gender Control in Seventeenth-Century England," *Rural History* 4 (1993), 5–21.

14. Quoted from Simon Shepherd, ed., *The Women's Sharp Revenge* (London: Fourth Estate, 1985), 116.

15. F. L. Utley, *The Crooked Rib: An Analytical Index to the Argument about Women in English and Scots Literature to the End of the Year 1568* (reprint, New York: Octagon Books, 1970).

16. F. O. Waage, "Social Themes in Urban Broadsides of Renaissance England," in *Journal of Popular Culture* 11 (1977), 731–41.

17. *RB* 1:93–8; *PG* 12; *RB* 3:634–7; *PB* 2, 78; *RB* 7:188–9; *PB* 2, 74; *Euing,* 289; *RB* 3:478–80; *Douce Ballads* 2, 144b; *RB* 3:301–6; *RB* 8:676–8; *RB* 8:673–5; *RB* 3:237–45; *RB* 3:245–8; *PG* 41; *PG* 42.

18. J. Sharpe (1986) sees evidence in the ballads for the possible existence of female subcultures.

19. Watt (1991), 37. F.G. Emmison, *Elizabethan Life: Morals and the Church Courts* (Chelmsford: Essex Record Office, Essex County Council, 1970), chapter 4, gives further examples of ballad-type rhymes with personal names inserted for the purposes of slander. See also Adam Fox, *Oral and Literate Culture in England 1500–1700* (Oxford: Clarendon Press, 2000), 321.

20. For other ballads on this theme, see "The benefit of Marriage," *Euing* 18, and "A Good Wife is a Portion every day," *RB* 6:332–5.

21. Ballads in praise of the single life (for men as well as women) are numerous. See those discussed by Wiltenburg, 65–7. She supposes their frequency to be partly the result of the fact that ballads were mainly

directed at a young audience and therefore its interests, a view I would question.

22. See Wurzbach, 190, and Robert Weimann, *Shakespeare and the Popular Tradition in the Theatre*, ed. Robert Schwartz (Baltimore: Johns Hopkins Press, 1978), 24, 185–6.

23. This ballad is characterized by H. R. Rollins, ed., in *A Pepysian Garland: Black-letter Broadside Ballads of the Years 1595–1639. Chiefly from the Collection of Samuel Pepys* (Cambridge, 1922), note on number 207, as a jig, though it is printed as a broadside. He notes the strong dramatic element. Similar in form and theme is "A Merry Dialogue between a Married Man and his wife," *RB* 2:158–63.

24. Another view is that the laughter aroused by comic ballads had a regulatory function. Foyster (6) sees it as "re-inforcing gender control." But her readings of the ballads assume that they are straightforwardly didactic, and she takes no account of the possibilities for subversion during performance. The same position is taken by the historian Laura Gowing in *Domestic Dangers: Women, Words, and Sex in Early Modern London* (Oxford: Clarendon Press, 1966), 207–8, 233.

25. This is a traditional formula for evaluating marital roles, and Utley exemplifies it from early Tudor ballads (see Index, no. 149a).

26. See also "A Merry Dialogue betwixt a married man and his wife," by Martin Parker (*RB* 2:158–63), which similarly presents a double perspective on marital duties, and "A new Ballad, Containing a communication between the carefull wife and the comfortable Husband" (*RB* 1:122–250).

27. Wurzbach, 97. But it is also important to remember that the terms of the medieval controversy about women allowed for the alternation of attack and defense, and sometimes their combination within a single text. See Utley, 52–3.

28. Wiltenburg, 150–56, gives further examples of ballads in which men's sexual failures lead their wives to look for satisfaction elsewhere.

29. For example, "Cuckolds' haven, Or, The marry'd man's miserie," *RB* 1:148–53; "My Wife will be my master," *RB* 7:188–9; "Mirth for Citizens: Or, A comedy for the Country," *RB* 8:699–700; "The Cuckold's Complaint: Or The turbulent Wives severe Cruelty," *RB* 7:431; "The Henpeckt Cuckold," *RB* 7:432; "The Cuckold's Lamentation of a Bad Wife," *RB* 3:634–7, "Household Talke, or: Good Councell for a Married Man," *RB* 1:441–6, "The Lancashire Cuckold," *Euing*, 200. Ebsworth has a long note on cuckoldry ballads, *RB* 7:194–6.

30. Wiltenburg, 157.

31. Utley, 50.

32. This ballad surely requires two performers.

33. "The Wiving Age. Or A great Complaint of the Maidens of London" (*PG* 41), by Martin Parker, is another in the series of 'Age' ballads,

beginning with "The Siluer Age, or, The World turned backward" (*PB* 1, 154). It satirizes the marriage of young men to widows. "The Poet" is Martin Parker, its author.

34. E.g., "A proverb old, yet ne'er forgot," *PG* 40; "The Wiving age" *PG* 41; "Nobody's counsel to choose a wife," *PG* 46; "A rich widow's wooing," *PB* 1, 43; "A fairing for Maids," *RB* 8:676–8; "Tobias' Observation," RB 7:155–6; "The Bachelor's delight," *RB* 3:423–6; "The Batchelor's Feast," *RB* 1:46–51; "The Bachelor's Triumph," *RB* 3:427–9.

35. See the comments of Wiltenburg, 50, on this ballad.

36. See Sharon Achinstein, "Audiences and Authors: Ballads and the Making of English Renaissance Literary Culture," *Journal of Medieval and Renaissance Studies* 22 (1992), 320 for figures.

37. Wurzbach, 79.

CHAPTER 6

"WEELE HAVE A WENCH SHALL BE OUR POET": SAMUEL ROWLANDS' GOSSIP PAMPHLETS

Susan Gushee O'Malley

In a preface to Samuel Rowlands' pamphlet *Tis Merry when Gossips meete*, printed in 1602, a gentleman discusses with a bookseller's apprentice what book he should buy. The gentleman says he knows of no new book that interests him. Perhaps the apprentice could sell him all of Robert Greene's works in one volume, or has he something by Thomas Nashe? The apprentice urges upon him a new book about "a Merrie meeting heere in London, betweene a *Wife*, a *Widdow*, and a *Mayde*." At first the gentleman demurs: he says that the title "Merrie meeting" is "stale." He knows other ballads and books with "merrie meeting" in the title. The apprentice assures him that this is a new work and that it has special properties. If the gentleman purchases the book, he will be able to carry the wife, maid, and widow in his pocket and let them out when he wants to listen to them talk. When he has heard enough of their gossip, he can repocket them. The apprentice further argues that the gentleman "may make vertious use of this Booke divers wayes." Because he may summon at will the bodies and voices of the three women in his room alone, the book may keep him "from Dice, Taverne, Bawdy-house, and so forth." One wonders what else the gentleman might do with the book in his pocket or what the apprentice meant by "and so forth." Convinced by the apprentice's sales pitch, the gentleman buys *Tis Merry when Gossips meete* for a sixpence. Thus, the book or pamphlet, *Tis Merry*, becomes a female commodity for the gentleman to own and listen to at his leisure and perhaps also a sexualized text to provide a private and renewable source of arousal.[1]

It could be argued that the pamphlet form was gendered female in the early modern imagination and had a special affinity for questions about women. In Samuel Rowlands' two gossip pamphlets, *Tis Merry when Gossips meete* and *A whole crew of kind Gossips,* published in 1609, the women gossips talk about men, courtship, husbands, pregnancy, and work.[2] Of course, these are Samuel Rowlands' representations of what he thinks women talk about when they are together out of the earshot of men. In giving voice to the three women in *Tis Merry* and the six women in *A whole crew,* Rowlands controls their speech by speaking for them and expresses the anxiety often felt by male writers of the early modern period when women congregated together.

Samuel Rowlands wrote thirty-two pamphlets, of which *Tis Merry* was the fifth to be published. Although the first pamphlet, *The Betraying of Christ,* published in 1598, was religious, Rowlands' second and third pamphlets, *A Merry Meetinge, or 'tis Merry when Knaves mete* (1600), to which the gentleman in the preface may be referring when he says that he has heard of the title "A Merrie Meeting," and *The Letting of Humours Blood in the Head-Vaine* (1600), were deemed so offensive that they were publicly burned by order of the censors in the kitchen of the Stationers' Company on October 26, 1600. Despite this, twenty-eight booksellers were fined 2s 6d for selling *The Letting* in March 1601 and a twenty-ninth the following March.[3] By the time William White entered *Tis Merry* in the Stationers' Register on September 15, 1602,[4] Samuel Rowlands had become, if not famous, at least a notorious writer. *A whole crew,* Rowlands' second gossip pamphlet, was first printed with the second edition of *Tis Merry* in 1609 and is believed to be a rewriting of the 1607 *Six London Gossips,* all copies of which have disappeared.[5]

Of Samuel Rowlands not much is known. The *Dictionary of National Biography* conjectures his dates as 1570?–1630? Edmund W. Gosse, who wrote the Memoir in *The Complete Works of Samuel Rowlands, 1598–1628,* assigns 1573 as Rowlands' year of birth, because it is the same year in which John Donne and Ben Jonson were born.[6] It is not known if Rowlands attended university, married, or worked at other employment to supplement the income that he received from writing the thirty-two pamphlets attributed to him. In a letter to George Gaywood, written in 1602 and quoted in the *Dictionary of National Biography*, he states: "My pen never was and never shall be mercenary," which may mean that he had another profession, or that he was professing modesty at having his work printed, or that he did not write only to make money. Sir Walter Scott conjectures that Rowlands spent time with the lower sort of people in London. In an advertisement for a nineteenth-century reprint of Rowlands' *The Letting of Humours Blood in the Head-Vaine,* Sir Walter Scott says, "It has been remarked, that his muse is seldom found in the best company; and, to have become so well acquainted with the bullies, drunkards, gamesters, and cheats, whom he describes, he must have frequented the haunts of dissipation."[7] A note later appended cites that such an accusation is unjust.[8]

Tis Merry is a verse dialogue among a Wife, a Maid, and a Widow who compare their situations in life while eating sausage and drinking claret and sack in a tavern. The dialogue is written in iambic pentameter and is worked into six-line stanzas rhyming ababcc. The dialogue is carefully individuated: each of the three women has a distinct voice that changes as the evening progresses. The Maid and Wife become more garrulous, the Widow more assertive. All three abandon their pretensions because they are together in a private room away from the judgment of men and do not have to pretend to drink like women. The Widow tells the Maid and Wife to "fill your Cup, / Wee'le have no pingling now we are alone, / If heere were men, I would not drinke it up / For twenty pounds my selfe."

The Widow, who is standing in front of the tavern door, asks the Wife, who is returning from the pawn shop, and the Maid named Besse, who is supposed to be visiting her brother, to drink a pint with her. At first they refuse. The Wife, who is called Grace, says that she must return to tend their shop; the Maid says she must be at home when her mother returns from church. The Widow insists, and the three women drink until "Bow-bell rings" or 9 P.M. According to John Stow's *A Survey of London* (1598), the five bells of St. Mary-le-Bow in Cheapside, London, were "to be rung nightly at nine of the clock" (229). The Widow pays the final bill of three shillings and a penny, which at 1602 prices for sack and claret is a lot of drink.[9]

That the Widow chooses a tavern, not an alehouse, for her drinking party may indicate her class aspirations. She orders only sack, a kind of Spanish white wine, and claret from the Vintner at the tavern. Taverns sold wine to the more prosperous, as opposed to alehouses, which sold beer and ale usually to the less prosperous. In a dialogue entitled *Wine, Beere, Ale, and Tobacco,* written in 1630, it is decided that wine is the drink of courtiers, gentlemen, and poetical wits; beer, the drink of citizens; and ale of those who live in the country (C2).

There is evidence that women did frequent taverns or alehouses in the early modern period. Thomas Platter from Switzerland comments on this in the account of his travels in England in 1599:

> women as well as the men, in fact more often than they, will frequent the taverns or ale-houses for enjoyment. They count it a great honour to be taken there and given wine with sugar to drink; and if one woman only is invited, then she will bring three or four other women along and they gaily toast each other; the husband afterwards thanks him who has given his wife such pleasure, for they deem it a real kindness.[10]

Keith Wrightson argues that the early modern alehouse was not a male-dominated establishment. Women often ran or worked in the alehouse; they went there with their husbands or friends. Young men and women often met at the alehouse, and marriages were celebrated there.[11]

In the tavern in *Tis Merry,* the three women gossip about their friend Jane, who has moved from Bucklers-berry to London-wall. The Widow, who was formerly in domestic service, reminisces about one summer when her mistress had left London to stay in Kent. Jane, their friend Roger, and she would drink, dance, and sing the latest ballads every evening. The conversation then turns to whether it is better to be a maid, a widow, or a wife. The Widow, who has been all three, asserts that being a maid is the best because of all the gifts suitors give a maid. The Wife says that when she was a maid she was given "twenty paire of Gloves" and "Garters, knives, Purses, Girdles, store of Rings, / And many a hundred dainty pretty things." The Widow says that maids do not have to worry about the smell of their breath after drinking in the tavern. The Wife says that she does not care what her husband thinks about her breath and defends her husband and the married state. The Widow admits that her first husband had other lovers besides herself, but that she is currently being "plied" by a "Gentleman of passing gallant carr'age." Both the Widow and the Wife trade stories describing how they pretend sickness to get what they want from their husbands. The Widow advises the Maid Besse to trust neither a red-haired nor a yellow flaxen-haired man; she should choose a man with nut-brown, auburn, waxen, or black hair and make sure that he has a full beard. When Besse asserts that she will be sixteen next March, the Wife and Widow advise her to get married even though her mother thinks she should wait. The Widow refers to a youth who loves both Besse and her sister, but Besse will not return his favor because he is too short and not handsome enough. The Widow insists that he will maintain her well, but the Wife says Besse should follow her inclinations.

At this moment an overpowering smell of tobacco smoke comes up the stairs and the women complain. This leads to a conversation about what foods make them sick: pig makes the Wife's "body loose," the Widow cannot stomach "woodcock," and the Maid cannot eat "grosse Butchers flesh" or poor cuts of meat. During her pregnancy the Wife wanted to eat only "a Partridge wing" or a "Cherry-pye." They then discuss their recent dreams: the Wife dreamed of a spurless and combless cock; the Widow of leaping cats. They refuse the fiddler's offer of a song and continue to school the Maid in how to control men. When Besse says that she "thought mens love must still be fed with kindness," the other two women disabuse her of this. The Wife responds, "God helpe thee *Besse,* not one among a score, / That poore opinion is but Maidens blindnesse. . . ." It is best "in strangenesse we our meanings hide, / Which makes them love, & give good words beside." By this time the women are quite drunk. The Maid is afraid that if she drinks anymore, her girdle will break. The Widow berates Will, the Vintner's boy, who laughs at the Maid's comment about her girdle. She assures Will that the three of them are *"London-Gentlewomen* borne" and that she will pay the entire bill.

What is meant by describing the three women as "gentlewomen" is unclear. In addition to the Widow using this appellation, the Vintner and Fiddler use this term to describe the three women. They may be simply flattering the women or perhaps mocking them, as they would not technically be considered gentlewomen because their husbands were not landowners.[12] They are the new middling sort, the wives and daughters of the merchant class, not the landed gentry. Rowlands also describes them as "citizens" in the 1602 preface to *Tis Merry,* dedicated to "Gentlemen." The Wife, Maid, and Widow, however, are citizens and gentlewomen of London, for the pamphlet is insistently localized. They drink London's best claret in a London tavern, hear the bells of St. Mary-le-Bow, refer to streets of London, and make fun of "clowns" from the country who do not know how to drink like Londoners.

In Samuel Rowlands' second gossip pamphlet, *A whole crew of kind Gossips, all met to be merry,* six women, drinking claret in a tavern, complain about their husbands' inadequacies and trade strategies about how to control them. Instead of a dialogue, each gossip speaks at length of her situation in heroic couplets. The wives are answered by their husbands in the second half of the pamphlet.[13]

In the early 1600s, "gossip" was not necessarily a derogatory term, although men sometimes used it as such. In the fifteenth and sixteenth centuries, "gossip" or "godsip" was used to describe godparents of either gender; in the sixteenth and seventeenth centuries the definition was expanded to include any close male or female friend. Gossip, or the exchange of information, was useful to a community in enforcing understood customs of morality and neighborliness.[14] Later when gossip started to apply only to women, the term began to lose respect. In the eighteenth century, Samuel Johnson's *Dictionary* defines "gossip" as "one who runs about tattling like women in a lying in." "Shrew" and "scold," however, were more negative terms; scolding could be a legally actionable offense, while gossip was not.

The first gossip in *A whole crew* accuses her husband of miserliness: "His mind's of Money bags, to fill them full: / Ther's nothing that comes from him with good will, / But he is ever grudging, grumbling still." She says that she has learned from her sister Sara to be sullen, feign illness, weep, and scold in order to get her husband to open up his purse. She concludes her section with the assertion "A Shroe is ten times better then a sheepe."[15] Wife Two laments that although her husband gives her money, he contradicts everything she says. To cure him of this habit, she learned a lesson from her mother, who used to strike her father. She took a "Faggot-sticke" and beat her husband until "blood ran downe about his eares apace" and "he pist."

The third gossip applauds her friend's violence toward her husband, but says she is unable to strike her man because he is too strong. Her husband's fault is drunkenness. To get the upper hand over him, she sets a stool in his path. When he returns from the tavern, he trips and hurts his shins, but he cannot figure out who put the stool in his path. Gossip Four's husband wastes his money on cards and ignores her. She wishes that he would play the card games, noddy (cribbage) and dublets (backgammon), with her, although she deplores his sexual inadequacies. She says that he is "no Cocke of game, / For I do find he doth his business lame, / In things (you know my meaning) scant worth praise." To solve her problem she has "kinde Gentlemen" friends who give her gifts such as a ruff of lawn. When she sees a hat in church that she wants to buy, her husband berates her for not concentrating on prayer. She responds by saying, "Is Dice and Cards become a Puritan?"

In addition to his drinking, the fifth wife complains that her husband smokes tobacco:

> With filthy leaves he smoakes his head with all,
> Such Weeds, as *Indians* do *Tobacco* call:
> But sure as *Black-amores* looke outward skin,
> So Collier-like are English-men within,
> That take such trash. . . .

She likes "a *Sir-reverence*," or human excrement, as much as she likes his stinking tobacco breath. He used to have "breath as sweet as any Rose," but now she says, "if I do kisse him I am sicke." To combat her problem she throws his tobacco into the privy or toilet. The sixth, and final, gossip declares her problem is the worst because her husband is "lewd"; he knows all the "Taffity Queanes, and fine light silken Whores" in London / That have the gift of pox in their owne pores." He sings bawdy songs that he has learned from them and spends all his money on his whores instead of buying his wife new clothes. She, however, has "laide a plot / Shall coole the Gentleman is growne so hot." The sixth gossip concludes the first half of the pamphlet by asking that they set a date when the six women will meet again. If any of the gossips fails to show up, she will owe the others five shillings in wine.

The response of the six husbands is slightly shorter and more somber than that of the six wives. The first husband accuses the six wives of telling lies about their husbands. What upsets him is the fact that the gossips have put their slanders "in print" and that the husbands' silence may cause "the world" to believe their wives and censure them. This is a curious reversal of the chaste, silent woman and the man who expresses his views in print. The first husband says it is time for the husbands to speak. He has endured his wife Joan's "Shrowes tongue" enough; she is always demanding more money for clothes even though she has six gowns. What's worse, she earns "not a penny in a yeere," but only wants more money. Although he assures the other husbands that he does not hit his wife, he asserts that he will rule in his marriage: "Ile be head, my title Ile not lose." Husband

Two repeats his wife's complaint that he crosses her in everything she does. He says that he pays her tailor's and mercer's[16] bills, but wonders why she has to spend so much on her clothing when she is supposed to dress to please only him. He does not mention his wife's beating him with a "faggot-sticke."

The third husband, "charged by his wife to bee hard and cruell," laments that he is married to a widow and warns all bachelor readers to marry only maids. He describes her as "most impudent, and shamelesse bold." Because she continually praises her dead husband and "wishes in his grave with him she lay," he proclaims that a man married to such a woman has only two happy days in his life: his wedding day and the day when his wife is carried to her grave. He has heard from a friend that it is rumored that his wife is a whore. If he can prove it, he will divorce her because he is "loth" "to weare a paire of hornes." Husband Four, "complained by his wife to be a common Gamester," says he rarely plays tables or backgammon, and he detests dice and cards. He accuses his wife of laziness, but says that

> Sometimes her lookes will carry such a sway,
> That for my life I cannot say her nay:
> Sometimes her teares do charme me in such wise,
> That I give credit to deceiving eyes.
> Sometimes her words in such great force do stand,
> I yeeld to every thing she doth demand.

Lately, however, his wife has been trafficking with "some Gallants," and he has been experiencing a headache and a swelling in his forehead. He says he will not be "a Wittoll" or a contented cuckold; if she has committed adultery, he will turn his wife "to grasse" next summer.

The fifth husband, whose wife charged him with being a drunkard, says he does drink, but that he rarely gets drunk. Besides, if he did drink too much, his wife should say to him in private, "Husband, last night you sung a pot to hye" or "In truth (Sweet-hart) you are a little in," not talk publicly about his drinking in a tavern with her sister gossips. He says he will tame his wife; if she insults him publicly again, he has "a tricke to mortifie her flesh." Charged by his wife of inconstancy and haunting whores, the sixth husband says he has been in a bawdy house only twice. Although he sometimes gives his female neighbors " a pinte" of ale and kisses them, he is innocent. Besides, he says concerning his wife, "I do not care a pin" and hopes that she will die soon.

Critical opinion of Rowlands' two gossip pamphlets has been mixed, with *Tis Merry* receiving better reviews than *A whole crew*. In an excellent discussion of the pamphlets in *Women and the English Renaissance*, Linda Woodbridge describes it as Rowlands' "best poem" and says "it fails to accomplish its satiric objectives and bumbles instead into being a work of art." Edmund W. Gosse in *The Complete Works of Samuel Rowlands* describes *Tis Merry* as "one of the best studies of *genre* we possess in all Elizabethan literature." Although Woodbridge terms *A whole crew* "a lifeless, mean-spirited piece of work," she says that *Tis Merry* makes Rowlands "England's laureate of gossip verse." Gosse is also critical of *A whole crew*, describing it as "one of Rowlands' failures."[17] Perhaps with the publication of *Custom Is An Idiot: Renaissance Pamphlet Literature on Women*, a collection of pamphlets that includes the Rowlands' gossip pamphlets, *A whole crew* will be assessed more positively.[18]

Both *Tis Merry* and *A whole crew* were popular pamphlets in the seventeenth century. *Tis Merry* went into seven editions from 1602 to 1675, and *A whole crew* into three editions from 1609 to 1663, making the Rowlands' gossip pamphlets very profitable to the bookseller or publisher. Writers did not make much money from writing a pamphlet and neither did printers. Payment to authors ranged from only a small fee and a number of copies of the pamphlet to about forty shillings for one pamphlet. Writers made no extra money for subsequent editions. Printers also did not fare well, because there was not enough work for them to do and not enough capital to finance new work. The more fortunate printers were also booksellers who could profit very nicely from pamphlets that went into several editions. The number of copies in a press run was from 1,250 to 1,500 copies.[19] If in 1602 William White paid Rowlands forty shillings for *Tis Merry* and sold each copy for sixpence as stated in "A Conference betweene a Gentleman and a Prentice," he would have made about thirty-three pounds for the first printing of *Tis Merry* minus the printing costs.[20] In 1609 bookseller John Dean would have also made about the same for the second edition, although he would have had to pay White for the publishing rights. He also had additional author costs, as Rowlands wrote another gossip pamphlet, *A whole crew*, which was bound together with *Tis Merry* in the 1609 edition. In any case, pamphlet printing was very lucrative to booksellers. In addition, the printing of pamphlets was also critical for printers because the turnaround time for printing a pamphlet was short. A printer could set the type, print a pamphlet, and realize a quick profit while he or she was setting the type and correcting the proofs for a longer work.

Because one of the major costs of production was paper, which was bought in great quantity, being able to get a quick return on the printing of a pamphlet helped solve the habitual cash-flow problem of printing houses.[21] William Jaggard, the printer of the 1609 edition of Rowlands' two gossip pamphlets, printed many pamphlets while his compositors were working on Shakespeare's First Folio.

With each reprinting, material was added or deleted in order to persuade the potential buyer that this was a new pamphlet and ought to be purchased again. "A Conference betweene a Gentleman and a Prentice" mentioned above appears only in the first edition in 1602. Perhaps the publisher thought that the dialogue no longer made sense in the 1609 edition because the pamphlet was too well known for the apprentice to be announcing its appearance to the gentleman. Also included only in the 1602 edition was a dedication "To All the Pleasaunt conceited [clever] London Gentle-women that are friends to mirth, and enemie to dull Melancholy." Using the same stanza form that is used in *Tis Merry*, Rowlands asserts that "this merry meeting" is written for London gentlewomen who like to drink, not for "peevish" women who take their "liquor by the dram and ounce / With Faith I cannot drinke, cry fie and frowne." Rowlands compares the drinking gentlewomen with Dido, who plied Aeneas with drink; Semiramis, who "dranke all her Nobles downe"; and Cato's wife, who also was a wine drinker.

A whole crew is also dedicated to women, but these women are not drinking women, but virginal maids of London who wish they were wives. The pamphlet is to instruct the maids how not to behave. Rowlands tells them:

> Abuse not HUSBANDS *at each gossips feast*
> *When they (good harmelesse men) offend you least:*
> *For if with any fault you can them touch,*
> *It onely is, their loving you too much.*

It is impossible to know how many women read these two pamphlets, but other pamphlets having to do with issues concerning women are also dedicated to women. For example, William Heale's *An Apologie for Women* (1609), on wife beating, is dedicated to Lady M. H., and Christopher Newstead's *An Apologie* (1620), on the superiority of women, is dedicated to Mary Beaumont, the countess of Buckingham, the mother of George Villiers, the favorite of James I. These pamphlets dedicated to women may point to female readership. Recent studies by Margaret Ferguson, Jacqueline Pearson, and Eve

Sanders suggest that literacy rates for women, particularly in London, were higher than previously thought.[22] Given the strictures on their time, women who could read may have been more likely to read a short pamphlet than a longer book. Or perhaps some women heard these pamphlets read aloud at household circles or social gatherings.[23] The short length of a pamphlet might have made it more likely for them to have been read aloud.

Pamphlet reading was often disparaged. Alexandra Halasz suggests that female readership of pamphlets might correlate with "the predilection among university men not to acknowledge pamphlet reading as a serious activity." Thomas Bodley wanted no pamphlets to defile the library he founded at Oxford in 1603. He called them "baggage books" and wrote to the librarian at the Bodleian: "the benefit therof will nothing neere contervaile, the harme that the scandal will bring unto the Librarie, when it shalbe given out, that we stuffe it full of baggage books."[24] In *Women and the English Renaissance,* Linda Woodbridge dispenses with the word "pamphlet." For her it is an "insidious term" that denotes "hasty composition, ephemerality, a popular and undiscriminating readership, and hack work."[25] I think it is important to reclaim the pamphlet as a critical part of the early modern print culture both in its role in the printing house and as a form that has a special affinity for questions about women.

Samuel Rowlands makes extravagant claims for his 1602 pamphlet *Tis Merry.* In a dedication to gentlemen that is omitted in later editions, he states, whether facetiously or not, that his pamphlet is an improvement on Chaucer's *Canterbury Tales* because he includes more women's voices. Rowlands compares Chaucer's pilgrims at the Taberd Inn to the Wife, Maid, and Widow, who "drinke like men" at their London tavern. Unlike Chaucer, however, who, according to Rowlands, "of blithe Wenches scarcitie he hath / Of all that Crue none but the wife of Bathe," Rowlands writes an all-women scene except for brief appearances by the Fiddler, the Vintner, and his Boy. Also printed only in the 1602 edition of *Tis Merry* was "In Commendation of this Booke," which advertises the pamphlet as a suitable work for the middling sort. I. S., the writer of "In Commendation," addresses *Tis Merry* as "not seated in a sumptuous Chaire, / Nor do thy Lines import of Majesty," but instead, "*A Gossips friendly meeting,* art thou named"; or, in other words, Rowlands consciously positions his gossip pamphlets to be read by the newly emerging and increasingly literate middle class. One such reader was John Manningham, a young law student of the Middle Temple. He

was so taken with the language of *Tis Merry* that a month after the
first edition was printed, he copied thirteen lines or passages that
were about drinking or that were particularly bawdy into his diary.
One such example is the description of a man that the widow warns
the maid to avoid, one "whose fore-frunt lookes like Jacke-an-Apes
behind."[26]

Other additions to the later editions of *Tis Merry* point to
women, also perhaps facetiously, as writers. The title of this article,
"Weele have a Wench shall be our Poet," is a line from a dedication
to the readers by the wife, maid, and widow that prefaces the 1619
and 1627 editions. The wife, maid, and widow, speaking in the first-
person plural, say, "weele have a Wench shall be our Poet." They
contend that men drink but have "no Bookes in Rime to show it."
By writing a pamphlet, the three women will "pay them [men]
home, because they doe provoke." In this preface the three women
also assert that they pay their bills. They claim, "*And there was no
man charg'd with our expense; / Unto a penny wee our reckning payd.*"
At the conclusion of *Tis Merry*, the widow also insists on paying her
tavern bill. She tells the Vintner's Boy that "weele pay your Maister
for the Wine we have." Often in the early modern period, patrons of
alehouses ran up large debts. Think of Christopher Sly in *The Taming of the Shrew*, who tells the Hostess that he will pay "not a denier"
for the glasses he has broken in the alehouse (Induction 9) or Mistress Quickly of the Boar's Head in *1 Henry IV* who tells Falstaff,
"You owe money here besides, Sir John, for your diet, and by-
drinkings, and money lent you, four and twenty pound"
(3.3.72–72). But these gossips are proud that they pay their bills.
The widow in *Tis Merry* was previously in domestic service, and the
wife tends her husband's shop, so they have some means. Although
the gossips in *A whole crew* also claim to pay their drinking bills, their
money is probably taken from their husbands. The first wife, according to the narrator in the beginning of the pamphlet, "spend[s]
her Crowne [in the tavern] / With any she that durst . . . / That
never plaide the Mizer in her life." The six husbands complain that
their wives do not earn money but spend their days gadding about,
playing with their lapdogs, and spending their husbands' money, a
common complaint of gossip literature.

Additional stanzas and ballads are added to later editions of *Tis
Merry* to make it a new work for potential buyers. One of the ballads
added to the 1613?, 1619, and 1627 editions again points to women
wielding the pen. *The Maydes bad choyce* is a ballad, "Pen'd by a Mayde
her selfe, whose constant truth / Was lately wronged by a Merchants

Youth." The woman author of the ballad states that despite being beautiful, ready-witted, and skillful in embroidery and dancing, she was taken advantage of by a merchant's youth. Although she is now pregnant, he has left her for another maid. She warns maidens to take heed, that because of her pregnancy, she is "not *Widdow, Wife, nor Mayd,* / But of another size." Other changes to later editions of *Tis Merry* are the additions of woodcuts of the wife, maid, and widow. The woodcut added to the 1627 edition differs from the woodcut in the 1613? and 1619 editions in that all three women wear hats, those of the widow and wife being considerably larger than the hats in the previous woodcut. The maid no longer wears a ruff, reflecting contemporary fashion, and the women are larger in comparison to the serving man, who has become smaller. The only addition to the 1613 edition of *A whole crew* is a dialogue between a maid and a bachelor in six-line stanzas in which they both agree to beware shrews and widows in marriage. Before they marry they will ask permission of their parents.

Besides making some money for the printer and author and more money for the publisher, the intended object of Rowlands' two gossip pamphlets probably was to satirize women who drink together in public taverns away from their husbands. Most likely Rowlands' male audience would have found the thought of women writing ballads, wenches writing poetry, and gossips' writing appearing in print, as charged by the first husband in *A whole crew,* hilarious, if not anxiety provoking. But how would women in the seventeenth century have read or heard these pamphlets? Would they have missed some of the intended jokes and, instead of looking at women's writing as a violation of chastity, be intrigued by the possibilities of women and print? Perhaps they would regard the representation of the women's friendships and their ability to gather together to talk and pay their own bills as something to be emulated.

Frances E. Dolan speculates on possible responses of women to Thomas Heywood's *A Curtain Lecture.* She suggests that "it is also possible to imagine a female reader who finds encouragement in all this female complaint or who picks up tips about things she might resent or insults she could level."[27] Pamela Brown echoes this contention when she says that some "satire [of women] raises to view scenes and pleasures that some might prefer to imitate rather than scorn."[28] In "Separate Domains? Women and Authority in Early Modern England," Bernard Capp uses *Tis Merry* as an example of how "ordinary women could create their own social networks and their own social space," in order to introduce his contention that women "were not the helpless, passive victims of male authority." According to Capp, women used their networks of gossips to obtain "some measure of support, independence and even power."[29]

Rowlands' probable intended joke, "weele have a wench shall be our poet," may not have been received so humorously by the women who read and listened to his gossip pamphlets. Perhaps these two pamphlets offered a space for women's speech, camaraderie, and agency. Probably contemporary women writers, such as Rachel Speght, Aemilia Lanyer, and Dorothy Leigh, welcomed the references to women in print.[30] And perhaps some women reveled in the antimasculinist humor and took pleasure in the women's bawdy speech and quietly applauded the independence of the Wife, Maid, and Widow who drink together, share gossip, and pay their own bills.

Notes

1. In *The Imprint of Gender: Authorship and Publication in the English Renaissance* (Ithaca: Cornell University Press, 1993), Wendy Wall uses "A Conference between a Gentleman and a Prentice," appended to the 1602 edition of Rowlands' *Tis Merry when Gossips meete*, to suggest "the conflation of [pamphlet] text and woman," 204. Alexandra Halasz in *The Marketplace of Print: Pamphlets and the Public Sphere in Early Modern England* (Cambridge: Cambridge University Press, 1997) discusses the preface to *Tis Merry* in her section on commodity pamphlets, 171–4.

2. Linda Woodbridge discusses the genre of gossip literature in *Women and the English Renaissance: Literature and the Nature of Womankind, 1540–1620* (Urbana: University of Illinois Press, 1986), 224–43. Some of the characteristics of gossip literature, according to Woodbridge, are the emphasis on drinking; the schooling of maids by experienced women on husband management; the debate on whether being a wife, maid or a widow is the preferred state; and the complaining of wives about the faults of their husbands. Among the works she cites are *The proude wyves Pater noster that would go gaye*, 1560; Edward Gosynhyll's *The Scole house of women*, ca. 1542; William Dunbar's *The Twa marrit wemen and the wedo (A Talk of Ten Wives on Their Husbands)*, ca. 1508; Henry Parrot's *The Gossips Greeting*, 1620; *The Batchelars Banquet*, 1603; and John Davies' *A contention betwixt a Wife, a Widdow and a Maide*, 1608, which was probably influenced by *Tis Merry*.

3. *Records of the Court of the Stationers' Co. from Register B.*, ed. W. W. Greg and Eleanor Boswell (London: The Bibliographical Society, 1930), 79. *A Transcript of the Register of the Company of the Stationers of London, 1554–1660 A.D.*, ed. Edward Arber (London, 1875),

2:832–3). *A Mery Meetinge* was reissued as *The knave of clubbes* in 1609; there are three surviving copies of the 1600 edition of *The Letting*. In 1599, the year before the Rowlands' pamphlets were burned, the official censors of the press, John Whitgift, archbishop of Canterbury, and Richard Bancroft, bishop of London, ordered many pamphlets and books by Thomas Nashe, John Marston, Christopher Marlowe, Gabriel Harvey, Robert Tofte, Sir John Davies, and Thomas Middleton, among others, to be burned by the Stationers' Company; see Lynda E. Boose, "The 1599 Bishops' Ban, Elizabethan Pornography, and the Sexualization of the Jacobean Stage," in *Enclosure Acts,* ed. Richard Burt and John Michael Archer (Ithaca: Cornell University Press, 1994), 185–187.

4. Arber, 3:216.

5. Edmund Gosse, "Memoir on Samuel Rowlands," in *The Complete Works of Samuel Rowlands 1598–1628* (Glasgow, printed for the Hunterian Club, 1880), 1:14–17.

6. Ibid.

7. Sir Walter Scott in Advertisement for *The Letting of Humours in the Head Vaine,* by Samuel Rowlands (Edinburgh: reprt. by James Ballantyne & Co. for William Laing and William Blackwood, 1815) in Gosse, *The Complete Works of Samuel Rowlands,* 1:7.

8. Thomas Campbell in Sir Walter Scott, Advertisement, 1:7, note 2.

9. In *The History of the Wine Trade in England* (London, Wyman & Sons, 1906), Andre L. Simon says that a gallon of sack cost from three shillings tenpence to four shillings eightpence in 1598–99, and a gallon of claret cost from one shilling eightpence to two shillings in 1600 (III, 291). A shilling was the daily wage of a building craftsman in 1600.

10. *Thomas Platter's Travels in England, 1599,* trans. and intro. Clare Williams (London: Jonathan Cape, 1937), 170.

11. Keith Wrightson, "Alehouses, Order and Reformation in Rural England, 1590–1660," in Eileen and Stephen Yeo, *Popular Culture and Class Conflict, 1590–1914* (Brighton: Harvester, 1981), esp. 6–7.

12. Although landed wealth was what was most important in determining gentleman status, the category "gentleman" (or "gentlewoman") was not legally defined: Keith Wrightson, *English Society, 1580–1680* (New Brunswick, N. J. : Rutgers University Press, 1982), 17–38.

13. In the 1613 edition of *A whole crew,* the wives and husbands alternate their comments; in the 1663 edition, as in the 1609 edition, the six wives speak first and are answered by their husbands.

14. Sara Mendelson and Patricia Crawford, *Women in Early Modern England, 1550–1720* (Oxford: Clarendon Press, 1998), 215.

15. Pamela Allen Brown's *Better a Shrew Than a Sheep: Jesting Women in Early Modern Drama and Culture* (forthcoming from Cornell University Press) discusses the importance of gossips in maintaining social order.

16. A mercer is a dealer in fabrics.
17. Woodbridge, 224–31; Gosse, 1:17.
18. Edited by Susan Gushee O'Malley, forthcoming, University of Illinois Press.
19. See Edwin Miller Haviland, *The Professional Writer in Elizabethan England: A Study of Nondramatic Literature* (Cambridge, Mass.: Harvard University Press, 1959); Sandra Clark, *The Elizabethan Pamphleteers: Popular Moralistic Pamphlets, 1580–1640* (London: The Athlone Press, 1983); H. S. Bennett, *English Books and Readers, 1603–1640,* vols. 2 and 3, Cambridge: Cambridge University Press, 1965); Phoebe Sheavyn, *The Literary Profession in the Elizabethan Age,* (New York: Haskell House Publishers, 1964 [reprint from 1909 edition]); Colin Clair, *A History of Printing in Britain* (London: Cassell, 1965).
20. Sixpence was considered a high price for a pamphlet. Perhaps this was wishful thinking on Rowlands' part. A more likely price was two- or threepence. See Miller, 151–64; Clark, 25; Bennett, 2:228. My figures are computed on a press run of 1,400 copies.
21. Halasz, 15; Tessa Watt in *Cheap Print and Popular Piety, 1550–1640* (Cambridge: Cambridge University Press, 1991), 262, states that paper was often 75 percent of the cost of production of a book, depending on length and whether or not it was the first edition.
22. Margaret Ferguson, "Renaissance Concepts of the 'Woman Writer'" in *Women and Literature,* ed. Helen Wilcox (Cambridge: Cambridge University Press, 1996), 147–50 and Jacqueline Pearson, "Women Reading, Reading Women," also in *Women and Literature,* 80–1. Eve Rachele Sanders, *Gender and Literacy on Stage in Early Modern England* (Cambridge: Cambridge University Press, 1998), 197, note 3, has a brief survey of articles on women's literacy.
23. See "Women's Household Circles as a Gendered Reading Formation: Whitney, Tyler, and Lanyer," in Louise Schleiner's *Tudor and Stuart Women Writers* (Bloomington: Indiana University Press, 1994), 1–29, and Barry Reay's chapter on "Orality, Literacy, and Print" in his *Popular Cultures in England, 1550–1750* (London: Longman, 1998), 36–70.
24. *Letters of Sir Thomas Bodley to Thomas James, First Keeper of the Bodleian Library,* ed. G. W. Wheeler, 22. Quoted in Halasz, 1. Despite Sir Thomas Bodley's wishes, the Bodleian library possesses the 1609 editions of *Tis Merry* and *A whole crew.*
25. Woodbridge, 7.
26. John Manningham, *The Diary of John Manningham of the Middle Temple, 1602–1603,* ed. Robert Parker Sorlien (Hanover, N. H.: University Press of New England, 1976), 98–9 (folio 45).
27. *The Taming of the Shrew: Texts and Contexts,* ed. Frances E. Dolan (Boston: Bedford Books of St. Martin's Press, 1996), 325.

28. Brown, chapter 2.

29. Bernard Capp, "Separate Domains? Women and Authority in Early Modern England," in *The Experience of Authority in Early Modern England,* ed. Paul Griffiths, Adam Fox, and Steve Hindle (New York: St. Martin's Press, 1996), 117, 139.

30. Rachel Speght wrote *A Mouzell for Melastomus,* 1617, a response to Swetnam's *Arraignment of Lewd, idle, froward, and unconstant women,* 1615; Aemelia Lanyer wrote *Salve Deus Rex Judaeorum,* 1611; and Dorothy Leigh wrote *The Mothers Blessing,* 1616, printed shortly after her death.

PART IV

GENERIC DEPARTURES:
FIGURING THE MATERNAL BODY,
CONSTRUCTING FEMALE CULTURE

CHAPTER 7

THE MAT(T)ER OF DEATH:
THE DEFENSE OF EVE AND
THE FEMALE *Ars Moriendi*

Patricia Phillippy

Describing Philip Stubbes's *A Chrystal Glasse for Christian Women*,
which presents "the godly life and Christian death"[1] of Stubbes's
twenty-year-old wife Katherine, Kate Aughterson suggests that the
work—as if against its author's will—becomes "complexly dialogic"
when it offers evidence not of "Katherine Stubbes's internalisation of
the ideology of womanhood," but of her "resistance to dominant
ideological discourses."[2] Apparently prompted by a desire to find in
the early modern woman's voice a subversive chord that would signal the work's feminism and frustrate Stubbes's authorial and patriarchal monologism, Aughterson portrays Katherine as an
autonomous speaker whose forays into extradomestic theological debate and public deathbed confession of faith (that is, both performed
before witnesses at her death and later published by Stubbes) run
counter to her culture's—and her husband/author's—insistence on
women's chastity, silence, and obedience. While Aughterson's motives may appeal to, and be shared by, many critics of early modern
women's writing, her interpretation is troubled by Stubbes's own
promotion of his subject as a "rare and wonderful example . . . who

whilst shee lived, was a Myrrour of womanhood and now being dead, is a perfect patterne of true Christianitie."[3] A husband's pride in his wife's accomplishments (which bespeak his own exemplary government of household subordinates)[4] occasions Stubbes's memorial act and discounts the possibility that Katherine's speech or actions transgress the strictures placed upon her by his authority. Moreover, the text's popularity (it appeared in thirty-four editions between 1591 and 1700) seems to attest not to Katherine's dialogic resistance to patriarchy, but to her effective exemplarity within it. More troubling, indeed, is the fact that Katherine Stubbes never truly *speaks* in *A Chrystal Glasse:* despite Stubbes's claim that her deathbed drama is "set downe word for word as shee spake," Katherine's voice is always represented for us by Philip.[5] Any dialogism contained in the text, therefore, would necessarily be that of Philip Stubbes's voice—a polyvocality that might, in turn, suggest feminist tendencies *within* dominant patriarchal and theological discourses themselves. The binarism of women's "monologic internalization" of masculinity versus their "dialogic resistance" to patriarchal discourse is in need of refinement in order to characterize more accurately the feminine voice in the period and to ask how the performance of femininity within a culturally sanctioned (that is, "masculine") genre might be given different inflections by the female writer than by the male. As such, *A Chrystal Glasse* might be read not as a primer on the restrictive masculine discourses against which early modern feminine (or feminist) speech continually struggled, but as an affirmation of more numerous, more productive generic and discursive options for early modern women than Aughterson's one-dimensional portrait of patriarchal monologism allows.

Such options, as Katherine Stubbes's deathbed performance implies, are clearly available to early modern women approaching the matter of death.[6] A surprisingly large number of texts written by early modern women concern themselves explicitly with death and mourning, and bespeak not only the widely perceived intimacy of women with death's physical ravishments but also the unusual license to write and publish afforded to women in proximity to death—from lamenting wives and mothers to women who spoke with the heightened authority granted by the deathbed. This essay examines two works that have the distinction of being the only female-authored *artes moriendi* of the period, Rachel Speght's *Mortalities Memorandum, with A Dreame Prefixed* (1621) and Alice Sutcliffe's *Meditations of Man's Mortalitie* (1634),[7] in order to characterize the feminine voice within the genre and to ask in what ways these women redirect generic conventions toward constructions of their gendered presence as authors. Like many male writers in the period, both Sutcliffe and Speght dedicate their death manuals to women, but in the case of these female-authored *artes,* their dedications establish intimate connections between women joined in mourning that constitute textual reflections of the communal character of early modern women's grief.[8] Both texts, moreover, are unusually concerned with questions of women's writing, education, and publication, and use the genre to theorize the possibility of women's public discourse and to realize that possibility. If the male-authored *A Chrystal Glasse* invites the question "Is there a woman's voice in this text?" so, too, do the female-authored *artes moriendi* of Speght and Sutcliffe: rather than marrying the gendered speaker to the sexual identity of the texts' authors, I suggest that the woman's voice resides in discernible sites and gestures within the works at which gender is understood as a cultural act or social construction not uniformly or directly linked to the biological sex of the body.[9] In Speght's and Sutcliffe's exercises in the art of dying, the figure of Eve proves to be such a site, at which rival versions of femininity are staged. For these authors, the legacy of the pamphlet debate's defense of Eve offers a potent image within which to focus not only a gendered narrative of Christian salvation but also a gendered "anatomy" of Christian consolation; a *raison d'être* for the *ars moriendi* itself that engages the commonplace, "Men live and learn to *die,* and *die* to live"[10] through the unique conflation of life, death, and knowledge in the female figure of Eve.

Joseph Swetnam's *Arraignment of Lewd, idle, froward, and unconstant women* opens with a grim portrait of Eve: "shee was no sooner made, but straightway, her mind was set upon mischiefe, for by her aspiring minde and wanton will, shee quickly procured mans fall, and therefore ever since they are and have beene a woe to man, and follow the line of their first leader."[11] In *A Mouzell for Melastomus,* Rachel Speght offers a narrative of the Fall and a defense of Eve's role within it that parallel and prefigure her treatment of Eden in her later work, *Mortalities Memorandum.* She begins her refutation of the charge "that woman, though created good, yet by giving eare to Sathans temptations, brought death and misery upon all her posterity," by admitting that Eve, "being the weaker vessel was with more facility to be seduced: Like as a Cristall glasse sooner receives a cracke then a strong stone pot."[12] The image of Eve as a crystal glass resonates with the literature of exemplarity (as suggested by its echo of Stubbes's title, *A Chrystal Glasse*) while, paradoxically, describing feminine weakness rather than virtue. This paradox begins the movement undertaken in *A Mouzell*'s narrative of the Fall from an essentialist casting of sex in the Garden to a historicized, contingent notion of gender as manifested in culture. Eve, "created good," is at once weak by nature and more attractive and refined than the "strong stone pot" that is man.[13] The double meaning of "glass" as both vessel and mirror invests Eve with significances that rest simultaneously in the material female body (a beautiful but imperfect container) and its social currency (a model of feminine behavior). Eve's troublesome exemplarity points to Speght's retrospective acculturation of the Creation story itself and a reading of gender within that narrative that consistently overrides the original "natures" of the sexes toward affirming the social functions of gender as established by the Fall. Thus Speght argues that despite their different prelapsarian natures, man and woman commit "parallel" offenses (*Mouzell* 14): although woman sinned first, man's transgression was more serious since he, as the stronger vessel, "should have yeelded greatest obedience to God" (*Mouzell* 15). Thus joined in sin, both man and woman arrive at the same fate—although it is a fate enabled by woman: "by *Hevah's* blessed Seed (as Saint *Paul* affirmes) it is brought to passe, that *male and female are all one in Christ Jesus*" (*Mouzell* 16).

Speght's assertion of the equality of the sexes in Christ engages the familiar typology of the Fall as a *felix culpa* that both initiates and enables Christian salvation. She exploits the gendering of that typology even as she describes its consequential eradication of gender. Grounded on the potentially radical restructuring of social hierarchies advocated by Galatians 3:28 ("There is neither Jew nor Greek, there is neither bond nor free, there is neither male nor female: for ye are all one in Christ Jesus"), Speght locates this merger of male and female within a chronology of the Fall that features woman in a complex central role as both cause and effect:

> the first promise was made in Paradise, God makes to a woman, that by her Seede should the Serpents head be broken: whereupon *Adam* calles her *Hevah, life,* that as the woman had beene an occasion of his sinne, so should woman bring foorth the Saviour from sinne, which was in the fullnesse of time accomplished. (*Mouzell* 15–16)

Speght's careful chronicle of events in Eden portrays this aftermath of the Fall as the founding moment not only of death, but of life as well—both intimately associated with the female body of Eve. Adam's "calling" of the woman by name, *Hevah* (in the Geneva Bible's rendering on which Speght, as a Calvinist, relied), inaugurates the redemptive march of Christian history. If the loss of Eden is a fall into death and mourning, it is also, Speght suggests, a fall into history, into culture, and the moment at which the prelapsarian sexes "fall into" gender.[14] Woman is the purveyor of death, but she is also *hevah*—the guarantor of life itself. Femininity finds its calling, as it were, in the consequences of events determined by the female.

Speght's defense of Eve by way of an indictment of Adam, while a strategy shared by other early modern women writers (not only those of the pamphlet debate, but Aemilia Lanyer as well), cannot be seen, in itself, as subversive of orthodoxy. The Church of England's *Certain Sermons and Homilies,* first published in 1562 and repeatedly reissued through the eighteenth century, instructed the faithful in its "Sermon of the State of Matrimonie" that "though a man had a companion in his fault, yet should he not thereby be without his fault. . . . For Adam did lay the blame upon the woman, and she turned it unto the serpent: but yet neither of them was thus excused."[15] "The Second Homilie Concerning the death and Passion of our Saviour Christ" further explains:

> When our great grandfather Adam had broken Gods commandement, in eating the apple forbidden him in Paradise, at the motion and suggestion of his wife, he purchased thereby, not onely to himselfe, but also to his posterity for ever, the just wrath and indignation of God, who according to his former sentence pronounced at the giving of the commandement, condemned both him and all his to everlasting death. . . . [B]y this offence of onely *Adam,* death came upon all men to condemnation.[16]

Philip Stubbes gives a similar interpretation to his wife when Katherine confesses her belief that "[man] had no sooner received the inestimable blessing of free will in innocency and integrity, but by hearkening to the poisoned suggestions of the wicked serpent, and by obeying his persuasions, he lost his free will, his integrity, and perfection."[17] Aughterson observes that this elision of "Eve as an agent of temptation" is more unusual than the inclusion (based on Galatians 3:28) of "all men and women in the generic (though gendered) man," but sees "this double revisionary reading" as carrying "radical implications for women's power to speak and act in a religious field." "The discovery of this space by Katherine Stubbes," she concludes, "gives *this account and her words* a poignant power, and *her* rereading of the historical Fall in ungendered terms both a spiritual and temporal significance" (my italics).[18] When read in light of the state-sanctioned Anglican sermons quoted above, Stubbes's elision of Eve seems slightly less revisionary, and when we recall that this rereading is technically Philip's rather than Katherine's, the exact location and quality of the woman's voice in this "radical" account is difficult to discern. Yet a comparison of the passage with Speght's defense is nonetheless instructive, since the texts' shared allusion to Galatians 3:28 suggests that both Stubbes's and Speght's textual performances of femininity (and perhaps Katherine Stubbes's nontextual deathbed performance) argue the eradication of gender differences to exonerate Eve, on the one hand, and to authorize their speakers on the other. Moreover, *A Chrystal Glasse* contextualizes this characteristically "feminine" gesture within the discourses of the *ars moriendi*, since Katherine "is on her deathbed occupying the literal space between a gendered and submissive present and an ungendered and equal future."[19] In doing so, the work implies that the figure of Eve—simultaneously the bearer of life and death—may offer a means of self-authorization for the woman's voice in female-authored arts of dying.

Three times in her brief corpus of written works Speght treats the story of the Fall, each time inflecting it with gendered terms that resonate throughout her defense of women against Swetnam's arraignment, her autobiographical "Dreame," and the consolatory *Mortalities Memorandum*. Since original sin marks the birth of death, Speght's *ars moriendi* begins with a six-stanza rehearsal of the events in Eden that echoes the narrative's gendering in *A Mouzell*: "Thus eating both," Speght reaffirms, "they both did joyntly sinne, / And *Elohim* dishonoured by their act; / Doth ratifie, what he had earst decreed, / That *Death* must be the wages of their fact" (*MM* 61). Again she points toward the translation of Eve from woman to "life" and from sex to gender: while "*In Adam all men die*," she states, "*Womans seede hath brooke the Serpents head*" (*MM* 61, 63). Finally, she associates the inaugural moment of mourning in the aftermath of the Fall with her own authorial project in *Mortalities Memorandum*:

> Considering then *Jehovahs* just decree,
> That man shall surely taste of *Death* through sinne,
> I much lament, when as I mete in mind,

> The dying state securely men live in;
> Excluding from their memories that day,
> When they from hence by *Death* must passe away. (*MM* 62)

As the epigraph that joins "A Dreame" to the *Memorandum* summarizes Speght's goal, "*Esto Memor Mortis*" (*MM* 60), the Fall into death
prompts Speght's lament and her writing of the text as an exhortation
to the Elect to "welcome *Death* with joy of heart" (*MM* 76).

In Speght's revision of Eden in "A Dreame," the uniquely gendered contours of her memorial project take shape and the characteristics of the female *ars moriendi* begin to emerge. In many ways,
Mortalities Memorandum is a conventional entry in the consolatory
literature of the period: Speght's handling of themes such as *contemptus mundi* (64, 66) and the good versus bad death (73–4, 76)
and her imagery—life as a loan that God justly calls in (87), as a
prison (64, 76), as a snake-filled garden (69)—are all consistent with
the many Protestant arts of dying that appeared before and after her
work (and, as we shall see, are all reiterated by Sutcliffe).[20] Her
avowed motives, too, are predictable and familiar: "from continuall
thought of *Deaths* assault"—prompted by the reading of her book—
"Doe sundry speciall benefits arise" (*MM* 85). Speght's work departs
from convention, however, by prefacing *Mortalities Memorandum*
with the autobiographical "Dreame," where we understand that this
author has personal motives for composing a text that is at once an
act of consolation and a work of mourning:

> But when I wak't, I found my dreame was true;
> For *Death* had ta'ne my mothers breath away,
> Though of her life it could not her bereave,
> Sith shee in glorie lives with Christ for aye;
> Which makes me glad, and thankefull for her blisse,
> Though still bewayle her absence, whom I misse. (*MM* 59–60)

Speght's lamentation for the postlapsarian condition of humankind
here takes on an authenticity of direct experience. Valuing grief by
experience, Speght unites the self-history recounted in "A Dreame"
with the teleology of fall and redemption that opens *Mortalities
Memorandum,* and returns to Eden to anchor the feminine art of
dying in the polysemous figure of Eve. Thus "A Dreame" rewrites
Eden in the image of "*Eruditions* garden" (*MM* 51), a second Paradise entered by way of *Experience* whose fruit, available to "both
man and woman" (*MM* 53), is lifesaving *Knowledge:* "'Tis life eternall God and Christ to *Know*" (*MM* 57).

Implicit in Speght's defense of Eve as "life" is an exoneration of women's desire for knowledge: thus "A Dreame" reverses the Fall by depicting her state of mind *prior* to her entry into Erudition's garden as "an irkesome griefe" (*MM* 51) that she later understands as Ignorance; a state of living death (*MM* 55) that Thought "pitie[s] much and doe[s] bewayle" (*MM* 50) even as the speaker will "bewayle" the death of her mother at the poem's close (*MM* 60). Upon entering "the place / Where *Knowledge* growes," Speght like a second Eve is tempted by "the vertue of the plant" (*MM* 55) and learns that it is "a lawfull avarice, / To covet *Knowledge* daily more and more" (*MM* 57). Speght's rendering of knowledge as life—that is, knowledge of salvation through Christ as the guarantee of life after death—licenses her revisionary treatment of the woman in the Garden and her reversal of the misogynist censure of Eve's desire for knowledge. Insofar as the *ars moriendi* instructs Christians in the knowledge that is a remedy not only for grief ("The onlie medicine for your maladie is *Knowledge*," *MM* 51) but also for death ("'Tis life eternall, God and Christ to *Know*," *MM* 57), Speght's deployment of Eve as a figure for life-in-death or life-through-knowledge rationalizes the genre itself by constructing femininity at the fruitful juncture of these terms.

Speght portrays her education as the experience of a redeemed Eve in a second Eden that cures rather than kills. This portrayal informs the construction of the woman's voice in her work. Like Lanyer's clever defense of Eve's desire for knowledge in *Salve Deus Rex Judaeorum* ("Yet men will boast of Knowledge which he tooke / From *Eves* fair hand, as from a learned Booke"),[21] Speght's defense of Eve is also an indictment of men's scholarly pretensions. Thus Speght's second work implicitly continues the feminist critique of "masculinity . . . as a product of written language"[22] that is carried out explicitly in *A Mouzell for Melastomus*. "A Dreame" traces Speght's educational history, including the unnamed "occurrence" (*MM* 57) that signaled the end of her studies, and records her foray into the pamphlet debate:

> But by the way I saw a full fed Beast
> Which roared like some monster, or a Devill.
> And on Eves sex he foamed filthie froth,
> As if that he had had the falling evil;
> To whom I went to free them from mishaps,
> And with a *Mouzell* sought to binde his chaps. (*MM* 58)

Speght's quasi-heroic encounter with Swetnam suggests that misogyny is a monster best vanquished with learning. The studies of

Speght's youth, although curtailed by the interruption that "made [her] rest content with that [she] had, / Which was but little, as effect doth show" (*MM* 57), are nonetheless adequate to enable her to defeat the vicious but untenable arguments of her opponent. The emphasis on experience as the source of knowledge in Speght's allegory of her education, as Simon Shepherd points out, opposes "the formal, received opinions of the 'authorities' and tradition," countering masculine authority with feminine experience as a defining feature of the woman's authorial voice.[23] But the appearance of this secular beast is immediately followed in "A Dreame" by Speght's portrait of a second, more ferocious monster who is less easily tamed:

> Thus leaving them I passed on my way,
> But ere that I had little further gone,
> I saw a fierce insatiable foe,
> Depopulating Countries, sparing none;
> Without respect of age, sex, or degree,
> It did devoure, and could not daunted be. (*MM* 59)

The encounter with Death introduces a new level of experience into the poem and its author's autobiography ("with pearcing dart my mother deare it slew," *MM* 59), and the painful knowledge derived from that experience retroactively interprets and redirects Speght's literary career. Unlike her battle with Swetnam, for which she was prepared by years of learning grounded in youthful experience, her mother's death and the speaker's consequent mourning are a struggle for which she was entirely unprepared: "Her sodeine losse hath cut my feeble heart, / So deepe, that daily I indure the smart" (*MM* 60). The result is *Mortalities Memorandum* itself, an effort to "blaze the nature of this mortall foe," written both in response to Death's "cruell deed" and as a cure for the speaker's pain: "The profit may and will the paines requite" (*MM* 60). Speght's "paines" reveal her gendering of authority, since they are at once the conventional pains experienced by male and female writers alike in bringing forth the text as "off-spring" (*MM* 45) and the more personal pain of a mourning daughter for her absent mother. Again Speght turns to Eve, whose punishments for seeking knowledge—the fall into mourning and pain in childbirth—are simultaneously the results of death and its remedy. In acquiring direct knowledge of death in the loss of her mother, Speght stages in "A Dreame" the lesson of the *Memorandum* that follows: that mourning can be overcome only with the knowledge enabled by Eve, the knowledge that "by Christs *Death* grim *Mors* has lost his sting" (*MM* 75).

Mortalities Memorandum is dedicated to Speght's godmother, Marie Moundford, a figure whose presence in the text underscores the absence of Speght's recently deceased mother and counterbalances that of her father, who is invoked in an oft-quoted passage in the dedication: "I am now, as by a strong motive induced (for my rights sake) to produce and divulge this off-spring of my indevour, to prove them further futurely who have formerly deprived me of my due, imposing my abortive upon the father of me, but not of it" (*MM* 45). Speght's concern to locate her authorial presence at the fertile juncture of maternity and mourning—that is, in the figure of Eve—acknowledges both the paternal legacy of textual erudition that produced the "abortive" *Mouzell for Melastomus* and the maternal heritage of experience, associated with the female culture of mourning of which *Mortalities Memorandum* and its dedicatee are both products and exempla. Thus she writes to Moundford, "I would not have any one falsely thinke that this *Memorandum* is presented to your person to implie in you defect of those duties which it requires; but sincerely to denote you as a paradigma to others; for what it shews to be done, shewes but what you have done" (*MM* 46).

The language of "duty" with which Speght describes the lessons of her work, like the personal experience of loss that inflects her *ars moriendi*, energizes the material body of women's mourning in post-Reformation England and exploits the period's common, and increasingly derogatory, association of women with the duties and rites attending the demise of the physical body. In the absence of professional undertakers,[24] early modern women were the most frequent and immediate attendants on bodies in death, fulfilling not only emotive rites of mourning but also the more mundane tasks of caring for the dying, washing and winding the corpse, watching the body during its period of laying out, serving as mourners for funerals, and donning mourning garments according to cultural rules of relation, sex, and class. In light of these necessary material practices, the figurative association of women with death takes on specific forms of ideological and affective power within the polemics of early modern male writers. As we have seen in the case of Stubbes's *A Chrystal Glasse,* Katherine's deathbed confession is both rich in pathos and consolatory, instructing onlookers—particularly her husband—patiently to endure loss: "And further she desired him that he would not mourne for her . . . affirming, that she was not in case to be mourned for: but rather to be rejoyced of."[25] While early modern *mourning* was usually considered women's work and the more doctrinally centered art of *consolation* the property of men (to be precise, of clergymen), Katherine Stubbes's deathbed performance, albeit male-authored, suggests that women writers such as Speght and Sutcliffe might find in feminine mourning—a recognized site of particularly volatile, powerful expression for women—fertile ground on which to establish their rights to public speech.

⸻

Like Speght's, Alice Sutcliffe's entry into the discourse of death takes place under the rubric of Experience: addressing her female dedicatees, Katherine and Susanna Villiers, widow and sister of the recently deceased George Villiers, duke of Buckingham, Sutcliffe writes:

> I have chosen a *subject* not altogether *Pleasing;* but my ayme is, that it may prove *Profitable,* having observed in this short course of my *Pilgrimage,* how apt *Man* is, not to thinke of his *Mortalitie,* which stealeth upon him as a *Thiefe in the night: Experience* teacheth mee, that there is no *Action* wisely undertaken, whereof the *End* is not fore-called in the first place, howsoever it bee last put in execution.[26]

This work born of observation and experience rather than textual erudition, again like Speght's, addresses itself to a surrogate mother: Sutcliffe says to Katherine Villiers, "you . . . have been more than a Mother to mee, I having onely from her received life, but next under God from your Grace, & your honorable *Sister* the being both of mee and mine" (A6v). She further cultivates the communal relationship between female mourners by pointing out that she as well as Buckingham's female family members, "In peerless woe . . . still lament [his] fate" (a1), casting herself and her patron as mother and daughter joined in mourning. Finally, like *Mortalities Memorandum,* Sutcliffe's conventional *ars moriendi* is unconventional in its decision to append to the death manual proper a poem exploring the specifically feminine aspects of her subject in the figure of Eve: the eighty-eight-stanza "Of our losse by Adam, and our gayne by Christ" returns to Eden not only to rehearse the female-authored origins of death ("Wicked woman," she writes, "to cause thy husband dye," 144) but also to vindicate Eve as the enabler of the lifesaving knowledge that her "Seed shall bruise the Serpents head" (150).

Meditations of Man's Mortalitie is similar to Speght's *Mortalities Memorandum* in tone and outlook. Sutcliffe also relies on the Geneva Bible and takes pains to distinguish between the "fearefull end of the Wicked" (1) and "the joyfull end of the godly" (57), who "feareth not Death, because through all [their] life [they] learned to dye"

(62).[27] Sutcliffe, like Speght, revisits the commonplaces of the *ars moriendi* throughout her work. Thus for Speght's "Life is but lent, we owe it to the Lord" (*MM* 87), Sutcliffe informs us that "after Death [man] must give account of his Stewardship, for [goods] are not his, but lent him of the Lord" (4). Speght compares life to "a Ship which swiftly slides the Sea (*MM* 86), and Sutcliffe urges the Christian to "prove the Pilot of thy owne Ship, which now lyeth floating on the seas of this troublesome World" (12).[28] While it is enticing to imagine that Sutcliffe may be directly imitating Speght, this supposition cannot be supported on the basis of these clichés, which were commonly employed in male-authored *artes moriendi* from the mid-sixteenth century forward.[29] Rather, both works give us female authors, on the one hand, utilizing and mastering the conventional, masculine discourse of the genre and, on the other, supplementing that discourse with textual gestures intended to define the specifically feminine characteristics of the *ars moriendi* in the woman's hands. In Sutcliffe's work, both a series of commendatory verses by male poets and the closing poem, "Of our losse by Adam, and our gayne by Christ," constitute such gestures.

To counterbalance the community of female mourners invoked by Sutcliffe's dedication to her female patrons, a community of male literati is established within the *Meditations* by commendatory verses by Ben Jonson, Thomas May, George Wither, Peter Heywood, and Francis Lenton. Sutcliffe juxtaposes the female culture of mourning, grounded in women's common experience of loss, with the male culture of textual production and its values. While the text assumes that Sutcliffe is naturally included in the former group, her uneasy relationship with the latter is, predictably, the primary subject of the commendatory verses. In fact, the relationship between Sutcliffe and these writers seems to have been virtually nonexistent: both Lenton and Wither state in their poems that they never met her, and Wither's address of his poem "To Mr. John Sutcliffe Esq. upon the receipt of this Booke written by his Wife" suggests that she may have gained only indirect access to this circle of male writers through her husband's court connections:

> Sir, I receiv'd your Booke with acceptation,
> And thus returne a due congratulation,
> For that good Fortune, which hath blest your life
> By making you the *Spouse* of such a *Wife*.
> Although I never saw her, yet I see,
> The *Fruit*, and by the *Fruit* I judge the *Tree*. (n.p.)

Indeed, Wither's description of the book as John's ("I receiv'd *your* Booke") and his offering of congratulations to husband rather than wife seem to announce Sutcliffe's exile from the community of male writers and to ratify her text only on the basis of her wifely obedience to a well-connected husband. The volume's title page, too, authorizes Sutcliffe's work by calling on her husband's presence and position: "Written, By Mrs. Alice Sutcliffe," it states, "Wife of John Sutcliffe Esquire, Groome of his Majesties most Honourable Privie Chamber" (A2).[30] Lenton's encomium agrees that it is Sutcliffe's identity as wife that most qualifies her as author: "Great Ladies that to vertue are inclin'd / See here the pious practice of a wife" (n.p.). As a group, the commendatory poems praise Sutcliffe and her text, but also definitively describe the learned woman as a rare exception rather than the rule. Wither condescendingly implies that women's writing can be of value only if it is "manly," while hinting (in the act of denial) that men may, in fact, have written these extraordinary works:

> I am not of their mind, who if they see,
> Some *Female-Studies* fairely ripened be,
> (With Masculine successe) do peevishly,
> Their worths due honour unto them deny,
> By overstrictly censuring the same;
> Or doubting whether from themselves it came,
> For, well I know Dame *Pallas* and the *Muses*,
> Into that *Sexe*, their faculties infuses,
> As freely as to *Men*. (n.p.)

Heywood, too, admits, "It seems to me above thy Sex and State, / Some heavenly Sparke doth thee illuminate," but insists that Sutcliffe "[l]ive still a praise, but no example to / Others, to hope, as thou hast done, to doe" (n.p.). Lenton concurs, "For she is Rara Avis in our *Nation*"; and May encourages readers, "nor disdaine to take / that knowledge, which a Womans skill can bring. / All are not Syrennotes that women sing" (n.p.).

If the commendatory verses exclude Sutcliffe from engaging in the masculine literary and cultural economies that they exemplify and espouse, her treatment of the Fall in her closing poem deploys the figure of Eve to respond to their exclusionary poetics and to authorize her publication in the *ars moriendi* genre. In this respect, the inclusion of the poem in the volume parallels Speght's feminist scripting of Eve's central role in the Christian teleology of salvation, as simultaneously the purveyor of death and the guarantor of life, and echoes her defense of women's education in "A Dreame." Like Speght, Sutcliffe describes the Fall as a lapse simultaneously into gender, mourning, and history. Addressing Eve, she writes:

> Now seizes on your sicknesse Griefes and Feares,
> Which night and day with trouble will torment;
> Your sweet Delights, are turned all to teares,
> And now what you have done with woe repent!
> Nothing but Griefes and Feares and sad annoyes,
> You now possesse, in stead of endlesse Joyes. (148)

Sutcliffe's Eden shares with Speght's the notion that sex is translated into gender as a result of the Fall, when masculine and feminine social roles are assigned in the gender-specific punishments meted out by God:

> For as thou now conceives thy seed in sinne,
> So in great sorrow thou must bring it foorth,
> The gaine which thou by that same fruit didst winne,
> Thou now dost find to be of little worth:
> Obedience to thy Husband yeeld thou must,
> And both must Dye and turned be to Dust. (145–6)

While Speght's vindication of women's knowledge emphasizes the naming of Eve (*Hevah*) in Genesis 3:20, Sutcliffe turns to Genesis 3:16 to stress woman's "great sorrow" in childbirth (an event in the early modern period that often claimed the lives of both mothers and infants)[31] and the imposition of the sentence of wifely obedience as concurrent with the appearance of death. In the same way that Speght's manipulation of the figure of *Hevah* as life enables her authorial presence in *Mortalities Memorandum,* Sutcliffe's performance of wifely obedience in *Meditations of Man's Mortalitie* depends upon her affiliation with postlapsarian Eve.

While Sutcliffe authorizes her textual performance throughout her "Glasse of . . . Mortality" by accepting a role much like Katherine Stubbes's as "a Myrrour of womanhood,"[32] she also stages an implicit challenge to the exclusionary masculine poetics of the volume's commendatory verses by, once again, returning to Eve to trace the origins of masculine erudition in feminine "pride." May's assurance that "All are not Syren-notes that women sing" resonates ironically throughout the volume's frequent episodes of *contemptus mundi,* where earthly temptations are compared to "the singing of Syrens" (82): as the closing poem states, Satan's "Mermaide Songs are onely sweet in sound, / Approach them not, lest Death thy life doth wound" (193). The misogynist reading of Eve as an agent of satanic temptation, of course, lies behind May's assumption that some, if not all, of women's speech tempts men to sin. This conventional rendering of Eve's guilt is rehearsed by Sutcliffe as well, when she informs the Eve of her poem, "T'is [sic] not saying, the Serpent thee deceiv'd / That can excuse the fault thou didst commit" (145). Although Sutcliffe here seems to accept a misogynist view of Eve's guilt, her admonition echoes the Church of England's orthodox position ("Adam did lay the blame upon the woman, and she turned it unto the serpent: but yet neither of them was thus excused") and argues, as do the sermons, the mutual guilt of Adam and Eve. It is *Adam*'s disobedience, she explains, rather than Eve's, that signals the Fall:

> This onely sinne on all Mankinde did draw,
> Gods heavy wrath, for this, we suffer still.
> By ADAMS breaking Gods commanded Law;
> Sinne with a poysned dart our soules did kill:
> For through the breach thereof there entered death,
> For so 'twas sentenced by Gods owne breath. (167)

Moreover, the intimacy of Sutcliffe's direct address to Eve serves effectively to tell the story of the Fall from Eve's point of view and emphasizes the relationship between the female author and her female protagonist as "learned" women—women experienced in death and knowledgeable of the means to life. Sutcliffe presents the events in Eden, from mourning to joy, through Eve's eyes:

> No, you are in a laborinth of woe,
> And endlesse is the maze in which you goe.
>
> Yet courage, Woman, whose weake spirit's dead,
> GOD in his love a helpe for thee hath found,
> Bee sure thy Seed shall bruise the Serpent's head,
> CHRIST by his Death shall Sathan deadly wound. (150)

Sutcliffe's invocation of the *felix culpa* serves, as it does for Speght, to emphasize woman's centrality in redefining death as "a True guide to Eternall blisse" and "Portall to Heaven, by which we enter must" (177). As such, the poem ends by reminding the faithful of the benefits of death ("Now ends all sorrowes, now all griefes are done," 180) and by offering the prayer that "[u]nto this

Happinesse and place of Joy, / In thy good time sweet Saviour Christ us bring" (199).

———

Sutcliffe's vindication of Eve's "syren-notes" takes one final turn that parallels Speght's indictments of masculine scholarly pretensions in her allegorical encounters with the "full fed Beast," Swetnam, and with the "insatiable foe," Death. As a result of the Fall, Sutcliffe explains, Satan's "Syren songs mans mortall Death intends; / And hee must Dye that thereto his eare lends" (162). More precisely, she describes this state of affairs as a direct result of Eve's desire for knowledge: "'Twas Pride, made EVE desire still to excell; / When Sathan said, as Gods, you then shall be; / Incontinent, she tasted of that Tree" (160). She continues with an etiology of death that is simultaneously a history of human knowledge, tracing the origins of both to Eve's transgression:

> This Lep'rous sinne, infected so the bloud,
> That through her off-spring, it hath wholly runne;
> Before the child can know, the bad from good;
> It straight is proud, Nature, this hurt hath done.
> A female sinne, it counted was to be,
> But now Hermaphrodite, proved is shee. (161)

Sutcliffe's image of an Eve Hermaphrodite repeats in contemporary secular terms the implications of the "parallel" offenses of man and woman in original sin. Recalling Lanyer's comment, "Yet men will boast of Knowledge which he tooke / From *Eves* fair hand, as from a learned Booke," Eve Hermaphrodite makes Sutcliffe's case that masculinity, as both a cultural commodity and a biological fact, is figuratively constructed in and dependent upon a woman. As concurrent results of the Fall, Eve's maternity not only causes but also cures death, while her transgressive desire for knowledge enables and authors the "masculinity . . . as a product of written language" that the volume's commendatory poems so ably embody. Eve Hermaphrodite, finally, is a figure for Sutcliffe's own hermaphroditic authorial voice, which combines (in Wither's terms) "*Female-Studies*" with "Masculine successe." For Sutcliffe, as for Speght, the "full fed Beasts" (Sutcliffe 157) of sin that threaten to consume humankind can be tamed only with the life-saving knowledge enabled by Eve, that "[woman's] Seed shall bruise the Serpents head" (150). Thus Sutcliffe provides an image of the Christian's battle against Satan that recalls Speght's struggles with her own full-fed beasts:

> Who on this Panther skinne doth gazing stand,
> Had need beware who lyes in wayte to catch,
> Who holdes a Woolfe by th'eares but with one hand,
> Must with the other muzzell up his chaps:
> If better thou dost get leave not off so,
> But of all meanes to hurt, deprive thy Foe. (171–2)

It is the duty of "Eve's sex" (*MM* 58), Sutcliffe and Speght argue, to capture, tame, and anatomize the body of death in the female-authored *ars moriendi,* not only for the consolation of Christians but also in defense of women's rights to acquire and display knowledge in overcoming the "mortall foe[s]" (*MM* 60) that would silence them.

For Speght and Sutcliffe, women approaching the masculine art of consolation in the *ars moriendi,* Eve offers a rich, productive figure for locating the woman's voice in the feminized merger of life, death, and knowledge that a feminist reading of the Fall affords. These women engage in the conventional, masculine discourse of consolation, but also suggest that they, as women, are uniquely qualified to treat the matter of death due to the cultural affiliation of early modern women with the physical body of death in the period's gendering of grief, and licensed by the legacy of Eve's fortunate fall into death, gender, and history in Eden. Their additions to the *ars moriendi* of poems that energize the female culture of mourning within the genre emphasize woman's experiential knowledge of death and her foundational role in enabling Christian salvation. Speght and Sutcliffe thus open the genre to the woman's voice, rooted not in the physical bodies of these authors but in their fruitful constructions of femininity in the body of Eve; a creation that allows them, in turn, to script their own performances of femininity as intimately tied to the mat(t)er of death.

NOTES

1. Philip Stubbes, *A Chrystal Glasse for Christian Women* (London: Richard Jones, 1592), A1.
2. Kate Aughterson, *Renaissance Woman: A Sourcebook* (London and New York: Routledge, 1995), 2–4.
3. Stubbes, A2.
4. Lorna Hutson, *The Usurer's Daughter: Male Friendship and Fictions of Women in Sixteenth-Century England* (London and New York: Routledge, 1994), esp. 1–51.

5. Stubbes, A1.

6. As forms of religious discourse, some types of writing on death were sanctioned for use by women writers. See Margaret Patterson Hannay, ed., *Silent but for the Word: Tudor Women as Patrons, Translators, and Writers of Religious Works* (Kent, Ohio: Kent State University Press, 1985), 1–14, and see Patricia Phillippy, *Women, Death and Literature in Post-Reformation England* (Cambridge: Cambridge University Press, 2002).

7. A first edition of Sutcliffe's work, entered in the Stationers Register on January 30, 1633, is no longer extant. Mary Sidney's translation of Philippe de Mornay's treatise is the best-known example of the genre in a woman's hands: see *A Discourse of Life and Death*, in *The Collected Works of Mary Sidney Herbert, Countess of Pembroke*, ed. Margaret P. Hannay, Noel J. Kinnamon, and Michael G. Brennan (Oxford: Clarendon Press, 1998), 1:229–254. Dorothy White's *A Lamentation Unto this Nation* (London: Robert Wilson, 1660) belongs more properly to the "jeremiad" tradition than to the *ars moriendi*. Lady Frances Norton's *Memento Mori* (London: John Graves, 1705) is the only other female-authored art of dying that I have found.

8. On the communal character of early modern women's mourning, see Phillippy, esp. chapter 1.

9. I rely on Judith Butler's description of the performativity of gender in *Gender Trouble: Feminism and the Subversion of Identity* (London and New York: Routledge, 1990).

10. Rachel Speght, *Mortalities Memorandum, with A Dreame Prefixed*, in *The Polemics and Poems of Rachel Speght*, ed. Barbara Kiefer Lewalski (Oxford: Oxford University Press, 1996), 84. All citations are to this edition and appear parenthetically.

11. Joseph Swetnam, *The Arraignment of Lewd, idle, froward, and unconstant women* (London: George Purslowe for Thomas Archer, 1615), B1.

12. Rachel Speght, *A Mouzell for Melastomus*, in *The Polemics and Poems of Rachel Speght*, 13. All citations are to this edition and appear parenthetically.

13. Eve's material refinement reflects the common argument of the *querelle des femmes* that Eve, created from Adam's rib rather than from dust, was "of a refined mould" (*Mouzell* 18).

14. For related readings of the consequences of the Fall, see Catherine Belsey, *Shakespeare and the Loss of Eden* (New Brunswick, N. J.: Rutgers University Press, 1999), and Amy Boesky, "Giving Time to Women: The Eternizing Project in Early Modern England," in *This Double Voice: Gendered Writing in Early Modern England*, ed. Danielle Clarke and Elizabeth Clarke (Houndsmills, Basingstoke, Hampshire: Macmillian, 2000), esp. 127–8.

15. Church of England, *Certain Sermons or Homilies Appointed to be Read in the Time of Queen Elizabeth I* (1623), facs. ed., Mary Ellen Rickey and Thomas B. Stroup (Gainesville, Fla.: Scholars' Facsimiles and Reprints, 1968), 243. I am indebted to Ken A. Bugajski for this reference. Interestingly, this rendering of the Fall occurs within a part of the sermon addressed specifically to wives, admonishing them to "bring not such excuses to me at this time: but apply all thy diligence to beare thine obedience to thine husband" (243–4). For Lanyer's defense of Eve, see *The Poems of Aemilia Lanyer: Salve Deus Rex Judeaorum*, ed. Susanne Woods (Oxford: Oxford University Press, 1993), 84–7.
16. Church of England, 181.
17. Stubbes, B2.
18. Aughterson, 4. I would argue that the narrative of the Fall can never be "ungendered"; rather, Speght and Sutcliffe deconstruct traditional genderings to replace them with radical new ones.
19. Ibid.
20. For a good survey of the early modern *ars moriendi*, see Nancy Jo Beatty, *The Craft of Dying: A Study of the Tradition of the "Ars Moriendi" in England* (New Haven: Yale University Press, 1970).
21. Lanyer, 85.
22. Simon Shepherd, ed., *The Women's Sharp Revenge: Five Women's Pamphlets from the Renaissance* (New York: St. Martin's Press, 1985), 15.
23. Ibid., 17. Although Speght's erudition is evident in the volume, her insistence on the primacy of experience over education as the foundation of her feminine abilities is a typical disclaimer put forth by many early modern women publishing in a variety of genres.
24. On the development of professional undertaking in the late seventeenth century, see Paul S. Fritz, "The Undertaking Trade in England: Its Origins and Early Development, 1660–1830," *Eighteenth-Century Studies* 28:2 (1994–5), 241–53.
25. Stubbes, C3v.
26. Alice Sutcliffe, *Meditations of Man's Mortalitie*, ed. Patrick Cullen, in *The Early Modern Englishwoman: A Facsimile Library of Essential Works*, part 1, vol. 7 (Aldershot: Scolar Press, 1996), A5-A5v. All citations are to this edition and appear parenthetically.
27. Germaine Greer, Susan Hastings, Jeslyn Medoff, and Melinda Sansone, eds., *Kissing the Rod: An Anthology of Seventeenth-Century Women's Verse* (London: Virago Press, 1988), 13, suggest that Sutcliffe's work "was probably published on behalf of the Puritan cause and as a tacit condemnation of the court of Charles I," since "the scriptural echoes in Sutcliffe's poetry are all from the Geneva Bible."
28. Other passages in which Speght and Sutcliffe share conventional imagery include: the figure of life as a prison (*MM* 64, 76; Sutcliffe 72,

96, 178); life as a shadow (*MM* 87; Sutcliffe 4); and life as a garden hiding a serpent (*MM* 69; Sutcliffe 82, 120, and 170).

29. Early modern *artes moriendi* are rife with examples, but perhaps one will suffice: Otto Werdmuller, *A Most fruitfull, pithie and learned treatyse, how a Christian man ought to behave himself in the danger of death* (London: William Blackwall, 1590), treats the life-as-loan image as follows: "yet much lesse cause have we to grudge against God our creditor when he by death taketh his owne again. For . . . all other thinges that wee have, what are they else but lent goodes" (198–9).

30. Further evidence of the lack of direct connection between Sutcliffe and the male writers appears in Jonson's poem, which, as Greer et alia state, "is so contorted, being no more than a versification of her chapter headings, that we might suspect an element of parody" (13).

31. The figurative and factual mergers of life and death in childbirth are frequently the subject of mothers' legacies in the period; see, for example, Elizabeth Jocelin, *The Mother's Legacie to her Unborne Childe* (London: F.K. for Robert Allot, 1635).

32. Thomas May, "Upon the Religious Meditations of Mrs. Alice Sutcliffe," in Sutcliffe, n.p., and Stubbes, A2v.

CHAPTER 8

"HENS SHOULD BE SERVED FIRST": PRIORITIZING MATERNAL PRODUCTION IN THE EARLY MODERN PAMPHLET DEBATE

Naomi J. Miller

In a variety of early modern texts, the physicality of the woman's body is represented in explicitly maternal terms and is closely tied to issues of production: the production of domestic goods, of marital satisfaction, of exemplary behavior, and, most obviously, of offspring. Powers of reproduction position women as producers of valuable goods in social as well as familial contexts. At the same time, maternity in the early modern period was associated with a doubleness of identity that only partially coincided with the doubleness commonly associated with femininity at the time. Whereas women in general were directed to be chaste, silent, and obedient in order to counteract the perceived power of their sexuality, mothers in particular emerged as figures who combined the sexuality required for procreation with considerable authority over their offspring, male as well as female.

Consequently, in early modern discourse, mothers offer the potential for both neglect and nurture, consumption and production.

Interestingly, some of the most virulent attacks on women attempt to construct them primarily as consumers of male goods and services, while going to quite remarkable lengths to avoid acknowledging the possibility that the conundrum of maternity might upset the rhetorical equation of male production and female consumption. For example, when Joseph Swetnam opens *The Arraignment of lewd, idle, froward, and unconstant Women* (1615) with the assertion that "I am weaned from my mother's teat and therefore nevermore to be fed with her pap," his assertion in fact highlights the very problem that he is trying so strenuously to dismiss: all men originate as consumers of maternal production.[1] As the female respondents to Swetnam's pamphlet so clearly recognized, the gentleman doth protest too much. For it is precisely upon the rock of maternity that the rhetoric of female consumption must founder. So when the suppressed power of maternal production breaks the surface of Swetnam's invective against women, there is no obvious rhetorical escape available:

> Amongst all the creatures that God hath created, there is none more subject to misery than a woman, especially those that are fruitful to bear children, but they have scarce a month's rest in a whole year, but are continually overcome with pain, sorrow, and fear. As indeed the danger of childbearing must needs be a great terror to a woman, which are counted but weak vessels in respect of men, and yet it is supposed that there is no disease that a man endureth that is one half so grievous or painful as childbearing is to a woman. Let it be the toothache, gout, or colic: nay, if a man had all these at once, yet nothing comparable to a woman's pain in travail with child. (213–14)

As this unexpected acknowledgment of the primacy of childbirth overtakes the sustained rantings of the pamphlet, it begins to appear that perhaps Swetnam was not quite as "weaned" as he so proudly asserted in his introduction. Despite the thrust of his critique of the opposite sex, Swetnam appears to believe that women do labor after all, and that no masculine efforts can ultimately compete with a mother's "travail with child."

Strikingly, while many of the male-authored advice books, sermons, and pamphlets assign significant value to material products of labor, whether by men or by women, the female-authored mother's advice books and pamphlets attend more consistently to the process of production itself, including conditions of and motivations for labor, and consequently expand the frame of evaluation for female production in particular from material goods to spiritual ends.[2] The primary roles of housewife and mother, which serve as loci for the gender debates on female behavior, receive strikingly different treatment, then, depending on the rhetorical focus of the texts in question. In conduct books, sermons, or pamphlets concerned with women as consumers of male goods and services or at best as subordinate producers, the tasks of housewife and mother are represented primarily in material terms, with emphasis upon physical chores such as tending poultry and mending laundry, birthing babies and brewing beer. In advice books and pamphlets that prioritize the process of female production, however, the responsibilities of housewife and mother are frequently merged in more comprehensively maternal terms, so that the housewife's care for the hens, themselves embodiments of maternal production, intersects with the mother's attention to the spiritual welfare not only of her children, but also of her household at large.

To offer some illuminating preliminary examples, Thomas Tusser advises women in *A hundred good points of housewifery* (1557) that "when hens fall a cackling, take heed to their nest," and offers the observation that "young children and chickens would ever be eating."[3] With more pointed emphasis on the importance of maternal production, Jane Anger declares in *Her Protection for Women* (1589) that "it is reason that the Hens should be served first, which both lay the eggs and hatch the chickens."[4] Attending to maternal tasks in *Mulierum Paean* (1542), Edward Gosynhill emphasizes the burdensome physicality of labor for women, where "hath the mother all the care, / All the labor and disease,"[5] while Elizabeth Clinton maintains in *The Countess of Lincolnes Nurserie* (1622) that the womb is only the starting point for a mother's responsibility to "*Beare* children, that is, not only to *Beare* them in the wombe, and to bring them forth, but also to *Beare* them on their knee, in their armes, and at their breasts: for this Bearing a little before is called nourishing, and bringing up."[6] Even as tending poultry can provide a rhetorical occasion for prioritizing maternity, so birthing babies can offer an opportunity for expanding the frame of maternal production beyond the womb. In these female-authored texts, the scope and significance of maternal production includes not only the feeding of chickens but also the rearing of souls.

While maternal responsibilities function in a number of male-authored conduct books and pamphlets to keep women in prescribed positions of subordination to men, the maternal rhetoric of the female-authored advice books and pamphlets thus serves to transform

and reorder accepted frames of patriarchal production, extending
women's authority in spiritual as well as material terms. Even as female authors of advice books, such as Elizabeth Clinton and Dorothy
Leigh, emphasize the strength and conviction that they bring to their
roles as mothers, allowing them to prioritize their speaking positions
in familial or social systems that would otherwise function to subordinate or suppress their voices, so female-identified participants in the
pamphlet debate, such as Jane Anger and Esther Sowernam, use
broad strokes to delineate maternal production and its concomitant
authority in countering misogynist attacks. Indeed, as Mary Thomas
Crane points out in her study of conflicting identities in early modern Englishwomen, "a woman's power as producer of offspring was,
like her potential to augment family income, a quality both desired
and feared."[7]

In this essay, I will trace the deployment of competing as well as
complementary representations of gendered production and consumption in conduct books, sermons, advice books, and polemical
pamphlets, in order to evaluate some of the strategic uses of the
rhetoric of maternity in early modern England. By examining ideal-
izations and caricatures of maternal roles, as well as variant conceptions and practices of maternal production, I hope to explore some
of the ways in which the rhetoric of production served variously to
delimit or to extend female authority, depending upon whether maternity was constructed as supplement to or source of the health and
well-being of the family. In both types of rhetorical circumstances,
expressing maternity can signify writing to excess, beyond the prescribed bounds of gender behavior, whether to reinscribe or revise
gendered categories of production.

In order to contextualize any consideration of maternal rhetoric in
the female-authored mothers' advice books as well as polemical pamphlets, it is important to consider the numerous prescriptions for female behavior outlined in male-authored conduct books and
sermons of the sixteenth and seventeenth centuries, which frequently
address housewifery and maternity in related terms. Early housewifery instructions typically appeared in books of husbandry, such as
John Fitzherbert's *The book of husbandry* (1534), in which wives are
enjoined against "idleness" at any time, even before any specific
"works" are outlined.[8] As in Tusser's slightly later book of housewifery, Fitzherbert outlines a long list of discrete tasks for the housewife to attend to, including the direction to "give thy pullen meat in
the morning, and when the time of the year cometh . . . take heed
how thy hens, ducks and geese do lay, and . . . gather up their eggs."[9]

It is against typical "poultry care" instructions such as these that one must read Jane Anger's assertion that "hens should be served first," which achieves an effective rhetorical emphasis on the priority of maternity in the unexpected context of domestic labor.[10]

The male authors of the conduct books consistently warn against female idleness, and exhort wives to "diligently" oversee material goods and services within their households, without suffering anything "to be unfruitfully and wastefully spent."[11] One of the most popular volumes of this type, John Dod and Robert Cleaver's *A Godlie Forme of Householde Government* (1598), maintains that the material prosperity of the husband depends directly upon the behavior of the housewife, so that "the husband that is not beloved of his wife, holdeth his goods in danger, his house in suspicion, his credit in balance and also sometime his life in peril."[12] From this emphasis on housewifely participation in material production, it is only a short step to the construction of the housewife herself as merchandise, as when Alexander Niccholes, in his *A discourse of marriage and wiving* (1615), warns the husband not to "set that to sale that he would not have sold (for who sets out his ware to be cheapened and not bought?)," and thus to adorn his wife "thriftily, not lasciviously."[13]

Lest it appear that the housewife's contribution to material production might carry enough weight that the woman should have a voice in ordering the household, William Whately takes care to explain in *A Bride-Bush, Or A Wedding Sermon* (1617) that "when the husband will be housewife and all, and be dealing with brewing, baking, washing, and the particulars of these and the like businesses, . . . when the man will bid and charge so eagerly in a thing of nothing, . . . this devalues his words, and makes his charge of no regard."[14] Women's work, in Whately's words, is a "thing of nothing," fitting for their charge, and housewifely production only "devalues" the voice of the laborer.

Expanding upon this same topic shortly thereafter in a sermon rather disingenuously entitled *A Good Wife Gods Gift* (1623), Thomas Gataker excoriates bad wives as poor investments, observing scornfully that "many have good skill in choosing of wares, in valuing of lands, in beating a bargain, in making a purchase, that are yet but blind buzzards in the choice of a wife."[15] In a list of progressively vitriolic similes, Gataker compares a bad wife first to an "artificial and equivocal limb," then to "a wart or a wen," and finally to "a wolf, or a cancer, that consumeth the flesh, wasteth the vital parts, and eateth even to the very heart" (35). He concludes with the comparatively restrained observation that by far the majority of housewives are nothing more than "drones" or "droils" (35). With supporters like these, in conduct books and sermons apparently dedicated to representations of feminine ideals, who needs enemies?

And yet enemies of women abounded, in the vituperative male authors of the pamphlet controversy. One of the first volleys in the pamphlet war, *The Schoolhouse of women* (four editions between 1541 and 1572), compiled many of the popular standard arguments against women, with a notable focus on the concomitant dangers of female speech and sexual voracity. What concerns the author of *Schoolhouse* is not so much what women say as the fact that their speech produces idleness, so that "play who will, the man must labor / And bring to house all that he may; / The wife again doth nought but glaver / And hold him up with 'yea' and 'nay.'"[16] Rather than fear any subversive content in women's speech, men must simply be concerned that the fruits of their labor will be consumed by the "chatter" and "babble" of "gossips" (140–1). As the pamphlet succinctly comments, "where many geese be, are many turds, / And where be women, are many words" (148). Extending the poultry care metaphor from female speech to sexual appetite, *Schoolhouse* offers statistical data on the fact that although one cock can supply fifteen hens, fifteen men will not be sufficient for a single woman (146). The opinion that "hens should be served first" quite evidently has no place in this pamphlet, where female production even among poultry is reduced from eggs to turds.

The most notorious of the popular pamphlets attacking women was of course Swetnam's *Arraignment,* which crammed together multiple grievances against all sorts of female behavior, with the common theme that "women are all necessary evils" (191). Identifying his subject population as not "the best nor yet . . . the worst, but . . . the common sort of Women," Swetnam nevertheless qualifies his acknowledgment of the existence of a few good women with the assertion that "there is no woman so good but hath one idle part or other in her which may be amended" (191). Idleness, once again, proves to be the common flaw of the female sex. Even a beautiful woman, no matter how desirable from a distance, "is for the most part costly and no good housewife" (196)—in other words, damaged goods, as far as domestic production is concerned.

Swetnam takes great care to detail the crafty practices that enable women to be such successful consumers of male goods and services:

> Women are called night Crows for that commonly in the night they will make request for such toys as cometh in their heads in the day, for

women know their time to work their craft. For in the night they will
work a man like wax and draw him as the Adamant doth the Iron. . . .
A man must take all the pains, and women will spend all the gains.
(199, 201)

Ultimately, Swetnam promises, "what labor or cost thou bestowest
on a woman is all cast away, for she will yield thee no profit at all"
(205). Beginning with the bottom line, then, it is the economic angle
that proves most compelling for many of the attacks on women, with
Swetnam's pamphlet simply serving as one of the most impassioned
examples of this rhetorical strategy. When women "spend and consume all that which man painfully getteth" (205), then women apparently have no practical "use." More alarmingly, women seem to
have the capacity not only to consume the fruits of male labor, but
even to consume men themselves: "eagles eat not men till they are
dead, but women devour them alive" (201).

Moreover, Swetnam resists the significance of maternal production, which counters his emphasis on female consumption, by focusing on domestic production in agricultural terms. Advising
against the need for any maternal production at all, Swetnam assures potential male customers for wives that "far better it were to
have two plows going than one cradle, and better a barn filled than
a bed" (206). He insists that even a woman with many good qualities will have "one ill quality or other which overthroweth all the
other, like unto that Cow which giveth great store of milk and
presently striketh it down with her foot" (207). Weaned from that
teat or (apparently) not, he promises that a woman's production of
any value will be subject to destruction by the same. And once
safely back in the fields of masculine labor, he closes his pamphlet
by musing over why he should "make so long a harvest of so little
corn," given that "the corn is bad," leaving no possibility for a crop
of praise (216).

In rhetorical terms, then, the male authors of the conduct books,
sermons, and gender debate pamphlets focus with remarkable con-
sistency on issues of production rather than companionship in cri-
tiquing female behavior. Indeed, where female insubordination
might have been expected to take primacy of place in the list of un-
acceptable practices faced by husbands, it turns out that female idleness receives more press. Chastity, silence, and obedience seem to be
valued more highly for their potentially limiting effect on female appetites than as virtues in and of themselves, at least where "the common sort of Women" are concerned (190). And in the examples

reviewed above, it becomes apparent that paeans to masculine labor are easier to sustain if the influence of maternity is obviated.

It is against this polemical background of insistent attention to the consumer practices of women and the labor products of men that the maternal rhetoric of the mothers' advice books and the female-authored debate pamphlets can be evaluated. The male-authored conduct books, sermons, and pamphlets, for instance, not only represent women as idle consumers of male production, but also focus on the material goods that mark the success of that production, from bread and beer to silks and servants, depending on the class of husbandry represented.[17] The female-authored advice books and pamphlets, by contrast, consistently attend to the process of maternal production as well as its products and by-products, and represent the significance of women's work in spiritual as well as material terms.

Given the nature of their subject matter, the mothers' advice books offer the most concentrated example of maternal rhetoric among the texts under consideration in this essay. Addressing advice books to their offspring, those mothers who dared to write their words down stand as examples of early modern women who claimed voices arising from the mother's authority within the family as a social system.[18] Given that many of the mothers, such as Elizabeth Jocelin, did indeed die in childbirth, their advice was often framed by an immediacy of mortality that enhanced the authority of their last words.[19] However, other maternal authors, such as Dorothy Leigh, appropriated not so much the literal occasion of impending death as the promise that their written production would outlast the lengths of their lives. Embracing topics as varied as poultry care and child care, marital relations and gender relations, the early modern women writing as mothers achieve a twofold output of maternal production: offspring and advice.

Despite their common topic of guiding the upbringing of their children, the advice books are by no means uniform in their approach or scope. Nevertheless, they share with the female-authored polemical pamphlets a number of common rhetorical strategies that prioritize the authority of maternal production. By considering not simply the results of labor but also the process of labor required to achieve those results, for example, the mothers' advice books address the practices of housewifery in more proactively enabling terms than do the strictures of John Fitzherbert or Thomas Tusser. Thus the anonymous author of *The Northren Mother's Blessing* (1597) advises her daughter to "be huswife good" and take the initiative in supervising men laborers in her husband's absence, "for they will do better if

thou by them stond."[20] Although Tusser likewise charges the housewife to "look to their labor that eateth her beef" (212), the *Northren
Mother's* advice encompasses not only material advantage in oversee-
ing production but also the well-being of the servants under the
housewife's care.

In *Miscellanea, Meditations, Memoratives* (1604, 1605–6), Elizabeth Grymeston appropriates housewifery advice about poultry care
in the service of instructing her son on the necessity of casting out
evil thoughts: "Break ill eggs ere they be hatched. / Kill bad chickens in the tread, / Fledge they hardly can be catched."[21] Not only
does Grymeston apparently feel free to instruct her son in domestic
terms that male authors would eschew, given their frequent directives
to the husband to stay away from housewifery as a "thing of nothing" that might "devalue" their authority in the household, but her
advice itself prioritizes maternal judgment in both tenor and vehicle
of the metaphor. "Ill eggs" and "bad chickens" as well as good sons
must come under the supervision of a good housewife and mother.
Moving beyond physical to verbal production, Elizabeth Jocelin's advice in *The Mother's Legacie to her Unborne Childe* (1624) conjoins
"good housewifery" not only with concrete domestic responsibilities
but also with "writing," leading her to observe that "where learning
and wisdom meet in a virtuous-disposed woman . . . she is like a well-
balanced ship that may bear all her sail."[22] Remarkably, then, Jocelin's attention to maternal writing as her culminating example of
female production explodes the frame of material domesticity within
which male authors of conduct books and polemical pamphlets at-
tempted to confine the significance of women's roles.

In each case, the concepts of housewifery that appear in the
mothers' advice books convey the maternal care of the author-
mothers for their children, so that domestic advice cannot be sepa-
rated from maternal responsibility. Passing on a legacy of maternal
instruction, the author of *The Northren Mother's Blessing* urges her
own children to "take heed to thy children which thou hast born"
(F3v), while Grymeston reminds her offspring of the legitimacy of
her maternal authority, "as ever the love of a mother may challenge
the performance of her demand of a dutiful child" (104). Dorothy
Leigh identifies her advice in *The Mother's Blessing* (1616) with the
"great care, labor, travail, and continual study which parents take to
enrich their children,"[23] while Elizabeth Clinton calls attention to
the exclusive power of maternal labor in advising mothers to nurse
their own children and "be no longer at the trouble and at the care
to hire others to do your own work" (158). From this "travail"

emerges both blessing and authority, once maternity is viewed not as the burdensome "labor and disease" represented in Gosynhill's seemingly celebratory *Mulierum Paean,* but rather as an empowering work-in-progress.

Attempting to divorce the female sexuality required to produce children from the authority required to raise them, male authors of medical treatises address maternity in purely physical terms, leaving advice on familial roles to the authors of the conduct books. Thus works such as Jacques Guillemeau's *Child-birth, or, The Happy Deliverie of Women* and *The Nursing of Children* (1612), which includes explicit descriptions, in some cases illustrated by woodcuts, of women's sexual organs, treat the issue of female sexuality apparently only in terms of medical concerns regarding pregnancy, labor, and delivery. While Guillemeau's nursing text opens with the straightforward recommendation that mothers nurse their own children, substantial space is devoted to discussion of the size, shape, and color of suitable breasts for nursing when wet nurses must be selected. By contrast, Elizabeth Clinton offers an explicitly maternal perspective on the same issue in *The Countess of Lincolnes Nurserie,* urging mothers to nurse their own children for reasons of spiritual as well as physical nourishment—without concomitant attention to breast size and nipple shape. Along similar lines, Dorothy Leigh promises her sons that no mother can "forget the child of her womb," but rather will "bless it every time it sucks on her breasts, when she feeleth the blood come from her heart to nourish it," even as she will "instruct it in the youth, and admonish it in the age, and pray for it continually" (292). Womb, breasts, heart, mind, and spirit: the female authors of the mothers' advice books refused to be anatomized as less than the sum of their parts, so that their words of advice collectively produce an authoritative rhetoric of maternity.

The authors of the mothers' advice books locate the origins of their authority in the irresistible force of maternal love. Elizabeth Grymeston, for instance, advises her son in the opening sentence of the prefatory epistle to her book that "there is nothing so strong as the force of love; there is no love so forcible as the love of an affectionate mother to her natural child," and promises him that in the written advice that she is leaving him "thou mayest see the true portrature of thy mother's mind" (100). Leigh not only announces the impetus for her writing as maternal love, stating that "the first cause of writing is a motherly affection," but even identifies those who might be threatened by such a force: "Therefore *let no man blame a mother,* though she something exceed in writing to her children, since *every man knows* that the love of a mother to her children is hardly contained within the bounds of reason" (293; italics mine). Far from documenting female instability or weakness, Leigh's claim establishes her right as a mother to speak her mind, and to inscribe her words so that "my mind will continue long after me in writing" (294). Not only do both Grymeston and Leigh have minds as well as wombs, but they apparently also feel empowered to make the connection explicit in writing words of advice to the children of those wombs.

Leigh asserts that her rhetoric has been shaped by the desire to "do no less for [my children] than . . . to write them the right way that I had truly observed out of the written word of God."[24] At several moments in her text, Leigh even associates the power of her written words with the text of the Bible, which her sons may learn to read "in their own mother tongue," under the direction of her "many words," so that they may gather food for the soul "out of the word as the children of Israel gathered manna in the wilderness" (295, 292). While Leigh takes care never to substitute the authority of her text for that of the Bible, the conflation of her maternal words with the "mother tongue" of the Bible suggests her power as a mother to provide verbal and spiritual nourishment for her children.

Maternal love "hardly contained within the bounds of reason" and yet writing "the right way" is a force for men to reckon with, and all the reasoned prescriptions of male-authored conduct books and sermons cannot begin to explain, let alone contain, such power. Paradoxically, one might argue that mothers were the figures most empowered, and even expected, to express passionate desire in the early modern period, apart from lovers. Combining the sexuality of generative wombs with the authority of generative words, the authors of the mothers' advice books found a receptive audience not only in their children, but also in an early modern society that called for their words to be printed and reprinted, extending their influence far beyond the boundaries of their immediate families, and intersecting with the concerns of the pamphlet debate. Maternal authorship, then, emerges as at once excessive and legitimate, reifying the authority of maternal production beyond the womb.

The "female-authored" pamphlets in the gender debate address the issue of women's production in comprehensive terms that share with the mothers' advice books the identification of maternity as a point of origin for all production, and extend the rhetorical strategies of the advice books by claiming maternity as a final justification for female authority not simply within the family, but more sweepingly within society at large. Even as authors such as Jane Anger and Esther Sowernam refute specific male criticisms of women, particularly on behalf of wives and mothers, they also expand the framework for the debate from the concern with material production and consumption that so preoccupied the male pamphlet writers to the labor process itself, viewed in spiritual as well as material terms.

Jane Anger's *Her Protection for Women,* which appeared almost thirty years before the pamphlets of Rachel Speght, Esther Sowernam, and Constantia Munda, is the first full-length defense purportedly written by an English woman author, using a pseudonym that conveys her combative stance.[25] Addressing herself "to the Gentlewomen of England," as well as "to All Women in General," Anger immediately constructs a community of "we women" whose shared experiences of masculine misogyny implicitly serve to validate the deliberate excess of her rhetoric.[26] From beginning to end, Anger's pamphlet is an exercise in labor that requires her to "stretch the veins of her brains, the strings of her fingers, and the lists of her modesty, to answer their surfeitings" (83). Women's work is never done.

Labor, indeed, receives significant attention in Anger's text as the author examines women's work in literal as well as metaphorical terms. Anger's first animal metaphor addresses the male slanderers of women, whose "conceits have already made them cocks," and whose primary claim to fame is "that coxcomb" (84, 86). Attributing the idle vanity of consumption to men, Anger observes that "they have been so daintily fed with our good natures that like jades (their stomachs are grown so queasy) they surfeit of our kindness" (85). Anger's pamphlet thus appropriates the rhetoric of consumption and production so crucial to the male-authored conduct books and sermons as well as pamphlets, and employs it to critique male consumption not only of women's products, but also of women's "good natures." From the start of Anger's *Protection,* the debate over gender behavior is no longer couched primarily in material terms.

Anger's adept manipulation of the rhetoric of consumption and production nevertheless enables her to underscore women's value to men in material terms that they must recognize, even as she insists upon the essentially spiritual nature of the conflict. Accordingly she characterizes women as "the greatest help that men have (without whose aid and assistance it is as possible for them to live as if they wanted meat, drink, clothing, or any other necessary)," but meanwhile observes that "because men are spurblind they cannot see into our natures," thus missing the level of existence according to which women "are contrary to men because they are contrary to that which is good" (87). When Anger writes of men as "ravenous hawks who do not only seize upon us but devour us" (87), her rhetoric of consumption links men's sexual voracity to their spiritual blindness.

The true value of women's production, argues Anger, can be estimated not simply in terms of material products such as bread and beer, but rather through a combination of housewifery and maternity that encompasses the ongoing process of both material and spiritual labor:

> Our bodies are fruitful, whereby the world increaseth, and our care wonderful, by which man is preserved. From woman sprang man's salvation. A woman was the first that believed, and a woman likewise the first that repented of sin. In woman is only true fidelity; except in her there is no constancy, and without her no housewifery. In the time of their sickness we cannot be wanted, and when they are in health we for them are most necessary. They are comforted by our means, they [are] nourished by the meats we dress, their bodies freed from diseases by our cleanliness, which otherwise would surfeit unreasonably through their own noisomeness. Without our care they lie in their beds as dogs in litter, and go like lousy mackerel swimming in the heat of summer. They love to go handsomely in their apparel and rejoice in the pride thereof; yet who is the cause of it, but our carefulness to see that everything about them be curious? Our virginity makes us virtuous, our conditions courteous, and our chastity maketh our trueness of love manifest. They confess we are necessary, but they would have us likewise evil. That they cannot want us I grant; yet evil I deny, except only in the respect of man who, hating all good things, is only desirous of that which is ill (through whose desire, in estimation of conceit, we are made ill). (91–2)

The fruit of maternity not only increases the world's population, but also provides for mankind's salvation. At one stroke, material and spiritual production are conjoined in the body of a mother, so that "from woman" springs both diurnal and eternal life. Not only that, but "a woman was the first that believed, and a woman likewise the first that repented of sin," so that Anger credits women, as represented by the New Testament Marys, not only with providing the means for salvation, but with recognizing the end of salvation as well.

From "fidelity" to "housewifery," women care for men, who are the recipients of their labor whether in sickness or in health. Comforting men with their "means" and nourishing men with their "meats," women meet both spiritual and physical needs of those

members of the opposite sex who regard them as "necessary evils."
Anger points out that it is men's "desire" for women (read sexual voracity) that constructs them as "ill," and thus drives home her message that male appetites at once consume the products of female
labor and devalue female production in the process. No wonder,
then, that Anger advises that "hens should be served first, which both
lay the eggs and hatch the chickens," while "the cocks which tread
them" must consume "meat" in their turn, epitomizing female production and male consumption in the poultry yard.[27]

   In the poem that closes the pamphlet, Jane Anger offers a
metaphorical fable of production that emphasizes the value of
women's work and represents the process of communication as the
labor of a community of women:

> Though sharp the seed by Anger sowed,
>   we all (almost) confess,
> And hard his hap we aye account,
>   who Anger doth possess,
> Yet hapless shall thou (Reader) reap
>   such fruit from Anger's soil,
> As may thee please, and ANGER ease
>   from long and weary toil;
> Whose pains were took for thy behoof
>   to till that cloddy ground,
> Where scarce no place free from disgrace
>   of female Sex was found . . .
> If to delight aught come in sight,
>   then deem it for the best,
> So you your will may well fulfill,
>   and she have her request.[28]

In this narrative of production engendered by the pamphlet, Anger
is at once sower, seed, and soil, and the work is ongoing. Far from
producing a single material "end-product" in the form of the pamphlet, Anger maintains that her words embody a process of production in which seed for thought is sown "by Anger," and fruit then
reaped from the soil of Anger's rhetoric by the female community of
listeners, who are empowered to take over the "long and weary toil"
initiated by Anger in order to find "delight." The several labors of
housewifery and maternity, sowing seed and reaping fruit, come together to free the female sex from "disgrace," and serve as a testament to female powers of production, so that an endeavor that
commenced in anger may conclude in delight.

The next outburst of the gender controversy, Joseph Swetnam's *Arraignment of Lewd, idle, forward, and unconstant women,* provoked responses from at least three female-identified authors: Rachel Speght, the nineteen-year-old daughter of a London clergyman, and two authors writing under the female pseudonyms Esther Sowernam and Constantia Munda.[29] As Barbara Lewalski points out, Speght is less concerned than Sowernam and Munda with refuting Swetnam's charges directly in *A Mouzell for Melastomus* (1617), addressing herself rather to a coherent and learned critique of gender ideology.[30] While Speght's response was criticized by Sowernam for the "slenderness of her answer," and praised by Munda for its "modest and powerful hand," Speght's approach can be seen to complement those of both Sowernam and Munda, specifically in her attention to the issues of female labor and maternal production.

In her opening address "to all vertuous Ladies Honourable or Worshipfull, and to all other of Hevahs sex," Speght sees fit to characterize Swetnam's scurrilous attack as "vomit" and "deadly poyson for women," against which she proffers the antidote of her own words (3). Identifying Swetnam's diatribe as "excrement," Speght further critiques the process of his production when she dismisses his argument for its "so disordered a methode" (7). Consistently expanding the terms of her discussion to embrace the process of maternal production, Speght observes that "the first promise that was made in Paradise, God makes to woman, that by her Seede should the Serpents head be broken: whereupon *Adam* calls her *Hevah, life,* that as the woman had beene an occasion of his sinne, so should woman bring foorth the Saviour from sinne, which was in the fullnesse of time accomplished . . . so that by *Hevahs* blessed Seed . . . it is brought to passe, that *male and female are all one in Christ Jesus*" (15–16). Salvation has its point of origin in the body of a mother. Maternal production then has significance not only, as the authors of the mothers' advice books maintain, because "bearing" a child entails "bringing up" offspring throughout their lives, but also because the labor and delivery of the mother of Christ initiates the process of salvation for all mankind, uniting the warring sexes through "Hevahs blessed Seed."

Unlike Jane Anger, Speght doesn't bother to make the case for the value of female production in terms of material benefits to men, but rather focuses on the spiritual as well as personal benefits of women's work, advising that "no power externall or internall ought woman to keep idle, but to imploy it in some service of God, to the glorie of her Creator, and comfort of her owne soule" (20). Moreover, in her consideration of domestic responsibilities, Speght argues that men and women be "yoakefellowes" in sharing the burden of work in marriage: "the other end for which woman was made, was to be a Companion and *helper* for man; and if she must be an *helper;* and but an *helper;* then are those husbands to be blamed, which lay the whole burthen of domesticall affaires and maintenance on the shoulders of their wives" (20). Explaining the justification for her position, Speght invokes the behavior of poultry in order to emphasize not the egg production of the hens, but rather the solicitous care of the male birds, as when "the crowing Cockrell helpes his Hen to defend her Chickens from perill, and will indanger himselfe to save her and them from harme" (21). Speght's rhetorical strategy of invoking a companionate mode of production unites the sexes through her language of labor as effectively as "Hevah's seed" may unite them in salvation, shifting the focus from competition to cooperation.

In the section entitled "Certaine Quaeres to the bayter of Women," which closes her pamphlet, Speght dismantles specific points from Swetnam's *Arraignment,* particularly with regard to scriptural misrepresentations or grammatical errors. In response to his general criticism that "a woman is better lost then found, better forsaken then taken," Speght remarks that it is a pity that no one advised Swetnam's father of that point of view before he married, so that "hee might not have begotten such a monster in nature *Asse* your selfe, who . . . defame and exclaime against women, as though your selfe had never had a mother, or you never beene a child" (34–5). Exposing the greatest insecurity in Swetnam's text, as evidenced by his unconvincing claim to be "weaned from my mother's teat" even as he acknowledges "nothing comparable to a woman's pain in travail with child" (191, 214), Speght reminds Swetnam of his origins in a woman's travail, effectively emphasizing that the output of his pamphlet can never compete with maternal production.

Moreover, when Speght found it necessary to repudiate the attempts of certain male readers to deny her authorship of *A Mouzell,* attributing it instead to her father, she responded in the prefatory letter to her subsequent work, *Mortalities Memorandum, with a Dreame Prefixed* (1621), by asserting the primacy of maternity in shaping her voice. Revealing that this verse meditation on death was prompted by the death of her mother, and dedicated to her godmother, Speght identifies both *A Mouzell* and *Memorandum* as her own "offspring."[31] Randall Martin points out that Speght's stated maternal relation to her work not only echoes the claims of other Renaissance women writers, but also enables her to assert her capability for "generating her own poetic lineage without male mediation."[32] Directly contrasting with Swetnam's denials of dependence on his mother, Speght's use of maternal rhetoric also serves to call attention to her origins as an author as well as a woman.

Despite her critique of the "slenderness" of Speght's answer to Swetnam, Esther Sowernam's *Esther hath hanged Haman* (1617) shares with *A Mouzell* specific metaphorical critiques of Swetnam as well as larger rhetorical strategies privileging the authority of maternal production.[33] Like Speght, Sowernam equates Swetnam's output with "vomit," and attributes value to women on their own terms, rather than primarily in relation to their usefulness for men: "You are women: in Creation, noble; in Redemption, gracious; in use, most blessed. Be not forgetful of yourselves nor unthankful to that Author from whom you receive all" (220). By acknowledging the source of all production to be God, Sowernam, like Dorothy Leigh, identifies the source of her words as an author with "that Author" of all.

Sowernam's rhetoric privileges the significance of female production from the start, as she points out Eve's role in completing God's creation: "Adam was not so absolutely perfect but that in the sight of God he wanted a Helper. Whereupon God created the woman, his last work, as to supply and make absolute that imperfect building which was unperfected in man, as all Divines do hold, till the happy creation of the woman" (224). Not only does woman represent the culmination of divine production, proceeds Sowernam, but her capacity for maternity initiates the process of salvation:

> Woman supplanted by tasting of fruit, she is punished in
>   bringing forth her own fruit.
> Yet what by fruit she lost, by fruit she shall recover.
> What more gracious a gift could the Almighty promise to
>   woman than to bring forth the fruit in which all nations
>   shall be blessed? (225)

In Sowernam's terms, as with Speght, maternity becomes a locus for empowered production, with female seed offering redemption to all mankind in the form of Christ. Significantly, what Eve lost as a wife she recovers as a mother, with the gift of redemption appearing not through femininity, but specifically through the promise of maternity.[34]

Throughout the pamphlet, Sowernam refutes Swetnam's charges of female consumption by focusing on the process of interaction between the sexes rather than simply the results. Thus Swetnam's position that women are "baits, nets, lures, charms to bring men to ruin" provides an opportunity for Sowernam to question how men might be "so idle, vain, and weak" as Swetnam's characterization of his sex as prey to female predators might imply (237). Using Swetnam's own words to expose men's power over the conditions of their interaction with women, Sowernam observes that "if a woman have froward conditions, they be none of her own; she was framed to them" (239), explaining that men who invest in the corruption of women's virtue cannot then blame others for their own consumption of female goods (241). Once again, it comes down to the problem of production and consumption, leaving Sowernam to conclude that "as Eve did not offend without the temptation of a Serpent, so women do seldom offend but by provocation of men" (242).

Just as Speght's reference to "Hevah" as the source of salvation celebrates the power of maternal production, so Sowernam's closing reference to Eve, whom she elsewhere terms "the mother of the living," recalls her iteration of the divine promise that Eve's "seed should break the Serpent's head" (225). Sowernam's final warning to Swetnam to "forbear to charge women with faults which come from the contagion of Masculine serpents" thus serves concomitantly as a threat that female descendants of Eve such as herself may break the heads of those "Masculine serpents" such as Swetnam who strive to poison society's perceptions of women through their critiques.

Constantia Munda's *The Worming of a mad Dog* (1617) asserts the power of maternity for authorial production from its very first sentence, as Munda dedicates the pamphlet "to the Right Worshipful Lady her most dear Mother, the Lady Prudentia Munda, the true pattern of Piety and Virtue."[35] The dedicatory poem that opens the pamphlet outlines the course of maternal labor, from childbirth through education:

As first your pains in bearing me was such
a benefit beyond requital that 'twere much
To think what pangs of sorrow you sustained
In childbirth, when mine infancy obtained
The vital drawing in of air, so your love
Mingled with care hath shown itself above
The ordinary course of Nature. Seeing you still
Are in perpetual labor with me even until
The second birth of education perfect me,
You Travail still though Churched oft you be. (245)

Munda constructs maternity as "perpetual labor," designated by an ongoing process of education and nurture rather than simply by the discrete production of an infant. Questioning "in recompense whereof what can I give / But what I take, even that I live?," Munda resolves upon the method of her repayment:

> Thus I pay
> My debt by taking up at interest, and lay
> To pawn that which I borrow of you: so
> The more I give, I take; I pay, I owe.
> Yet lest you think I forfeit shall my bond,
> I here present you with my writing hand . . .
> Although this be a toy scarce worth your view,
> Yet deign to read it, and accept in lieu
> Of greater duty, for your gracious look
> Is a sufficient Patron to my book. (245–6)

By framing her "worming of a mad dog" as a repayment of her debt to her mother's "perpetual labor," Munda at once honors the origins of her authorship in her mother's ongoing production of herself, and legitimates her participation in the pamphlet controversy with reference to the authority of maternity. Moreover, like Elizabeth Jocelin, Munda unabashedly identifies her "writing hand" as the prime instrument of her production.

The second dedicatory poem, which locates its impetus in Swetnam's attack, sets the stage for an examination of men's debts to women by identifying maternity as the originary point for every man:

> Woman: the crown, perfection, and the means
> Of all men's being and their well-being, whence
> Is the propagation of all humankind;
> Wherein the body's frame, the intellect and mind,
> With all their operations do first find
> Their Essence and beginning; where doth lie
> The mortal means of our eternity. (246–7)

In short, men's material "being" and spiritual "well-being" depend on a process of maternal production that extends from "the body's frame" to "the intellect and mind," and encompasses not only "their Essence and beginning," but their ultimate fate as well: "where doth lie / The mortal means of our eternity." In the shared rhetoric of Munda, Sowernam, and Speght, which builds on the rhetorical courage represented by the mothers' advice books, maternity becomes the alpha and the omega of human existence, and all that is left for men to do is offer thanks for an irredeemable debt. Swetnam's petty critique of women's alleged appetites pales by comparison before the immensity of men's reception of everything from breast milk to salvation via the operation of maternity.

The actual text of *The Worming of a mad Dog* shares with both Sowernam and Speght the characterization of Swetnam's verbal product as "vomit," and more pointedly describes such pamphlets as the illegitimate offspring of "base phrenetical brainsick babblers" (247). Munda's subsequent observation that "woman, the greatest part of the lesser world, is generally become the subject of every pedantical goose quill" (248) might even be reaching back to reverse the alleged equation of "women's words" and "goose turds" in *The Schoolhouse of women* (148). Warning Swetnam not to confuse the product and process of his vituperation, Munda proceeds to predict that "if your scurrilous and depraving tongue break prison and falls to licking up your vomited poison to the end you may squirt out the same with more pernicious hurt" (254).

Throughout the pamphlet, Munda insists upon respect for men's maternal point of origin, magnifying Swetnam's debt with reference to his dismissal of maternal authority:

> But your barbarous hand will not cease to ruin the fences and beleaguer the forces of *Gynaecia,* not sparing the mother that brought forth such an untoward whelp into the world as thyself, playing at blindman's buff with all, scattering thy dissolute language at whomsoever comes next. (250)

Indeed, even more precisely than Sowernam, Munda locates Swetnam's greatest weakness in his allegations of independence from his own mother:

> Is there no reverence to be given to your mother because you are weaned from her teat and nevermore shall be fed with her pap? . . . If she had crammed gravel down thy throat when she gave thee suck or exposed thee to the mercy of the wild beasts in the wilderness when she fed thee with the pap, thou couldst not have shown thyself more ungrateful than thou hast in belching out thy nefarious contempt of thy mother's sex. (254)

Every woman, Munda reminds Swetnam, represents "thy mother's sex," and thus each attack that he launches is a repudiation of his debt both to his own mother and to the maternal production that frames his opportunity for salvation. At the same time, Swetnam's inability to produce more than "the offscourings of other writers" (256) compels Munda to observe that even "the most pregnant place in your book" is "worthy laughter" (261), revealing his authorship to be lacking the productive authority that marks her own.

Whereas Joseph Swetnam's *Arraignment* effectively exaggerates women's powers by vilifying their seemingly successful victimization of men, himself included, the rhetorical strategies of Rachel Speght, Esther Sowernam, and Constantia Munda in effect diminish the significance of Swetnam's authorial product as vomit and excrement, refuse and excess, while magnifying the authority of maternal production in its stead. Jane Anger's insistence upon the eternal as well as diurnal fruit of maternity enables her admonition that "hens should be served first" to be read in light of the biblical promise that the last shall be first (Matthew 19:30), exposing the flawed confidence of the male authors of the conduct books and pamphlets regarding masculine primacy over the female sex.

Perhaps the most constructive as well as courageous outcome of the early modern debate over gender relations can be located in Dorothy Leigh's maternal advocacy of equality between the sexes, in her advice to her sons. Leigh's characterization of the marriage relationship stresses the woman's position as equal to the man, for "if she be thy wife, she is always too good to be thy servant and worthy to be thy fellow" (302). Furthermore, Leigh assures her sons that "if you get wives that be godly and you love them, you shall not need to forsake me," whereas "if you have wives that you love not, I am sure I will forsake you" (302). Leigh's decision to exert her maternal authority to safeguard the marital positions not only of her sons but also of her future daughters-in-law links her perspective with Elizabeth Clinton's advice to her daughter-in-law, as well as with Rachel Speght's and Constantia Munda's dedicatory acknowledgments of their debts to their own mothers. At once discursive strategy and survival mechanism, the maternal rhetoric of the early modern advice books and pamphlets elevates women's work and legitimates female authorship by identifying maternal production as both physical origination and spiritual culmination of women's authority in the early modern world.

NOTES

1. Joseph Swetnam, *The Arraignment of Lewd, idle, froward, and unconstant women* (1615), in Katherine Usher Henderson and Barbara

F. McManus, eds., *Half Humankind: Contexts and Texts of the Controversy about Women in England, 1540–1640* (Urbana: University of Illinois Press, 1985), 191. Subsequent references to this edition will be cited by page number in the text.

2. I should note for the record that while the actual female authorship of the mothers' advice books is documentable, I use the term "female-authored" in association with the polemical pamphlets as a convenient shorthand for the "female-identified speaking positions" of pseudonymous authors such as Jane Anger, Esther Sowernam, and Constantia Munda.

3. Thomas Tusser, *The Points of Housewifery, United to the Comfort of Husbandry* (1580; collated with 1573 and 1577), in Joan Larsen Klein, ed., *Daughters, Wives and Widows: Writings by Men about Women and Marriage in England, 1500–1640* (Urbana: University of Illinois Press, 1992), 219, 224.

4. *Jane Anger, Her Protection for Women* (1589), in Henderson and McManus, eds., *Half Humankind,* 184. Subsequent references to this edition will be cited by page number in the text.

5. Edward Gosynhill, *The praise of all women, called Mulierum Paean* (1542?), in Henderson and McManus, 162.

6. Elizabeth Clinton, *The Countess of Lincoln's Nursery* (1622), in Randall Martin, ed., *Women Writers in Renaissance England* (London: Longman, 1997), 152. Subsequent references to this edition will be cited by page number in the text.

7. Mary Thomas Crane, "'Players in your huswifery, and huswives in your beds': Conflicting Identities of Early Modern English Women," in Naomi J. Miller and Naomi Yavneh, eds., *Maternal Measures: Figuring Caregiving in the Early Modern Period* (Aldershot: Ashgate, 2000), 215.

8. John Fitzherbert, *The book of husbandry* (1534; first edition 1523), in Kate Aughterson, ed., *Renaissance Woman: A Sourcebook* (London: Routledge, 1995), 196.

9. Fitzherbert, in Aughterson, 197.

10. Lena Cowen Orlin points out in her introduction to *Elizabethan Households: An Anthology,* ed. Orlin (Washington, D.C.: Folger Shakespeare Library, 1995), 23, that "we must read these documents against the grain and we must look elsewhere for life as it was lived."

11. Thomas Becon, *The book of matrimony* (1564), in Aughterson, 113.

12. John Dod and Robert Cleaver, *A Godlie Forme of Householde Government: for the Ordering of Private Families, According to the Direction of Gods Word* (1598), in Orlin, 25.

13. Alexander Niccholes, *A discourse of marriage and wiving* (1615), in Aughterson, 123.

14. William Whately, *A Bride-Bush, Or A Wedding Sermon* (1617), in Orlin, 39.

15. Thomas Gataker, *A Good Wife Gods Gift: and, A Wife Indeed. Two Marriage Sermons* (1623), in Orlin, 35. Subsequent references to this edition will be cited by page number in the text.

16. *The Schoolhouse of women* (1541?), in Henderson and McManus, 140. Subsequent references to this edition will be cited by page number in the text.

17. See Crane, "'Players in your huswifery,'" for more detailed consideration of class issues in the husbandry and huswifery texts.

18. For additional discussion of the mothers' advice books, see Elaine Beilin, *Redeeming Eve: Women Writers of the English Renaissance* (Princeton: Princeton University Press, 1987), 247–85; Joan Larsen Klein, "One Woman's Voice: Dorothy Leigh," in *Daughters, Wives, and Widows*, 287–91; Wendy Wall, *The Imprint of Gender: Authorship and Publication in the English Renaissance* (Ithaca: Cornell University Press, 1993), esp. 283–96; and Edith Snook, "'His open side our book': Meditation and Education in Elizabeth Grymeston's *Miscelanea Meditations Memoratives*," in Miller and Yavneh, eds., *Maternal Measures*, 163–75.

19. For more detailed consideration of the implications of maternal legacy in these texts, see Wall, *Imprint of Gender*, 283–96.

20. *The Northren Mother's Blessing* (London, 1597), E8, F1. Subsequent references to this edition will be cited by page number in the text.

21. Elizabeth Grymeston, *Miscellanea, Meditations, Memoratives* (1604, 1605–6), in Martin, 102. Subsequent references to this edition will be cited by page number in the text.

22. Elizabeth Jocelin, *The Mother's Legacie to her Unborne Childe* (1624), in Martin, 39.

23. Dorothy Leigh, *The Mother's Blessing: or, The Godly Counsel of a Gentlewoman not long since deceased, left behind her for her children* (1616), in Klein, 292. Subsequent references to this edition will be cited by page number in the text.

24. Leigh, dedicatory preface to *The Mother's Blessing*, sigs. A2-A5, in Linda Pollock, ed., *A Lasting Relationship: Parents and Children over Three Centuries* (London: Fourth Estate, 1987), 174.

25. See Martin, introduction to *Jane Anger, Her Protection*, 80–1, for more detailed consideration of the conditions of Anger's authorship. Martin points out that whether Jane Anger was a real woman or a ventriloquizing man, her arguments "anatomise the patriarchally encoded nature of everyday language, in which 'woman' is a discourse constructed from masculine moral and aesthetic values that denies real women any authentic sense of agency" (81).

26. *Jane Anger, Her Protection for Women* (1589), in Martin, 82–83. Subsequent references to this edition will be cited by page number in the text.

27. *Jane Anger, Her Protection*, in Henderson and McManus, 184.

28. Ibid., 187–88.

29. See Barbara Lewalski, ed., introduction to *The Polemics and Poems of Rachel Speght* (Oxford: Oxford University Press, 1996), xi-xix, for a thorough and thoughtful review of Speght's biographical details.

30. Lewalski, xxii. References to Rachel Speght's *A Mouzell for Melastomus, the Cynicall Bayter of, and foule mouthed Barker against Evah's Sex* (1617) will be drawn from Lewalski's edition, and will be cited by page number in the text.

31. Rachel Speght, dedicatory epistle to *Mortalities Memorandum, with a Dreame Prefixed* (1621), in Lewalski, 45–46. Subsequent references to this edition will be cited by page number in the text.

32. Martin, footnote 15 to Speght's dedicatory epistle, 32.

33. *Esther hath hanged Haman; or, An Answer to a lewd Pamphlet entitled* The Arraignment of Women, *With the arraignment of lewd, idle, froward, and unconstant men and Husbands* (1617), in Henderson and McManus. Subsequent references to this edition will be cited by page number in the text.

34. Sowernam cites exemplary mothers other than Eve throughout her pamphlet, including a reference that recalls Elizabeth Clinton's insistence on the conjunction of nourishing breast milk and maternal instruction, in an allusion to Margaret of Richmond, mother of Henry VII, "from whose breasts he may seem to have derived as well his virtues as his life, in respect of her heroical prudence and piety whereof" (230).

35. Constantia Munda, *The Worming of a mad Dog; or, a Sop for Cerberus, the Jailor of Hell* (1617), in Henderson and McManus, 245. Subsequent references to this edition will be cited by page number in the text.

CHAPTER 9

CROSSED-DRESSED WOMEN AND NATURAL MOTHERS: "BOUNDARY PANIC" IN *Hic Mulier*

Rachel Trubowitz

In *A Godly Form of Household Government* (1621) Robert Cleaver and John Dod underscore the virtues of maternal breast-feeding by comparing "naturall mothers" to trees: "As therefore every tree doth cherish and nourish that which it bringeth forth, so also it becometh naturall mothers to nourish their children with their own milke."[1] For Cleaver and Dod, and other guidebook writers, maternal breast-feeding provides a way to define "woman" as governed by natural law. This appeal to nature is notable for, among other things, its coincidence with what Stephen Orgel sees as the "new anxiety" about female cross-dressing registered by *Hic Mulier*,[2] published one year before Cleaver and Dod's text—an anxiety also articulated in King James's admonition to the London clergy in 1620, that they "inveigh vehemently and bitterly in their sermons against the insolency of our women, and their wearing of broad-brimmed hats, pointed doublets, their hair cut short or shorn, and some of them stilettos or poniards."[3] For Orgel, the "new anxiety" about cross-dressed women has to do with both the sexual license suggested by the female transvestite's blurring of gender boundaries and the commonplace association of female cross-dressing with prostitution. Through their transvestite attire, early modern English women, Orgel argues, advertised their "masculine" sexual freedom, i.e., their whoredom. They had, as the anonymous author of *Hic Mulier* puts it, "laid aside the bashfulnesse of [their] natures, to gather the impudence of Harlots."[4] Pointing Orgel's intriguing observations in a somewhat different direction, this essay argues that while a response to the sexual liberty sartorially proclaimed by female cross-dressers, the "new anxiety" about transvestite women also reflects the period's revaluation of maternity—what Ruth Perry terms "the invention of motherhood." This "invention," as I read it, newly naturalizes maternity, thereby inscribing new cultural roles not only for mothers but also, more implicitly, for whores and transvestites.[5]

INTRODUCTION: INVENTING MOTHERHOOD

Driving the "invention of motherhood," in part, was the desire of physicians like the eminent William Harvey to find scientific explanations for the "archaic mystery" of conception and birth, the "literal blind spot" of medical investigation, as Richard Wilson observes.[6] Visible only at the microscopic level, conception failed to reveal itself to the penetrating gaze of early modern anatomists of motherhood. Cultural convention also closed off the maternal body to scientific observation. Men customarily were banished from the exclusively female and, hence, "invisible" birth room, over which midwives and nurses presided. In order to "see" motherhood by what Francis Bacon termed the "dry light" of reason, the maternal body, hitherto the subject of folklore, superstition, and other "vulgar errors," required naturalization. Shrouded in darkness under the "old" prescientific regime, motherhood compelled enlightenment in the new scientific era; it would be made known by and, hence, subject to natural law, thereby disclosing its secrets to the scientific reformers of knowledge.

Installing the new figure of the "natural" mother thus proved crucial to Baconian efforts to discredit the foundational authority of classical philosophy and to establish the Jacobean "present" as the originary moment for the advancement of "true" knowledge. But, as we shall see, "natural" motherhood also came to play an important role in the period's new narratives of national origin, more specifically, its expansionist myths of England reborn as the greater "Britannia." In this context, the "natural" mother represents a source of authentic Englishness, which, as transmitted by breast-feeding from mother to child, would remain intact no matter what expanded territorial shape the English body politic might assume. "Good women," as the author of *Hic Mulier* maintains, not only are "Seminaries of propagation" but they also "give life to [English] society."[7] But "natural" motherhood could not cover up all traces of its unknowable antecedents. In the Jacobean imaginary, these irrepressible remnants of archaic motherhood find expression as the monstrous antimaternity that is mapped onto not only whores, transvestites, witches, etc., but also foreign worlds and peoples, destabilizing the Jacobean vision of a greater Britain, a subject to which we shall shortly return.

The enhanced attention to the maternal nature of origins and the origins of "natural" maternity transforms the wearing of sexually inappropriate garments, as decried in *Hic Mulier*, into a resonant register of the new disquietude about transvestite women's "whorish" display of sexual freedom. As I shall show, under the reinvented "natural" standards for idealized maternity, the maternal body appears in the domestic guidebooks in a state of complete (social) undress—as, so to speak, a redeemed Eve, and thus as a way back to the unsullied Edenic state of origins. If the whore—the anti-mother—can be recognized by her sexually and socially ambiguous garments, maternal purity is the imprint of a chaste, socially transcendent notion of "the feminine," of "woman" stripped of both postlapsarian "vice" (sexual and intellectual) and class and other social titles and markings, and so, socially divested, denuded, and de-eroticized, restored to her "pure," originary virtues. It is this "undressed" state that manifests women's "natural" maternal character. By contrast, by artfully constructing and displaying her own social character through her transgressive attire, the female transvestite allies sartorial deviance with nonmaternal female unnaturalness, which *Hic Mulier* equates with both the origin of evil and evil origins.

Complicating these issues is that early modern oppositions between "natural" and "unnatural" bleed into the (porous) dichotomies not only between "mother" and "whore," "undressed" and "cross-dressed," "pure" origin and "impure," but between "home" and "world" as well. As Stephen Greenblatt maintains, it is precisely at this historical moment that "the natural" came to replace "the sacred" as the conceptual category through which England articulated the relationship between its normative identity as national "home" and the "deviance" it detected in the foreign worlds to which it increasingly came into contact. Greenblatt writes: "the sixteenth and seventeenth centuries also saw the beginning of a gradual shift away from the axis of sacred and demonic and toward an axis of natural and unnatural . . . but the natural is not to be found . . . among primitive or uncivilized peoples. . . . The stage is set for the self-congratulatory conclusion that European culture, and English culture in particular, is at once the most civilized and the most natural."[8] This emergent conflation of "deviance" with "the primitive," "the unnatural," and "the non-English," I suggest, informs the "new" in the "new anxiety" about the errancy of female cross-dressing. As the *Hic Mulier* author maintains, female cross-dressing is "barbarous, in that it is exorbitant from Nature."[9] The transvestite controversy articulated in *Hic Mulier,* in short, forces consideration of the relationship not only between "mother" and "whore," but between "mother" and "other" as well.

It is in light of these concerns that I propose that the "new anxiety" about female cross-dressing intermixes with the "boundary panic," to borrow Janet Adelman's apt term, that issues from expansionist Jacobean efforts to transform Elizabethan England's inviolate island-kingdom into the greater "Britannia."[10] As suggested, the shift between English and British identity required new national narratives and hence also new parameters for domesticity and foreignness—rewritings that, as Kim F. Hall argues, helped to initiate the racializing of "difference": "It is England's anxiety about losing its traditional insularity that provokes 'racialism.'"[11] I contend that the "invention of motherhood"—of nursing motherhood, more specifically—is concomitant with these proto-racialized efforts to build a new British national identity. I argue further that the construction of the idealized "natural" nursing mother is intertwined in surprising ways not only with revisionist narratives of British national origin but also with heightened Jacobean interest in gaining access to and ownership of the mysterious beginnings (historical and biological) of human existence—a project crucial to the new Britain's imperial ambitions.

In its most ambitious scope then, this essay reads *Hic Mulier* in relationship to both Jacobean expansionism and its reconstructions of both "exotic" antimaternal difference and "natural" maternal origins. The "new anxiety" that Orgel detects in this pamphlet thus may be understood as a symptomatic response not only to the "masculine," and hence nonmaternal, sexual license flaunted by women in male attire, but also to the "exotic" allure, and repulsion, of the transvestite as "unnatural" and, as such, uncivilized and so, not English. The "new anxiety" is, in short, a form of "boundary panic." I show that *Hic Mulier*'s alliance of whoredom and transvestism with exoticized "difference" places the pamphlet's degradation of women cross-dressers in line not only with travel-narrative accounts of gender perversion in foreign worlds but also with the antimaternal imagery that accrues to submerged or displaced "foreign" subcultures within England. Such antimaternal imagery—and the idealized figurations of "natural" nursing motherhood against which such images come to be read—encode Jacobean efforts not only to fix the present as a pure point of national origin but also to gain access to and political control over the ever elusive "Beginning" itself and so to rewrite world history in British terms. The "whorish" female transvestite disrupts this new British narrative because, though a feature of the national landscape, s(h)e, as the author of *Hic Mulier* suggests, cannot be historically and hence nationally situated: her "like [is] not found in any Antiquary's study."[12]

CONTEMPLATING THE BREAST

Perhaps the clearest point of overlap between *Hic Mulier* and guidebook reconstructions of motherhood is the attention both focus on the breast. It strikes me as telling that while the fashion decried in the pamphlet flaunts the accouterments of masculinity, most notably the sword, it also provocatively bares the female breast. (Transvestite attire, in short, creates odd contiguities between sword and breast.) The costume consists of "ruffianly broad-brimmed hat and wanton feather . . . the loose, lascivious civil embracement of a French doublet, being all unbuttoned to entice ["to reveal naked breasts," as Orgel glosses this], most ruffianly short hair," and a sword.[13] Domestic guidebook writers also contemplate the exposed female breast in their energetic arguments for the virtues of maternal breastfeeding over the viciousness of wet nursing. If the author of *Hic Mulier* attributes unnatural sexual aggression to women whose breasts voluptuously burst out of a "masculine" French doublet, William Gouge and others bare the lactating breast as the key to women's "natural" maternal character.

This general fixation on the breast stems in part from the exceptional, and uncontainable, character of maternal lactation within Galenism's "one-sex" model of human sexual and reproductive physiology.[14] Both men and women were thought, for instance, to have "seed," or sperm, and breasts. But, as Kathryn Schwarz has argued, while the breast was understood as shared by both sexes, lactation was designated an exclusively "female" bodily function. In Thomas Vicary's *The Anatomie of the Bodie of Man,* "the generation of milke" categorically distinguishes the female breast from its male counterpart.[15] By gendering the unisex "pap," maternal lactation disrupts Galenism's mirror-model of human sexuality and reproduction. As Schwarz puts it in her gloss on Vicary's *Anatomy:* "And even if, as in the Galenic model, women's genitals are imagined to mirror those of men, producing some degree of reproductive mutuality, the maternal breast is an inescapable site of difference."[16]

It is in the interest of the guidebook writers and, I argue, the *Hic Mulier* author to sustain this emphasis on the definitive ways in which the maternal breast not only naturalizes the differences between the two genders but also reduces "woman" to her reproductive role as nursing mother, the source of food and succor, physical and spiritual, for children, husbands, and the nation. Toward this end, guidebook defenses of maternal breast-feeding sweep clean all culturally determined distinctions among women. Placing mothers on the same universalist plane, these *tabula rasa* considerations of "Woman" in her God-given, "natural," and original state divest women not only of "sin" (sexual desire and intellectual curiosity) but also of the social titles and sartorial badges that give "the feminine" cultural particularity.

Guidebook defenses of maternal breast-feeding sort themselves into two main kinds: exegetical and empirical. On the one hand, Cleaver and Dod, to note but one example, impugn wet nursing by suggesting that Sarah's nursing of Isaac in Genesis 21:7 must be read as divinely mandating maternal breast-feeding for all women regardless of class. Sarah "nursed Isaak though she were a Princess; and therefore able to have had others to have taken that paines."[17] On the other hand, they also appeal to "experience," claiming that maternal breast-feeding is the function of inductively derived natural laws: "We see by experience, that every beast and every fowle is nourished and bred of the same that beare it: onely some women love to be mothers, but not nurse.[18] By describing maternal breast-feeding as a divine impulse and natural instinct operative in all women, guidebook writers helped to reconceive maternal nurture at once as a manifestation of both providentially inspired love and bodily need (and hence subject to both moral suasion and medical intervention), responding to no "outward" obligations or imperatives, and hence unmeasurable as "proper work" in socioeconomic terms—hence, the guidebook's degradation of wet nursing. As Robert Pricke writes in

The Doctrine of Superiority, "no outward business appertaining to a mother can be more acceptable to God then the nursing of her childe: this is the most proper work of her speciall calling, therefore all other businesses must give place."[19]

Stripped of its "outward," socioeconomic features, maternal nurture helped secure mothers' place within the reformed English home, itself reimagined as a transcendent realm of moral purity and spiritual refuge outside and above the *polis.* But even while facilitating the enclosure of women in private, domestic spaces, the effacement of nursing motherhood's socioeconomic character simultaneously integrated women into England's nation-building project by placing "natural" mothers at the service of the family and the nation. The idealized "natural" nursing mother shores up normative English identity by interpellating her children into the natural order and thus, in the same gesture, also into the English nation as civilized subjects. By contrast, "unnatural" mothers and maternal surrogates, typically the lower-class wet nurse, undermine the intactness of English identity by estranging children not only from their "natural" mothers, but from their families and, by extension, the nation-state as well.

One key medical/moral concern registered by the guidebooks was that breast milk physically transmitted the moral and bodily character of the nurse to her charge, ideally complementing but more often compromising the familial identity that the child had inherited from its parents. "We may be assured," maintains James (Jacques) Guillemeau in *The Nursing of Children,* "that the Milke (wherewith the child is nourish'd two years together) hath a power to make the children like the Nurses, both in bodie and mind; as the seed of the Parents hath a power to make children like them."[20] The same perception of nurse milk's competition with and perversion of parentally transmitted identity surfaces as well in Shakespeare's plays, especially at heightened moments of familial conflict. When, to take a well-known example, Lord Capulet disowns Juliet for refusing to marry Paris, he but formalizes the familial estrangement and loss of hereditary identity that his daughter has experienced not only through her love for Romeo but also through the likeness she bears to the bawdy Nurse—and the Nurse bawdy/body—who suckled her.

As this example suggests, children put out to wet nurses or breastfed by unfit mothers not only were thought more likely to die than those offered "tender" maternal care and nourishment—"The number of nurse children that die every yeare is very great"—but they were also believed to experience a social "death" unknown to their

properly suckled counterparts.[21] To the extent that they were transformed by the noxious qualities of unfamiliar, and unfamilial, breast
milk, they were forever estranged from their families. "Such children
as have sucked their mothers breasts, love their mothers best," writes
William Gouge, "yea we observe many who have sucked others
milke, to love these nurses all the daies of their life."[22] David Leverenz nicely encapsulates the divide in the guidebooks between "tender mothers" and "strange milk": "Tender mothers and tender
children go together. Mothers should not be surprised, ran the
warnings, when they deny children the breast early in life. Strange
milk would lead to strange manners."[23] The affective ties between
nurse and child, in short, were thought to generate strangeness and
breed strangers, and to interrupt the genealogical transmission of fa-
milial-national identity—hence, the emphasis in the guidebooks on
creating synonymity between maternal love and maternal breast milk.
For Cleaver and Dod, women acquire "the sweet name of
Mother . . . full of incredible love" by breast-feeding, their first and
most important maternal duty.[24] Love and milk, affective ties and familial bloodlines, maternal duty and desire all cohere at the idealized
breast of "natural" mother.

Closely allied to these concerns about lactation and identity was
the widely embraced notion of breast milk as white blood. "[N]oth-
ing else but blood whitened," as Guillemeau writes.[25] If nurse milk
can, through the powerful affective ties it creates, pervert or even
eradicate familial identity and social bonds, it is also a blood carrier
of color-coded character—a conception that generated concerns
about the pollution of bloodlines through morally and physically
tainted milk. "Now if the nurse be of an evil complexion" ["complexion," in the period, denoted both moral character and skin
color],[26] write Cleaver and Dod, " . . . the child sucking of her breast
must need take part with her."[27] The emphasis on "evil complexion"
is striking, for it encapsulates an incipient slide from an ethical to a
proto-racialized notion of identity that paints both the spirit and the
skin color of the wet nurse in diabolically dark hues. Put another way,
proto-racialized anxieties about Jacobean England's shifting borders
are displaced onto the familiar and more easily regulated site of the
maternal breast and its identity-sustaining milk/blood, as represented in and circulated by the domestic guidebooks and affiliated
texts. But such attempts to monitor the maternal breast tend less to
cure the "boundary panic" that, as Hall suggests, generated proto-
racialized difference in the Jacobean period than to restate this
"panic" in gendered terms. While serving as an affecting icon of

"pure" English domesticity, the "natural" (or normative, English) maternal breast threatens to lapse into its "unnatural" (i.e., deviant, foreign) but perversely more appealing counterpart, despite the best efforts of the guidebook writers to compartmentalize them.

BARED BREASTS AND SARTORIAL BARBARISM

It is the exotic allure/threat of the "unnatural" or deviant breast that I suggest is literally exposed by the protuberant globes that burst forth from the French doublet decried in *Hic Mulier*. If cross-dressing highlights the "masculine" sexual liberty or "Harlotry" deviantly proclaimed by the bare-breasted female transvestite, it also underscores the exotic nature of the cross-dressed woman's appropriation of men's erotic freedom. As the author of *Hic Mulier* maintains, the gender boundaries transgressed by the cross-dressed garments of the female transvestite signal the sexual, moral, and political unruliness of "wild" and "rude" (anti-)nations: "If this [i.e, female cross-dressing] be not barbarous, make the rude Scythian, the untamed Moor, the naked Indian, or the wild Irish, Lords and Rulers of well-governed Cities."[28]

It seems telling in this respect that early modern travel-narrative accounts of "rude," "untamed," and "wild"non-English peoples betray anxieties about gender transgression and female excess similar to those registered by *Hic Mulier*. Indeed in Leo Africanus' *A Geographical Historie of Africa,* cross-dressing (in men) is linked to sexual license (moral cross-dressing) in women. In his description of Fez, for example, Leo notes that the innkeepers "goe apparelled like women," an inversion of costume that paves the way for the licentiousness of their female concubines who are "notorious for their bad life and behaviour." Also disgracing Fez are its women soothsayers— homoerotic "women-witches," who "burne in lust towardes [fair women] no otherwise then lustie yoonkers doe toward yoong maides."[29] Hall's comments on the semiotics of race and gender in early modern travel narratives are most pertinent: "the chief sign of cultural disorder is gender, specifically a sense of the instability of gender, thus allowing for an easy slippage between the concerns about the alienness of race and the unruliness of women."[30]

Most relevant here is that fashionable dress forms a key site for such "easy slippage[s]." The interplay between foreignness and haute couture English fashion finds especially clear expression in the writings of John Bulwer, the obscure seventeenth-century natural philosopher, as Greenblatt points out in a fascinating recent essay:

Bulwer "argues that contemporary English clothing at its most fashionable actually reproduces many of the transformations that are carried out in other cultures on the flesh itself."[31] That is, fashionable English dress replicates the "exotic" markings, and mutilations, of the foreign body. Take for instance, the doublet, a garment noted several times in *Hic Mulier,* and especially relevant here as the sartorial frame for the female transvestite's exoticized bare breasts. Bulwer writes, "the slashing, pinking, and cutting of our Doublets, is but the same phansie and affection with those barbarous Gallants who slash and carbonado their bodies."[32]

To some degree, the anonymous author of *Hic Mulier* might be said to anticipate Bulwer's equation of English fashion with (mutilated) foreign bodies, although the pamphlet's rendering of this equation carries clearer antifemale valences than does Bulwer's text. The "foreignness" that *Hic Mulier* imputes to female haute couture cross-dressing, in turn, helps to disclose why the social/cultural denuding of "Woman" is linked to lactational "naturalness," which purifies and stabilizes identity and so insures the continuity of intact national character so crucial to England's successful "evolution" into the expanded Britain during this historically specific moment of Jacobean nation-building. "Nation" and "lactation," in short, prove to be interanimating concepts. But, given the easy slide between the "good" breast and the "bad," the "deviant" breast displayed by women in cross-dressed couture threatens to destabilize this alliance between nursing and nation-building. As such, it also exposes the fault lines in the utopian pure milk/pure nation matrix that early modern reformations of "mother" and "mother country" put into place. Hence, if female cross-dressing evokes the commonplace affiliation of transvestism with harlotry, it also taps into unsettling, if still emergent, linkages between early modern (dis)figurations of mother- and nationhood. In other words, the female transvestite decried in *Hic Mulier* forces consideration not only of mothers and transvestite/whores, but of mothers and "others" as well.

While travel narratives and ethnographies of the "exotic" peoples and traditions of Asia, Africa, and the Americas thus might seem to be literally at a distance from the English household, they can be seen in fact as allied with the domestic guidebooks of Gouge, Guillemeau, and others discussed above. All help their readers establish a clear sense of their Englishness and to secure their personal and national boundaries. Just as the domestic guidebook is perhaps most interesting in its proximity to the travel narrative, i.e., when it reveals its fascination with and anxieties about places and people outside the familial and national home, so too the travel narrative or ethnography is especially revealing when read as a kind of domestic guidebook that defines the English domestic "norm" in opposition to the "deviance" visible in foreign worlds. *Hic Mulier* can be situated at this intersection between the domestic guidebook and the travel narrative—its detailing of female cross-dressing makes the transvestite the exemplar of an exoticism that is also English, of a strangeness situated within the national *domus*. The nexus between female cross-dressing as the sartorial badge of "the whore" and female cross-dressing as a chief sign of the moral perversity imputed to foreign cultures, furthermore, broadens the scope of *Hic Mulier*'s very localized concerns to include a larger and more global perspective.

Monstrous Motherhood and Split Subjectivity

The broader scope of the pamphlet is most relevant here, for it helps to reveal the precision with which the "new anxiety" about female cross-dressing overlaps with the "boundary panic" that, as noted above, issues from Jacobean attempts to expand England's borders, most notably, by union with Scotland. As Claire McEachern points out, James I's unionist campaign heightened his kingdom's xenophobic aversion to Scotland: "Whatever its roots . . . prejudice against Scotland was rampant."[33] But fear of foreign attachment not only was affixed to the Scottish or other peoples outside of England's traditional insular borders. It was driven as well by long-standing anxieties about the divided loyalties attributed to "foreign" subcultures (past and present, mythological and real) within England, most notably, Catholics and Jews. The charge of divided loyalties was leveled most aggressively against Catholics, who were accused, among many other things, of putting the pope and the papal order above the English Church and crown and, as such, serving the various "Romish" plots against English monarchs and subjects—the Gunpowder Plot of November 5, 1605, is the most notorious example. But Jews too (who had no "official" presence in England since the Expulsion of 1290) were imagined to have ties to a globally dispersed, but nevertheless still threatening, Israelite nation, ties that rendered the Jews unintegrable and, hence, deportable.[34] If Catholic "plotting" within England was linked to the external threat explicitly presented by Spain and France, Jewish "crime," i.e., well poisoning and ritual murder, was associated in the early modern anti-Semitic imaginary with a secret and diseased netherworld, situated within but also outside of England, insinuating itself into and ever threatening to overpower the dominant Christian culture.

A full discussion of Catholics and Jews is quite obviously well beyond the scope of this essay. I also can do no more here than suggest that Protestant homologies between these "unstable" groups reflect a cultural paranoia about global, or even cosmic, anti-English conspiracies—nightmares in which England's small island-kingdom is threatened with being engulfed by either one or both of these diabolical world orders. (I would conjecture further that it is this same nightmare of engulfment that partly shapes England's efforts to expand its own territorial and cultural borders.) I would nevertheless like to document one related issue highly relevant to my concerns here: that is, that the divided loyalties between world and home that English Protestants imputed to Catholics and Jews are feminized through the same signs of maternal perversity and gender transgression that *Hic Mulier* attributes to transvestite women. Put another way, the split subject position ascribed to these recusant, secret, or wholly imaginary subcultures within England finds gendered expression in the form of the female transvestite. In turn, female transvestites, I would suggest, literally in-habit submerged Catholic or displaced Jewish hybridities within the nation, thereby symbolically cross-dressing as well the threat of foreign engulfment. The specter of monstrous maternity, in short, aligns (real and imagined) Anglo-alien hybridities with *Hic Mulier*'s fashionable female cross-dressers. In unveiling her "unnatural" breast, the female transvestite not only announces her whoredom, but also takes on the same errant maternity and malevolent motherhood stereotypically imputed to Catholics, Jews, and other domestic "exotics."

⤞⥢

Even a brief review of these stereotypes offers considerable insight into how the figure of the monstrous mother provides a nexus for seemingly disparate English cultural anxieties about gender, national, and religious instabilities. Of these stereotypes, the depiction of the Catholic Church as "the Whore of Babylon," the scarlet prostitute from Revelations 17:4, is without doubt the most commonplace— Spenser's Duessa providing the most compelling example. Especially relevant to my concerns here is the "good breast/bad breast" dichotomy that Thomas Dekker in *The Whore of Babylon* makes between his Duessa-like Empress of Babylon and her counterpart, Titania, the Faerie Queen. If life-sustaining "Soueraigne mercie" flows from Titania's breast (2.1.232), debased (Catholic) kings "suck treason" from their "Empres bosome" (1.2.255).[35] This same, and quite predictable, conflation of perverse maternal succor with Catholic "treason" supplies the theme for "*A pitiless Mother*," a popular reportial pamphlet published four years before *Hic Mulier*. "*A pitiless Mother*" tells the cautionary tale of Margaret Vincent, an English gentlewoman of "good parentage" who, having fallen "into the hands of Roman Wolves," proceeded to kill her two youngest children in a misguided act of religious enthusiasm.[36] Not unlike the female transvestite of *Hic Mulier*, Margaret's perverse maternity—her life-denying rather than life-sustaining nurture—is measured against the axis of "natural" and "unnatural," which as we have seen newly dominated the English cultural imaginary, especially its conceptual formulation of national, and foreign, identity. The very title of the pamphlet spells out how "most unnaturally" Margaret, as a Catholic, came to murder two of her children. "And therefore, to save their soul (as she vainly thought)," the anonymous author goes on to recount, "she purposed to become a Tigerous Mother and so wolfishly to committ the murder of her own flesh and blood, in which opinion she steadfastly continued, never relenting according to nature." A tigress that eats her children and a she-wolf (the female mate of the very same Roman wolves who converted her to "a blind belief of bewitching heresy"), Margaret, as a Catholic zealot, loses the "natural" maternal instinct to nourish her children with her own body—an instinct she had acted upon when she was still a Protestant.[37] Not unlike Dekker's contrast of his Empress and Faerie Queen, the author of *A pitiless Mother* equates Margaret with the (papist) anti-Christ, while contrasting her to the "natural" mother, emblematized christologically as the self-sacrificing pelican: "By nature, [Margaret] should have cherished them with her own body, as the Pelican that pecks her own breast to feed her young ones with her blood, but she, more cruel than the Viper, the envenomed Serpent, the Snake, or any Beast whatsoever, against all kind takes away those lives to whom she first gave life." Margaret is both exoticized as more savage than "the Savages" and "the Cannibals" (the stock-icon of the uncivilized New World) and debased as more bestial than "every beast and fowl," which all "hath a feeling of nature and according to kind will cherish their young ones." Having been "nursed by the Roman sect," Margaret perverts her "natural" and hence English Protestant maternity by murdering rather than nursing her children and, even worse, by believing these to be the same deed.[38]

A similar monstrous (and sometimes marvelous) maternity was imputed to Jews, who through their reverence for "carnal" Hebraic

law sometimes occupied the same subject position as idolatrous
Catholics in the English Protestant imagination. As recent studies
have shown, long-standing anti-Semitic perceptions of Jewish manhood as impaired and degenerate helped to code the social construct
of "the Jew" as "female"—a perception reinforced by the commonly
held assumption that Jewish men menstruated. Jewish male bodies,
like those of women, were thought of as leaky vessels, which dis-
charged a monthly flow of unclean blood. Thus the Spanish physician
Juan de Quinones wrote "a special treatise to prove that male Jews
have a tail and, like women, a monthly flow of blood."[39] Extending
this image of "leaky" Jewish manhood is the "marvel" of Jewish male
lactation that Samuel Purchas recounts in *Purchas His Pilgrimage*—a
depiction no doubt informed by the belief that mothers' milk was
formed from menstrual blood. "If you believe their *Gemara* (can you
choose?)," Purchas writes, "a poor Jew having buried his wife and
not able to hire a nurse for his child, had his breasts miraculously
filled with milk, and became nurse himself." Purchas also alludes to
the figure of a breast-feeding Mordecai represented in a Midrashic interpretation of the Book of Esther.[40] If the tale of Margaret Vincent
associates infanticide with depraved Catholic motherhood, depictions
such as Purchas' of marvelous, repellent Jewish male nurses were
closely intertwined with the perception of Jews as Christian-child
killers. The leakage of blood/milk from Jewish men was perceived as
both symptom and explanation for what was thought to be the Jews'
insatiable thirst for Christian blood. It was this blood-thirst that supposedly drove Jews to abduct, forcibly circumcise, and ritually murder young gentile boys and drink their blood. This signature Jewish
crime—the so-called "blood-libel"—also finds a point of origin in the
cluster of presumed ritual murders in medieval and Renaissance Europe, all following the same pattern—the "case" of Simon of Trent
(1472) is perhaps the most notorious example. The enduring
strength of English belief in the "reality" of these Jewish "crimes"
cannot be overestimated. As James Shapiro poignantly notes: "Not
even the Holocaust put to rest such allegations [of Jewish ritual mur-
der] in England."[41] As I have argued elsewhere, these enduring anti-
Semitic assumptions about blood, sucking, and Jewish men form an
important if lurid subtext for the guidebooks' and other idealized images of the Christian mother suckling her child with her "white
blood."[42] I would add here that as the "evil" and "unnatural" counterpart to this idealized nursing maternity, the bare-breasted whorish
female transvestite decried in *Hic Mulier* stands in close proximity to
the allied mythological figures of the Jewish ritual child killer (the

male Jewish anti-mother) and the savage Catholic "Whore of Baby-lon" and she-wolf. All conjure up the specter of unknowable, and un-containable, "archaic" maternity (and by extension, the untraceable but still powerful influence of England's murky prehistorical origins), repressed by "the invention of motherhood."

TRACKING THE SOURCE

The repetitive and almost reflex deployment of antimaternal images such as those outlined above thus helped to turn the specter of mon-strous motherhood into a stock expression of English xenophobia and cultural paranoia about Catholics, Jews, and, as I have suggested, female transvestites. But, while these images, and the "boundary panic" they encode, bespeak English fantasies about pure national identities and origins, they also imply broader, but interrelated, cul-tural preoccupations with the very nature of origin and identity itself. Such preoccupations, driven by visionary Reformation rewritings of Christian history, inspired campaigns to demystify and control hu-mankind's murky and mythologized "prehistorical" beginnings, thereby extending Britain's intellectual—and, subsequently, its polit-ical—reach both backward before the very advent of time as well as eastward, and westward, to the ancient ruins or living simulacra of early cultures in the Old and New Worlds.[43]

In this last section, I would like to return to, and gesture beyond, "the invention of motherhood" noted at the beginning of this essay. This event, as we recall, gains conceptual energy from the rise of ob-stetrical science, under the governance especially of William Harvey, as it peers into the maternal womb and breast in order to locate the precise biological origin of human life, a project doomed to failure. I return, by way of closure, to what Wilson describes as Harvey's "manic search" for the beginning of life, since we are now in a bet-ter position to place the new science's "invention of motherhood" (i.e., the effort to translate the primal scenes of conception and birth into the new master narrative of the new science) in alliance not only with pamphlets like *Hic Mulier* but also with Renaissance travel liter-ature, ethnography, historiography, and other genres, which inscribe and describe, explicitly or implicitly, originary sites and insights.[44] In-deed, while seemingly disparate, a variety of discursive efforts to chronicle and chart how and where humankind began (by mapping classical or scriptural precedents, geographical starting points, bio-logical or "natural" beginnings) in fact come together into what might be an inaugural moment of intersection when for the first time obstetrical attempts to anatomize the reproductive matrix intermix with ruling cultural desires to locate and control "the Beginning." It is this multivalenced interest in and anxiety about finding an absolute point of pure origin that *Hic Mulier* allows us to glimpse, however obliquely.

But before returning to the pamphlet, it is important first to note that while the cultural project of recuperating "the Beginning" took many forms, none was more crucial than the effort to chart the territorial site of the lost Garden of Eden. As John Michael Archer's important recent study makes clear, discursive efforts to situate the Garden in the fallen world acquired considerable force during the seventeenth century. Such determination to place Paradise on the map of the modern world carried considerable political weight, since nothing less than the translation of empire from the prelapsarian past—when divine decree granted humankind imperial dominion over God's new created world—to the redeemed present of Reformation England, ready to inherit and act on man's originary imperial prerogative, was linked to the regaining of Paradise. In an astute reading of both popular travel narrative and learned antiquarian efforts to locate Paradise, Archer details the "imperial rationality" that informs these texts, aptly summarizing the political *raison d'être* that drove such exploration and research: "By locating paradise, then, one will also gain access to the original "planting" or colonizing of the fallen world, to the Fall as a continued event of diaspora, renaming, and nation-building."[45]

The quest for Paradise is very much worth our attention because it is possible to detect the same imperial desire to gain access to and control over "the Beginning" in the obstetrical drive to decode the female mysteries of conception, birth, and maternal nurture. It is this desire—excessive because totalizing—that helps to turn the seemingly neutral and disinvested dissection of maternal wombs and breasts into a "manic search" for the biological beginning of life and nourishment. It is important to remember that the first obstetrical and gynecological explorations took place in the political context of incipient centralizing absolutism. The scientific project of translating the mystery of birth into rational discourse—that is, of creating obstetrics as a "discipline"—is concurrent with the emergence of the bureaucratic nation-state, with the formal institutionalization of hitherto unorganized, undocumented cultural experience.

By way of illustrating these issues, I turn once again to Richard Wilson's recent essay, especially his highly insightful analysis of the petition for a midwives' charter presented to James I in 1616 (the same year as Harvey's first anatomy lecture and four years before the publication of *Hic Mulier*). For Wilson, this petition forms a material context for the conceptual translation of the "old" maternity to the "new"—a rewriting that would bring conception and birth out of the untutored, female birth room into the professional chambers of the physician and, finally, up to the halls of "enlightened" government. While supposedly drafted by London midwives themselves, this petition appears to have been promoted by Peter Chamberlen, head of a Huguenot family that invented the obstetric forceps—a family that ardently campaigned for the state licensing of midwifery. The Chamberlens' professed aim in promoting the licensing of midwives was to avoid the dire "consequences for the health and strength of the whole nation if ignorant women, whom poverty or the game of Venus hath intruded into midwifery, should be insufficiently instructed." But, as Wilson aptly notes, the unspoken ambition behind the drafting of the midwives' petition was less improvement of the material conditions and practices of birthing than "the paternal licensing of fertility itself."[46]

As a coda to Wilson's illuminating discussion, I would add that domestic guidebook efforts to dismiss wet nurses from the English home and to establish "natural" mothers as the normative source of maternal nurture represents a threshold moment similar to that marked by the petition for the midwives' charter. Furthermore, like the licensing of midwifery, the guidebooks' campaign to promote maternal breast-feeding forces attention to the ways in which the attempt to reform and normalize maternal nurture—the source, as we recall, of personal and national identity—can mask absolutist, imperial desires to control originary sites and experiences that could not be wholly rationalized.

These issues, and more, come into especially resonant conjunction in James I's self-representation as a "nourish king." In *Basilikon Doron*, James reminds Prince Henry that monarchy displays both fatherly power and motherly nurturing: "it [is] one of your fairest styles to be called a louing nourish father" who provides his subjects with "nourish milke."[47] James's "nourish father[hood]—his equation of patriarchal imperial sovereignty with maternal nourishment—emblematically encapsulates the "invention of motherhood," that is, the "paternal licensing" of (nursing) maternity, which this essay has tried to chronicle. Recalling the ways in which "lactation" and "nation" impinge upon one another in this period, it is possible also to read James's self-image as nursing father as an affecting, and politically expedient, icon of the new "Britannia," an England made "greater" through the attachment of Scotland and other acts of colonization, domestic and foreign. Resistance to national attachment was made literally in the name of Mother Country, that of Elizabethan "England" rather than Jacobean "Britain" of "Albion." On April 25, 1604, a Mr. Percyvall urged in Parliament "the Name of our Mother Country to be kept: Our desire natural and honorable—she hathe nurst, bred, and brought us up to be men."[48] Most relevant here are the ways in which Percyvall's remarks place the received trope of England as maternal nurse in service of an imagined English insularity. It is in part to wrest control over this affecting antiunionist equation between "nation" and "lactation"—and the "natural" desires from which it derives justification—that James chooses to represent his sovereignty as nursing kingship. He addresses, and represses, the milk-memory of the idealized Elizabethan island-kingdom by substituting the greater breast of a masculine maternal Britain for the lesser one of a simply feminine "Mother England." By offering his subjects his own all-encompassing fount of social nourishment, James not only rewrites the attachment of Scotland to England as a bond of enduring mutual affection and never-ending sustenance, but he also, through the conversionary power of breast–milk (which "whitens" blood), bestows the same purity of "complexion" on two peoples who were perceived as morally and corporeally distinct.

The lactational powers of James's royal person thus projects national union by establishing the king as the sole source of his subjects' social nourishment, and so as the abolut(ist) origin of a greater British identity that would override subversive "local"attachments to Scotland or sub-nations/cultures within England. But while the androgynous king could project all-encompassing "oneness," his double gender also raised the specter of division and so also the risk of opening up crevices in the national surfaces that he endeavored to make literally labile. It is this specter of division, this potential for political instability and national disjunction, that is evoked by the androgynous "masculine-feminines" decried in *Hic Mulier*—the same cross-dressed women against whom, as we recall, James, in the same year, issued his admonition to the London clergy. We are now better able to appreciate how much ideological freight both the pamphlet and the admonition had to bear. The haute couture cross-dressed woman, with her bare breasts and sword—this whorish carrier of "foreign" difference, this "Miscellany or mixture of deformities"[49]—threatened foreclosure upon not only James's self-proclaimed nursing fatherhood but also the political fantasy of an undifferentiated, seamlessly unified "Britannia," the issue of the king's sovereign paternal-maternal nurture.

Hic Mulier's alliance of whoredom and gender transgression with the alienness of "difference" is thus finally notable for the ways in which it reveals, and intervenes in, the surprising nexus between the "invention of motherhood" and the expansionist fantasies, and xenophobic anxieties, of Jacobean Britain. As already noted, the reformation of motherhood—and allied attempts to (re)claim the maternal source—played itself out in sartorial terms through a social undressing of "Woman," a denuding that damned "unnatural" maternity by aligning unfit mothers with perverse "others," including female transvestites. It is precisely this "foreignness" that both *Hic Mulier* and "the invention of motherhood" were meant to suppress as part of a larger nationalistic project of historical revisionism. If this massive project, which ultimately helped to underwrite the supremacy of British empire, generated patriotic pride in the nation's emergent global preeminence, it also triggered anxieties about the intactness of English identity.

We have seen that such anxieties attached themselves both to the hybrid subgroups that England tried, and partly failed, to repress or deport and to the spectral threat of monstrous maternal engulfment and the return of repressed archaic motherhood that were imputed to these absent/present minority cultures, real and imagined. By contrast, in the domestic guidebook and affiliated literature, the civilizing powers imputed to "natural" motherhood are situated most importantly in the maternal breast, which, by transmitting and preserving originary Englishness, could stay the threat of engulfing barbarous maternity. *Hic Mulier* allows us to see the "deviant" breast protruding from the female transvestite's manly attire as the fetishized site of the "boundary panic" and obsession with origins that rule this historical moment—as the site, that is, of the "new anxiety" about cross-dressed women.

NOTES

1. Robert Cleaver and John Dod, *A Godly Form of Household Government: for the ordering of Private Families, according to the Direction of God's Word* (London, 1621), sig. P4r.
2. Stephen Orgel, *Impersonations: The Performance of Gender in Shakespeare's England* (Cambridge: Cambridge University Press, 1996), 119.
3. Angeline Goreau, *The Whole Duty of a Woman: Female Writers in Seventeenth-Century England* (Garden City, N. Y.: Doubleday, 1985), 91.
4. *Hic Mulier . . .* , in *Half Humankind: Contexts and Texts of the Controversy about Women in England, 1540–1640*, eds. Katherine Usher

Henderson and Barbara F. McManus (Urbana: University of Illinois Press, 1985), 266.

5. Ruth Perry, "Colonizing the Breast: Sexuality and Maternity in Eighteenth-Century England," *Eighteenth-Century Life* 16 (1992), 185.

6. Richard Wilson, "Observations on English Bodies: Licensing Maternity in Shakespeare's Late Plays," *Enclosure Acts: Sexuality, Property, and Culture in Early Modern England,* eds. Richard Burt and John Michael Archer (Ithaca: Cornell University Press, 1994), 126, 125.

7. *Half Humankind,* 265.

8. Stephen Greenblatt, "Mutilation and Meaning," *The Body in Parts: Fantasies of Corporeality in Early Modern Europe,* ed. David Hillman and Carla Mazzio (New York and London: Routledge, 1997), 230, 236.

9. *Half Humankind,* 268.

10. Janet Adelman, *Suffocating Mothers: Fantasies of Maternal Origin in Shakespeare's Plays,* Hamlet *to* The Tempest (New York and London: Routledge, 1992), 29.

11. Kim F. Hall, *Things of Darkness: Economies of Race and Gender in Early Modern England* (Ithaca: Cornell University Press, 1995), 3.

12. *Half Humankind,* 266.

13. Ibid., 267; Orgel, *Impersonations,* 119.

14. See Thomas Laqueur, *Making Sex: Body and Gender from the Greeks to Freud* (Cambridge: Harvard University Press, 1990), esp. 25, 37, 38, 171–4. Laqueur's study is contested by, among others, Gail Kern Paster, *The Body Embarrassed: Drama and the Disciplines of Shame in Early Modern England* (Ithaca: Cornell University Press, 1993), esp. chapters 2 and 4.

15. Thomas Vicary, *The Anatomie of the Bodie of Man,* issue of 1548 as reissued by the Surgeons of St. Bartholomews in 1577, ed. Frederick J. Furnivall and Percy Furnivall (London: Early English Texts Society, 1888), 55.

16. Kathryn Schwarz, "Missing the Breast: Desire, Disease, and the Singular Effect of Amazons," *The Body in Parts,* 147.

17. Cleaver and Dod, sig. P4r.

18. Ibid.

19. Robert Pricke, *The Doctrine of Superiority, and of Subjection, contained in the Fift Commandment* (London, 1609), section K.

20. James Guillemeau, *The Nursing of Children. Wherein is set downe, the ordering and gouernment of them from their birth;* affixed to *Childbirth, or the Happie Deliverie of Women* (London, 1612), sig. Ii4.

21. William Gouge, *Of Domesticall Duties. Eight Treatises* (London, 1622), 518.

22. Gouge, 512.

23. David Leverenz, *The Language of Puritan Feeling: An Exploration in Literature, Psychology, and Social History* (New Brunswick, N.J.: Rutgers University Press, 1980), 72.
24. Cleaver and Dod, sig. S4v.
25. Guillemeau, *The Nursing of Children*, preface, I.i.2.
26. See "complexion" (entry 4) in *Oxford English Dictionary*, which dates the term's first reference to "the natural colour, texture, and appearance of the skin, *esp.* of the face" to 1568.
27. Cleaver and Dod, sig. P4v.
28. *Half Humankind*, 269.
29. Johannes Leo Africanus, *A Geographical Historie of Africa*, trans. and ed. John Pory (London, 1600), 130–1, 148–9.
30. Hall, *Things of Darkness*, 25.
31. Greenblatt, "Mutilation and Meaning," 236.
32. John Bulwer, *Anthropometamorphosis: Man Transform'd* (London, 1653), quoted in Greenblatt, "Mutilation and Meaning," 235.
33. Claire McEachern, *The Poetics of English Nationhood, 1590–1612* (Cambridge: Cambridge University Press, 1996), 143.
34. For commentary on early modern Anglo-Christian perceptions of Jews as a nation, see James Shapiro, *Shakespeare and the Jews* (New York: Columbia University Press, 1996), 173–80.
35. Thomas Dekker, *The Whore of Babylon*, in *The Dramatic Works of Thomas Dekker*, 5 vols., ed. Fredson Bowers (Cambridge: Cambridge University Press, 1953–61). References are noted in the text.
36. *A pitiless Mother* in *Half Humankind*, 361, 362.
37. *Half Humankind*, 363, 362.
38. Ibid., 364, 367.
39. Quoted in Shapiro, 38.
40. Samuel Purchas, *Purchas His Pilgrimage* (London, 1626), 182.
41. Shapiro, 101. On the "blood-libel," see Shapiro, 100–11, and Ronnie Po-Chia Hsia, *The Myth of Ritual Murder: Jews and Magic in Reformation Germany* (New Haven: Yale University Press, 1988).
42. See my essay "'But Blood Whitened': Nursing Mothers and 'Others' in Early Modern Britain," *Maternal Measures: Figuring Caregiving in the Early Modern Period*, ed. Naomi J. Miller and Naomi Yavneh (Ashgate, 2000), 82–104.
43. These ambitions are meticulously documented in John Michael Archer's illuminating study, *Old Worlds: Egypt, Southwest Asia, and India in Early Modern English Writing* (forthcoming, Stanford University Press). I am grateful to Professor Archer for allowing me to read his book in manuscript.
44. Wilson, "Observations on English Bodies," 126.
45. I quote here from the manuscript of *Old Worlds: Egypt, Southwest Asia, and India in Early Modern English Writing*, ch. 2.
46. Wilson, 138–9.

47. C. H. McIlwain, ed., *The Political Works of James I* (Cambridge: Harvard University Press, 1918), 24.
48. *Common Journals* (London, 1803), I (1547–1628):184. See McEachern for discussion of Percyvall and participants in the debate over the naming of the united England and Scotland, 140–5.
49. *Half Humankind*, 276.

PART V

POLITICS, STATE, AND NATION

CHAPTER 10

Monstrous Births
and the Body Politic:
Women's Political Writings
and the Strange and Wonderful
Travails of Mistris Parliament
and Mris. Rump

Katherine Romack

Gynocritics attempting to chart a genealogy of English feminism
commonly take as their point of departure the *querelle des femmes.*[1]
The early modern period constituted a turning point in the long-
standing print controversy over the nature and status of women because, as Katherine Henderson and Barbara McManus point out,
"for the first time in England women began to write in their own defense and for the first time anywhere significant numbers of women
begin to publish defenses."[2] From broadside ballad to the Swetnam,
Hic Mulier/Haec Vir, and Juniper/Crabtree controversies, female
participation in the *querelle des femmes,* inaugurated on the Continent by the fifteenth-century work of Christine de Pizan, steadily
grew in force and intensity in England throughout the late-sixteenth
and early-seventeenth centuries. In 1589, Jane Anger boldly wrote of

the misogynist attackers of the female sex, "their slanderous tongues are so short, and the time they have wherein they have lavished out their words freely hath been so long, that they know we cannot catch hold of them to pull them out and they think that we will not write to reprove their lying lips."[3] Two decades later, Constantia Munda also wrote scornfully of men, "And Printing, that was invented to be the storehouse of famous wits, the treasure of Divine literature, the pandect [compendium] and maintainer of all Sciences, is become the receptacle of every dissolute Pamphlet, the nursery and hospital of every spurious and penurious brat which proceeds from base phrenetical brainsick babblers."[4] In 1640, "Mary Tattlewell" and "Joan Hithim-home" penned *The Women's Sharp Revenge* in response to the Juniper, Crabtree, and Wormwood "lectures" to "prove presently out of the best Authors that ever lived that women have been, and are, and will be, must be and shall be either men's betters or their equals or (at the least) not to be so much undervalued, as . . . to be abused, vilified and traduced by every idle and paltry potcompanion."[5]

Following Tattlewell and Hit-him-home, there is a curious cessation of Englishwomen's involvement in what Linda Woodbridge terms "the formal controversy about women" that persists until the restoration of the monarchy.[6] Between 1640 and 1660, despite a spectacular rise in the sheer volume of print and proliferation of thousands of pamphlets—many of these written by women—not a single formal defense of women is penned by a member of the "female sex."[7] This is intriguing given both the continued attacks on women by male misogynists and the striking political visibility of women in the period. If the debate among men about the "woman question" reached a fevered pitch during this period, women, it seems, left men to their own devices, not dignifying their writings with the effort of a response. As I will suggest here, women of the midcentury sought out different grounds upon which to represent themselves.

The swift expansion of information networks in the midcentury, especially through the large-scale dissemination of print, was conducive to both the development of an increasingly commercial system and the radical transformation of the conceptual means through which the rights and obligations of individual (male) subjects were envisioned.[8] On this topic, the contributions of women to the print debate over political representation remains a subject in dire need of explication. Between absolutism and the development of the "political" state (in its modern enlightenment sense), the collapse of structures of authority that had traditionally enforced women's subjection allowed them to come close to articulating a program of political and cultural entitlement. Such a program never finally materialized, yet the mass collectivization of women in the protests of the 1640s and 1650s, the midcentury petitions by women that declare their "equal share" with men in the commonwealth, and the activities of sectarian women in preaching, missionary work, and issuing prophetic warnings to the nation indicate that the explosion of information networks opened up a window of opportunity for the mass mobilization of women and their reenvisioning of themselves as citizens with specific political rights and obligations.

The absence of women's participation in the formal controversy surrounding gender had, I am suggesting, everything to do with the changing terrain of representation in the period. The temporary instability of political representation made it possible for women to strategically invert residual (socially engrained) and emergent (newly configured) cultural and political ideas. This transformed women's feminist strategies from those limited to a reactive politics of cultural "opposition," "protection," and "defense" to a politics of enactment which commonly subverted and sometimes completely ignored the classical, biblical, and aesthetic grounds upon which the debate about gender had traditionally taken place.

The title of my essay refers to a long-standing early modern commonplace, that is, the attachment of the female body (especially its reproductive capacity) to monstrous deformations of the state. I will examine the redeployment of this trope by midcentury women writers to demonstrate some of the ways in which women during this period subverted the conventional meaning of such residual images in an attempt to establish a language of political entitlement for women. Specifically, I look at Elizabeth Poole's use of the monstrous birth trope to ground her addresses to the Army Council of War concerning the fate of Charles I. Her addresses force us to attend to the fact that such women came extremely close to calling for equal access to representation in the years between the outbreak of civil war and the restoration of the monarchy. Because I am also interested in accounting for why such women were ultimately unsuccessful in their bids for political entitlement, I will also examine a number of misogynist satires that deploy the monstrous birth trope to achieve radically different ends. A permanent feminist refiguration of gendered representation never materialized, I will argue, not simply because women were excluded and oppressed by their misogynist counterparts—though this is of course true—but also because the dominant language through which women expressed political aspirations would be, by 1660, effectively rendered superfluous.

II

On December 29, 1648, Elizabeth Poole, a seamstress from Abington, first appeared before the General Council of the Army to reveal a vision that came to her after reading the army's *Remonstrance*. Poole's vision is remarkable because it was solicited by and delivered to what was, at that moment, the most powerful political body in England—directly engaging its most urgent debates over where political power was to reside—and also because of its direct insistence on Poole's own place in the body politic, "a member in her body."[9] In her address, Poole worked to provide prophetic "evidence" validating the transfer of political authority from king to the army council: "Kingly power is undoubtedly fallen into your hands . . . take heed to improve it," Poole warned.[10]

Poole would come before the council twice. The written statement she submitted during her second appearance on January 5, 1649, again foregrounds the sovereign nature of the authority vested in the military and asks that Charles I be brought to trial, "that he may be convicted in his conscience."[11] This time, however, to the horror of many members of the council, she qualified her initial justification of the army's actions with a warning: "touch not his person."[12] This imperative resulted in the repudiation of her political statements through the generation of sexual scandal, a response she resisted tenaciously in print.[13] The transcripts of her addresses appeared in print five days after her second appearance, in a pamphlet entitled *A Vision: Wherein is manifested the disease and cure of the KINGDOME. . . .* (1649).

Poole's vision employs the enthusiastic rhetoric so common to sectarian literature by women in the period, a language frequently used to enter public political debate. It was a distinctly feminized poetics, complete with its own formal conventions, intimately connected to women's social and political place in early modern culture, and crucially, characterized by the gendered inversions wonderfully described by Natalie Zemon Davis in her foundational essay "Women on Top."[14] Enthusiastic writing is a distinct literary genre, complete with its own formal and topical conventions, the most salient of which consist of the spatial disembodiment of the seat of authorship (allowing for the author to simultaneously occupy multiple locations from which to speak and allowing the speaker to change gender— sometimes midsentence). It is marked by the coexistence of internal (human) and external (divine or satanic) voice, a conflation of the literal and metaphorical, of the material and the symbolic, of thing and idea, a "stuttering" style (not unlike "stream of consciousness" or postmodernist writing), and a multivalenced revelatory logic. Crucially, this approach to language involves a profound awareness of the inadequacy of language to express God's word and will.[15] This qualifies any simple equation of the use of existent patriarchal themes and language with acquiescence to patriarchy, for with full cognizance of the inadequacy of the conventional language surrounding gender, women could and did bend this language to their wills. Enthusiastic literature is forward-looking and commonly utopian, typically employs leveling images (mountains leveled, the proud rendered low, the clothed divested of their garments, the poor being raised to the position of the most high and so forth), and always incorporates direct biblical and classical citation and gendered sententia (while strategically subverting the meanings of these) to present an often millenarian—and potentially feminist—vision. It is analogically rather than narratively driven, giving it the appearance of saying a variety of things at once.

Reproductive "labor" is a central motif in Poole's texts, as it is in countless other sectarian texts by women in the period. Her repeated use of the image is interesting, given the historical reduction of women to their procreative role in the family and the *querelle*'s longstanding preoccupation with the dangers and virtues of reproduction. Poole's use of this trope illustrates the strategies by which women drew on a residual language to achieve political ends. Regarded as "the weaker vessel" throughout the early modern period, women's public speech was commonly associated with divine impregnation. Both female and male prophets in midcentury England, for example, consistently deploy the trope of labor to describe the generation of prophecy—from the Lady Eleanor Davies' prophetic "babes" to Abiezer Coppe's highly erotic and maternal textual "deliverances." As Stevie Davies puts it, "all of this panging was perfectly in keeping with a prophetess's necessary birth-throes."[16] Just as prophetic men and women swapped their figurative bodies at will, Poole's use of the woman in labor operates on multiple registers; she simultaneously claims the status of part of the body politic in travail, midwife to the body politic, and mother of a vision. This rhetorical divorce of embodied and figural subjectivity cannot be underestimated, for here Poole uses the trope of childbirth not only to ground the very act of addressing the army council, but also to depict herself as a member of the body politic.

From the times of classical antiquity, political theory had commonly employed the human body to represent the configuration, function, and health of the polity. Centuries of political theorizing drew equally upon the classical feminization of tyrannical rule and biblical assertions of divinely sanctioned patriarchal authority. From the "fable of the belly" to the monstrosity of a headless nation under monarchical tyranny, the status of sovereign "bodies" (as well as those of other corporate political associations) were an integral part of the language of politics and a constant source of debate in early modern England. The use of the female body to depict the nation's health had similar historical antecedents. As might be expected, these "feminized" figurations of the body politic were fraught with anxiety and contradiction even if they did not exhibit the predominantly hostile attitude toward "feminized authority" best exemplified by Knox's 1558 invective against the "monstrous regiment":

> For who can denie but that it be repugneth to nature, that the blind shal be appointed to leade and conduct such as do see? That the weake, the sicke, and impotent persones shal norishe and kepe the hole and strong, and finalie, that the foolishe, madde and phrenetike, shal gouerne the discrete, and give counsel to such as be sober of mind? And such be all women, compared unto men in bearing of authority.[17]

Heavily impacted by the vicissitudes of the reigns of two female monarchs and the progressive association of Stuart rule with the tyranny of unchecked, sovereign exercises of arbitrary power—the association of the female body with monstrosity appears with ever-increasing frequency as a political commonplace in seventeenth-century England.

In the radical reconfiguration of the body politic marking the Civil Wars and Interregnum, women's bodies become a privileged site of contest for competing representations of the Commonwealth. Throwing the analogical relation of body to body politic into complete disarray as they did, the debates surrounding the war against and regicide of Charles I were especially conducive to such heavily gendered figurations as the "monstrous birth." These images spill over into the numerous "true reports" and "strange occurrences" published in the newsbooks of the period. In 1642, Mary Witmore gave birth to a headless child with a cross upon its breast after she had allegedly asserted that she would rather have a child with no head than have it signed with the cross in Baptism. The same year, English diurnals report monstrous births in Boston, Savoy, Ravenna, Paris and other cities across Europe and in the New World. In 1645, Mistress Brown gave birth to a stillborn monster without head or feet, and a hollow between its shoulders from which a tiny child emerged. In 1646, Mistress

Hart bore a noseless, legless, handless, hermaphroditic "monster" with a single ear attached to its neck. In 1656, eleven officials attested to Mary Adams' delivery of a "toad-like stillborn monster with claws." A year later, an anonymous woman in Yorkshire, characterized as "daft," bore three feline creatures after being given a potion by a mysterious stranger.[18] Midcentury subjects understandably exhibited a heightened preoccupation with the relationship between the deformed body (especially the deformed female body) and the body politic. Both women and men seized upon the residual images attached to the female body in labor to advance a spectrum of political agendas.[19]

Poole's address to the army opens with the image of a "weak and imperfect" woman in labor—"a woman crooked, weak, sick, & imperfect in body"—cured by "A man who is a member of the Army."[20] She opens her December address with the following justification:

Sirs,

I have been (by the pleasure of the most high) made sensible of the distresses of this Land, and also a sympathizer with you in your labors: for having sometimes read your *Remonstrance,* I was for many daes made a sad mourner for her; The pangs of a travelling woman was upon me and the pangs of death oft-times panging mee, being a member in her body, of whose dying state I was made purely sensible.[21]

In her vision, the council, as well as the nation, is depicted as a woman in labor. Insisting that "the gift of faith in me" can deliver the army of the difficult decision it faces—whether Charles I can lawfully be brought to trial—Poole positions herself not only as midwife, but as fellow "laborer" as well. Poole inserts herself into the body politic by describing her own "panging," a panging both sympathetic and metonymic (a product of both her sympathy for and proximity to the "labor pains" the army suffers and her "membership" in the body politic). Her use of the figure of the woman in labor to depict the "distresses of the land" is suggestive of the complexity of the midcentury debates over where political authority was to reside.[22] The king's position as *pater patriae* and *sponsus regni* to the nation and, simultaneously, *sponsa Christi* to God were some of the primary grounds upon which royal prerogative was understood both legally and figuratively. The implications of Poole's first address to the army council are neatly summarized as follows:

Here was the weaker vessel (woman) instructing a larger vessel (the Army) that, though it (the Army) was a weaker vessel in relation to the

stronger vessel (king as *sponsus regni*), he had himself become a weaker
vessel through infidelity to the Almighty (God as Bridegroom), thus
releasing the initially weaker vessel (the Army) from its conjugal oblig-
ation, to exercise a corrective function to the Body Politic.[23]

Poole's December justification of the army's de facto rule was reversed by her second army council address—which immediately followed the Rump's decision to bring Charles I to trial. Twenty-five
days before the regicide, Poole's matrimonial politics reverts to a
more conventional understanding of the sovereign's relationship to
Parliament: "The King is your Father and husband, which you were
and are to obey in the Lord. . . . And although this bond be broken
on his part. You never heard that a wife might put away her husband,
as he is the head of her body, but for the Lords sake suffereth his ter-
ror to her flesh, though she be free in the spirit to the Lord."[24] She
would make this point even more strongly in her *Alarum of War,
Given to the Army,* a defense of her vision and attack on her detractors, published soon after the execution of Charles I. In the *Alarum,*
she likens the army and the Rump to a murderous "strumpet . . . not
a faithful wife."[25] The army council was "understandably irked. Having not only divorced a king, but [also having] abolished matrimonial monarchy altogether, it did not take kindly to being accused of
being a 'strumpet.'"[26] It took no more kindly to Poole's suggestion
that in their decision to execute the king, what might have been the
easy delivery of a healthy child assisted by Poole was in reality the
profane product of failing to follow her directives, a monstrous
abomination. In the *Alarum,* Poole praises those who took no part
in the regicide by converting the conventional derision of female in-
fertility into a virtue: "I have a word from the lord to speake to your
better part . . . when your carcasse, or the body of your confederacy
is slaine: it is this, Rejoyce thou barren that bearest not, shout for joy
thou desolate woman."[27]

In 1648, the year Poole first appeared before the army council, the
first in a series of Mistress Parliament pamphlets penned by "Mercurious Melancholus" appeared in London. As its title, *Mistris Parliament Brought to Bed of a Monstrous Child of Reformation,*
indicates, childbirth looms large in this scatological parody depicting Parliament as a whore in labor. Published between 1648 and
1660, the Mistress Parliament satires commonly follow a stock format consisting of the strange and wonderful travails of "Mistris Par-

liament" or, by 1660, "Mris. Rump" [sic] The birth chamber attendees consist of such figures as Nurse Sedition, Mrs. Faction, and London. Fairfax, Rainsborough, and others occasionally appear in petticoat as well.

As Alvin Kernan has demonstrated, early modern satire is usually set in the busy streets of the city, "a dense and grotesque world of decaying matter moving without form in response only to physical forces and denying the humane ideal which once molded the crowd into society and the collection of buildings into a city."[28] What is striking about the Mistress Parliament satires is that they abandon this convention to turn a misogynist gaze upon the spectacle of childbirth. The early modern birthing chamber was the most privatized space imaginable, complete with its own hierarchy and rituals, and most importantly, exclusive to women. In *Mistris Parliament Presented in her Bed* (1648), the satiric speaker in the induction opens his speech by registering his physical reaction to the terrible spectacle of Parliament in labor:

> Oh sick! Oh faint! alas my sight doth faile,
> My Members tremble and my Spirits quaile;
> Oh what a chilness doth my heart oppresse,
> But what is the cause of 't is, I know you'le guesse
> 'Tis the most hedious Birth doth me a maze,
> And *much* torment me when on it I gaze:
> But *more* when as I thinke what men will conster,
> To see th'expected *Babe* of *Grace* prove Monster.[29]

Mercurious Melancholus inverts, as it were, the standing spatial conventions of satire in his feminization of Parliament. Unlike the hectic, crowded environs of Jonson's city comedy, the Mistress Parliament "tragedies" are claustrophobic, cloistered. These satires seek to publicize the private world of the birthing chamber not only by disseminating its image in print, but also by assuming the generic guise of the public theatre. The pamphlets commonly assume the formal conventions of a play, often including prologue, epilogue, and dialogue as well as acts, scenes, stage directions, and, in the case of *The Famous Tragedie of the Life and Death of Mris. Rump* (1660), occasionally an invitation to view for a price:

> Ring the Bells backwards; lusty bonfires make
> Of purest straw that from pist beds you take;
> Your musick be the screeching of a Cart,
> And your shrill Songs, sound sweeter than a——

> For joy that Mistris Parliament's brought a bed;
> Pray see the issue of her Maiden-head:
> Tis but 3 half-pence in: The sight will please ye,
> And of your Grief and melancholy ease you.[30]

In the first of these pamphlets, Parliament prepares to deliver her "precious babe of Grace," after a seven-year gestation. Mrs. Synod enters first, to relate the gossip surrounding Parliament's pregnancy. Among other things, Parliament is rumored to have "followed the *camp*" and become an "Ammunition W [whore]," turning "up her tayle to every lowly *Independent* Rascall in the *Army*" from Cromwell and Fairfax to "Broom-men" and "Tinkers."[31] After being given some "strong-waters" by her nurse, Mistress Parliament proceeds to vomit forth blood, gold, ordinances, votes, and "the accursed declaration" against the king.[32] Mistress London, the midwife, arrives only to refuse to help the strumpet: "languish still, till thou hast brought forth the bastard Issue of thy own Lust."[33] Unable to be delivered, Parliament writes a "confession" to the people, admitting that her lust-driven tyranny has caused deformation instead of reformation. She asks the people to pray for her: "so I may still Rule, Reign and Tyrannize over you, *Parliament everlasting,* Impositions, Assessments and Taxations without end. *Amen.*"[34] "Mrs. Priviledge," remarking on Parliament's sad condition, advises her to make peace with God, for "I cannot priviledge thee from dissolution."[35] As Priviledge speaks, Mistress Parliament gives birth to a hideous monster.

The Mistress Parliament pamphlets clearly work to undermine women's bid for political entitlement by appropriating the residual language of monstrosity and labor to deflate women's claims to membership in the body politic. They negate women's engagement in the arena of public politics by ridiculing the specter of female collectivity and aligning the undesirable elements of statecraft with the bodies of women so that they might be eliminated from the healthy body politic. This negation and alignment thus consolidates the emergent gendered division of labor and public/private dichotomy, and "deforms" (mystifies) women's political activity by transforming women from actors in the commonwealth to sexualized stand-ins for the disorder that results from allowing private interest to dominate the political arena. Mistress Parliament bears a monster because she panders to everyone from "privilege," "faction," and "London" to "broom-men," "tinkers," and "independent Army rascalls" for private profit. She bears a child of "deformation" because of the *plu-*

rality of voices that engender her progeny. "Melancholus'" satiric reduction of women to representatives of private interest thus contributes to the privatization of social gender difference within the consolidation of the modern political state.

III

The feminist movement in France, especially the theorizations of *écriture feminine* in the groundbreaking work of Cixous, Irigaray, and Kristeva, teaches us the importance of breaking with the language of patriarchy. Viviane Forrester writes: "Women will have to defend themselves against an accumulation of clichés, of sacred routines which men delight in or reject and which will frequently trap women as well. . . . They will have to see, instead of an old catalogue, fresh, new images of a weary world."[36] Forrester's call for the production of "new images of a weary world" reminds us of the continuing need for women to break away from the conventional language of patriarchy—its logic, clichés, tropes, and correspondences—if they are to alter their place in the world.

The problem with not attempting to invent a new discursive logic is demonstrated by the failure of the *querelle* to produce a recognizably feminist consciousness. As clever and vivacious as women's engagements in the pre-1642 debate about gender may have been, it is clear that any attribution of feminism to such texts requires serious qualification. "Women writing before the revolution," write Christine Berg and Philippa Berry, "unlike many of their European counterparts, had invariably chosen the most conventional of current literary formulae for their nervous—and usually very brief—excursions into the treacherous domain of a male-dominated literary practice."[37] Diane Purkiss similarly asserts that the formal defenses put forth by Englishwomen between 1540 and 1640 do not "mark a clean or revolutionary break with patriarchal figurations of femininity" as they invoke "equivocally and sometimes simultaneously the bifurcated figures of female virtue and vice on which the woman debate always depended."[38] As Joan Kelly succinctly puts it: "Caught up in opposition to misogyny, the feminists of the *querelle* remained bound by the terms of that dialectic. What they had to say to women and society was largely reactive to what misogynists said about women."[39] The debate about women in the Renaissance was constrained by the stock classical and biblical images of women that had perennially set the conceptual terms of the debate. Standardized narrative conventions and rhetorical strategies limited it as well.

Women's responses to their misogynist counterparts rarely stepped outside the logic of the debate itself to pressure its terms, framing their responses *not* as systematic attempts to reimagine their status by attacking the political, religious, and cultural institutions grounding their subjection, but rather as "defenses" that, though gradually increasing in sophistication, could not ultimately shatter the terms of the dialectic itself.

The language and form that political writings by women took during the midcentury stand in sharp contrast to the containment of women within the language of the pre-1642 *querelle*. Berg and Berry draw attention to the similarity between women's sectarian writing in the midcentury and *écriture feminine:* "it is notable that prophecy . . . has much in common with that phenomenon described by Luce Irigaray as 'the language of the feminine,' and by Julia Kristeva as the semiotic."[40] While "a feminine language is one both sexes may possess," they argue, this "non-rationalist discursive mode made entry into the domain of the politico-religious debate easier for a number of women."[41] Their observation is useful for understanding both the limitations of the early female defense and its absence during the English Revolution, for it helps us to identify the multiple strategies by which women like Poole, unlike her Renaissance forebears, abandoned the conventional logic of the debate about gender in their pursuit of political ends.

Feminist scholars have tended to downplay women's sectarian writing in the mid-seventeenth century. A focus on "royalists, Anglican and Catholic, like Lanyer, Wroth, Cary, Philips, Cavendish and Behn, who wrote in more conventionally literary genres," James Holstun observes, has obscured the fact that sectarian writings, in fact, "constitute a substantial proportion" of the catalogue of works penned by women in the period.[42] Berg and Berry's comparison of sectarian women's writings to *écriture feminine* also helps to account for the relative neglect of these works. The critical dismissal of these works, in spite of their sheer volume, has everything to do with their frustration of contemporary formal and aesthetic expectations of what early modern writings by women should look like.

Not only have these works resisted interpretation because of their generic or linguistic alterity, they have also resisted interpretation because their rationale does not conform to what is commonly associated with proto-feminism. "Proto-feminism," to be useful as an analytic concept, needs to be defined in relationship to practices that facilitate a program of equitable access to/allocation of labor, resources, and rights for women. Linda Woodbridge, in her instrumental study of the pre-1642 formal controversy about gender, marks a tension between the advocacy of sexual equality by contemporary feminist scholars and the insistence upon sexual "difference" by the early modern subjects of their inquiry. "Modern feminism," she argues, necessarily involves a "belief in the essential intellectual, emotional, and moral equality of the sexes, an equality which underlies apparent differences which feminists believe are mainly attributable to cultural influences, and the concomitant belief that this equality of essence makes logical and just the demand for equality of rights and opportunity for women."[43] However, the Renaissance defenses of the female sex penned by women in response to the *querelle*—commonly invoked in inaugural gestures by modern feminists and *unlike the writings of their midcentury counterparts*—"consistently emphasize the *differences* between women and men, make assumptions about female nature, ignore cultural influences on female behavior."[44] On the contrary, Elizabeth Poole, Mary Cary, Anna Trapnel, Eleanor Davies, Hester Biddle, and others attacked the grounds of patriarchal absolutism by tearing apart its terms, by using conventional language to achieve unconventional ends. They deconstructed the standing conceptual premises of patriarchy by strategically exploiting its contradictions as the female "defenders" of women—both in the Renaissance and in the Restoration—did not. Despite this, histories of feminist activity typically break off with "Tattlewell" and "Hit-him-home" on the eve of the outbreak of civil war only to resume with the Restoration and dominant "Tory feminism" of such writers as Bathsua Makin, Mary Chudleigh, and Mary Astell.

To claim that the *querelle* inaugurated feminist practice can all too easily lend itself to a genealogical narrative that asks feminists to accept the essentialism of the early debate about gender as coextensive with modern feminisms. This has resulted in a blindness to alternative forms of early modern political activity. A number of prominent studies of the activities of women in the Interregnum print arena, for example, warn against the easy identification of sectarian political writings with female agency.[45] What seems to underlie the widespread underestimation of the feminist potential of such texts is a misunderstanding of the representational premises grounding the language that sectarian women deployed. For example, it is commonly claimed that sectarian women were not "feminist" because they so often subsumed their identity to corporeal and noncorporeal patriarchs and seemingly ungendered political objectives. The unwillingness of scholars to recognize that naturalized assertions about gendered subjectivity are incompatible with feminism goes a long way toward explaining why women's political writings during the English Civil Wars and Interregnum—writings that make no attempt to "defend" the female sex as such—have not been regarded as early feminist texts.

I do not mean to suggest here that it is sufficient to attend to the linguistic and generic dimensions of female sectarian texts. Such an analysis must be conjoined with an attention to the institutional grounding of feminist practice. The danger of Berg and Berry's comparison of women's seventeenth-century prophetic writing to *écriture feminine*, for example, is that it risks obscuring the historical contingencies that made the language that sectarian women used necessary. Post-structuralist "difference" can all too easily come to resemble the essentialist logic of liberal humanism, which is premised upon inexplicable (*a priori*) assertions about what constitutes feminine identity. What aligns essentialism with the post-structuralist attention to "difference" is their equal reluctance to account for the historical contingencies that delimit representations of gendered identity. This problem constitutes a paradox by which gestures toward "democratic inclusivity" undercut themselves when they are not consistently grounded in material difference—*by which I mean the inequitable distribution of labor, resources, and rights through which differences in representation, in every sense, are engendered.*

Crucially, the early controversy about gender was "hardly a proletarian gesture."[46] To engage in it required the type of learning denied to a majority of the female population. Further, the overwhelming majority of Renaissance and Restoration defenses of the female sex were profoundly classist, carefully distinguishing between women of the "better sort" and their "vulgar" contemporaries. It was precisely when poor and middling women began to enter the print arena, as the more learned sort retreated to the Continent, that the traditional debate was eclipsed. When women abandoned the traditional *querelle*, gender took a back seat, in their writings, to discussions of the impact of poverty, war, legal process, government, tithes, and taxation on human beings. In short, women like Poole seem to have been more concerned with citizenship and society as universal questions than with the position of women in particular, and they tended to regard women's oppression as subsidiary to the working out of these questions. If, for women of the "better sort," class privilege allowed them to make claims for their sex at the expense of their less fortunate contemporaries, the more inclusive discourse of sectarian women was marked by a refusal of sexed claims.

Clearly, the achievement of equal political representation for *all* human subjects is feminism's end. Although sectarian women did not achieve this end, they did make remarkable advances toward it by refusing bifurcated conceptions of gendered capacity, distinctions between the cultural and the political, and the weight of institutional tradition in favor of responding to the social inequity of the day. James Holstun is right to qualify Berry and Berg's characterization of female sectarian writing as *écriture feminine* by noting that these women "struggled not so much to destroy male language as to appropriate it."[47] What distinguishes women's sectarian writings of the period from *écriture feminine* is that their writing was not bound up with naturalized conceptions of female subjectivity. The way sectarian women drew upon the residual language of the Renaissance tradition constituted a politics of enactment by which women assumed citizenship—a place in the body politic—by rejecting their subordinate place under patriarchal absolutism even as they simultaneously drew on its commonplaces.

Within the heated contest over political representation that occurred between 1642 and 1660, the contours of the modern political state began to materialize. This had a direct bearing on the status of women's midcentury relationship to representation. With the post-Restoration codification of the modern political state, the contradictions endemic to its universalized rhetoric of citizenship would become entrenched. Misogyny would persist in the emergent liberal political state as a host of prepolitical assumptions about gender rendered resistant to examination—hidden from view—by the modern state's ideological and material relegation of social gender difference to the private sphere. Patriarchy, as always, was to prove remarkably adaptable. Women's strategic use of a superannuated political language would ultimately be rendered the subject of ridicule and derision, reduced to a sign of antic eccentricity, lunacy, and extremism.

IV

Poole's and "Melancholus'" use of the monstrous birth trope suggests a much broader preoccupation with women's increased representational power in the midcentury political arena. Within the hierarchical structures of the early modern absolutist state, women were figured as the deformed, imperfect counterparts of men. Misogynists could assert the fundamental inferiority of women and justify their subordinate place in society as part of a divinely structured plan, an unknowable—hence unexaminable and incontestable—order of things. With the development of the modern political state, the irrational commonplaces surrounding "defect" and "anomaly" continue to accrue to women as the privileged male subject of liberal patriarchy is elevated to the status of "universal subject" and as all that diverges from this abstract subject of citizenship is expelled from the political register. What is expelled includes not only female subjects but a whole host of privatized differences that ground material social inequity. As Cora Kaplan has recently argued, "human anomaly . . . the wide range of visual differences that have historically elicited a reflexive repulsion, continues to trouble the rhetoric of liberal individualism, testing both its ethics of tolerance and its fetishization of autonomy and agency as a condition of human status and civic participation."[48]

Poole's political activity renders visible the contradictions endemic to both a residual and an emergent political economy. The disordered and disorderly grotesque speech, the stuttering tongue, of enthusiasm is a formal device endemic to the genre of enthusiastic literature that works to destabilize the anchoring of gender to sex. Its supposed "irrationality," its refusal to conform to more stable generic conventions, must be regarded as existing in direct generic opposition to the misogynist satires of the period—in both style and content, it is a literature that looks forward to the millennium, calls for destabilization, experimentation, social change. The sheer repetitiveness of misogynist pamphlets that ridicule the political activities of women—appearing with increasing frequency as the political crisis of the midcentury intensifies—not only attests to the profound anxieties evoked by the engagement of women in the political arena, but also constitutes attempts to stabilize, through ridicule and disavowal, the language through which women expressed political aspirations. In direct opposition to the politicized enthusiasm of the midcentury, the misogynist pamphlets satirizing women in the period work to impose order, to stabilize meaning; it is the "genre of a social order in shambles."[49] Typically "conservative," the satirist "calls not for experimentation and social change but for a return to the time-tested virtues and 'good old ways' which have been perverted or abandoned."[50]

As enthusiastic language comes to pervade political polemic, systematic efforts to stabilize meaning appear. For example, between 1640 and 1670, anxieties surrounding language manifested themselves in a Universal Language Movement, a body of literature dedicated to the creation (or "discovery") of a common language.[51] Such a language could not only, it was hoped, anchor words to things and

concepts, but also eradicate political and social confusion, controversy, conflict. Similarly, the misogynist pamphlets of the period are
obsessed with rendering the body hypervisible in order to stabilize its
meaning, to anchor the female body to patriarchal commonplaces
(only to expel both from serious political consideration), and by so
doing, to naturalize them. The language of enthusiasm, by contrast,
denaturalizes the association between gender and sex and subsumes
gender to political ends as opposed to foregrounding "gender" as
political end.

In a stunning refutation of the existing scholarship on Poole,
Manfred Brod makes a compelling case for the political intelligibility
of Poole's addresses. Taken in the context of disintegrating relations
between Levellers and officers in the army, far from the "rantings of
a demented female," Poole, in fact, "voiced opinions that would have
had significant support from both sides."[52]

> Poole's line could be seen as a very reasonable attempt at a compro-
> mise between the two camps that would enable them to continue the
> dialogue that had been broken on 15 December when Lilburne had
> abandoned the Whitehall discussions on the Agreement. . . . Poole's
> failure marked a stage in the final defeat of the Leveller cause and ini-
> tiated the period of uneasy cohabitation between Army and Parliament
> that would characterize the Interregnum.[53]

The reports of the arrest of one "Mistris Poole" in 1653 for preaching in spirited defense of Lilburne and again in 1688 for operating an
illicit press substantiate Brod's claim that Poole had republican lean-
ings and did not easily acquiesce to her early political defeat. Here, it
is important to note that republican politics were not in theory patriarchal, although they often were in practice. The *logic* of republican political theory did not subordinate women, its implementation
did; it was only through contradiction, through the failure to conform to its own logic, through the insertion of faulty *a priori* misogynist premises that republican politics was patriarchal. This
disjuncture between theory and practice is similar to the "mixed mes-
sages," as Kaplan puts it, that exist within the emergent liberal state:

> Viewed from a long-term perspective, the continuing debate about
> the rights of citizens, and the price of increased agency for them, is it-
> self a legacy of liberalism's historically mixed messages about auton-
> omy and social justice, an ongoing paradox that remains radically
> unresolved in the liberalisms that characterize late-twentieth-century
> social democracies.[54]

Kaplan's description of the paradoxes of modern liberalism reminds
us that the contradictions endemic to the emergent liberal state persist today.

In their struggle to find a language through which to articulate
representational right on the basis of sexual equality, the democratic
potential, *in theory*, of republicanism (advocated as imperfectly as it
was by the Levellers) must have held considerable attraction for
women like Poole. Representation is not seamless; it does not operate uniformly, and this is nowhere more clear than in the representations generated by people attempting to come to grips with
transformations that are not yet understood, that are yet unnamed,
in times of rapid social and economic change. Sexual difference was
so bound up with the standing conceptual premises surrounding
gender that women were required not only to strategically destabilize
gender's attachment to sex but also to abandon sex as a category altogether if they were to undermine the conventional social position
accorded them. It may well be that women did not ground their representational entitlement in arguments for or defenses of the female
sex because of a certain reluctance to act "as," or "for," "women," as
bound up as this term was with the long-standing misogynist tradition. Perhaps women's refusal to engage the woman question had to
do with a certain awareness of what the continued anchoring of
women to their patriarchally occupied "gender" might mean for the
future. Given the public nature of women's political activities in the
period, it could very well be that women like Poole believed that an
improvement in women's status would be the logical conclusion of a
more general redistribution of political authority. It was, after all, the
emergent "bourgeois formation of individualized female subjectivi-
ties, which occurred on the basis of an unquestioned and fully naturalized equation of gender with differences of sex," that would
ultimately come to neutralize women's midcentury engagements
with the state.[55]

Poole's *Vision* is suggestive of the strategies by which women
commonly inverted conventional ideas about the nature of women to
claim representational right. In other words, Poole's strategies for
representation index the much more widespread tactics by which
many women in the midcentury authorized their writing to a variety
of political ends. Her work, in short, opens up a number of potentially feminist opportunities, even if these possibilities were to be shut
down by post-Restoration political developments. Englishwomen
would not come close to the degree of representational agency exercised by women such as Poole for a long time to come. The Restora-

tion and first half of the eighteenth century saw the continued proliferation of satires against women. Women once again took up "defenses" of the female sex.[56] The debate about gender continued.

NOTES

1. See the work of Joan Kelly, Linda Woodbridge, Katherine Henderson
   and Barbara McManus, Hilda Smith, Angeline Goreau, Betty Travitsky, Elaine Beilin, and Ann Rosalind Jones.
2. *Half Humankind: Contexts and Texts of the Controversy about
   Women in England, 1540–1640* (Urbana: University of Illinois Press,
   1985), 4.
3. Jane Anger, *Her Protection For Women* (1589), in Henderson and
   McManus, 175.
4. Constantia Munda, *The Worming of a mad Dog* (1617), in Henderson and McManus, 247.
5. Mary Tattlewell and Joan Hit-him-home, *THE WOMEN'S SHARP
   REVENGE Or an answer to Sir Seldom Sober that writ those railing
   pamphlets called the JUNIPER AND CRABTREE LECTURES . . .*
   (1640), in Henderson and McManus, 318.
6. For Woodbridge "[w]orks of the formal controversy possess certain
   features in common. All foster a sense of genuine debate, positing an
   opponent whose probable arguments the author anticipates and re-
   buts. . . . These works do not merely lash out at women in bitter-
   ness . . . but argue a thesis about Woman, with the help of logic and
   rhetoric." They all "deal exclusively with the nature of Woman," "use
   exempla," "argue their case theoretically," and are commonly presented as "oration" or "dialogue"; Linda Woodbridge, *Women and
   the English Renaissance: Literature and the Nature of Womankind,
   1540–1620* (Urbana: University of Illinois Press, 1984), 3.
7. A brief look at Hilda Smith and Susan Cardinale's guide to the Wing
   Short-title Catalogue reveals a proliferation of women's pamphlet literature beginning in the 1640's. None of the works catalogued written by women between 1642 and 1659 constitute a female
   engagement in the formal controversy about gender. Smith and Cardinale, eds., *Women and the Literature of the Seventeenth Century: An
   Annotated Bibliography Based on Wing's Short-title Catalogue* (New
   York: Greenwood Press, 1990).
8. While these connections are well documented by current theorists of
   seventeenth-century culture—primarily in the context of the political
   theories of Filmer, Harrington, Hobbes, and Locke—the Levellers,
   such as Lilburne, and the Diggers, most notably Winstanley, are only
   beginning to be regarded as political theorists in their own right with
   radical contributions to the seventeenth-century discussion of individual rights.

9. Elizabeth Poole, *A Vision: Wherein is manifested the disease and cure of the KINGDOME. Being the summe of what was delivered to the Generall Councel of the Army, Decemb. 29 1648. TOGETHER With a true copy of what was delivered in writing (the sixth of this present January) to the said General Councel* ... (London 1649), 1.

10. Ibid., 2.

11. Ibid., 6.

12. Ibid.

13. "Through his friend William Kiffin's manipulation of the Baptist network, Cromwell seems to have brought his heel down on the annoying prophetess by spreading scandal about her sexual reputation." Stevie Davies, *Unbridled Spirits: Women of the English Revolution, 1640–1660* (London: The Women's Press, 1998), 141.

14. Natalie Zemon Davis, "Women on Top," in Davis, *Society and Culture in Early Modern France, Eight Essays* (Stanford: Stanford University Press, 1975), 124–51. Although both male and female sectarians employed this rhetoric, I am insisting that the adversarial relationship of the language of enthusiasm to the dominant languages of the seventeenth century aligns it strongly with women's position of representational alterity.

15. This linguistic failure of correspondence between sign and referent has direct implications for the "woman question" because the recognition of the instability of language allows for the potential disruption of the conventional meanings attached to "woman." This disruption of the correspondence between women and the conventional attributes assigned to them not only allows for a utopian destabilization of patriarchal values, it grants Poole the authority to address the reading public as a citizen of the commonwealth.

16. Davies, *Unbridled Spirits,* 138.

17. John Knox, *The First Blast of the Trumpet Against the Monstrous Regiment of Women* (Geneva, 1558), 9v.

18. On miraculous occurrences in the early modern period, see the work of Katherine Park and Lorraine Daston, Jean Ceard, David Cressy, Kathryn Brammall, and Dudley Wilson.

19. "Monstrous birth" is in this sense a highly charged *topos,* an object that can evoke a number of competing discourses at once, that provides a locus through which a variety of competing claims may be made, and which stands, not in a static relationship to history, but rather in a dialectical relationship to it.

20. Poole, *Vision,* 1.

21. Ibid.

22. Ibid.

23. Davies, *Unbridled Spirits,* 140.

24. Poole, *Vision,* 4–5.

25. Elizabeth Poole, *An [other] Alarum of War Given to the Army, and to their High Court of Justice (so called) by the will of God; revealed in Elizabeth Poole* ... (1649), 7.

26. Davies, *Unbridled Spirits,* 141.
27. Poole, *Alarum,* 17.
28. Alvin Kernan, *The Cankered Muse: Satire of the English Renaissance* (New Haven: Yale University Press, 1959), 14.
29. Mercurious Melancholus [pseud.], *Mistris Parliament Presented in Bed, after the sore travail and hard labor which she endured last weeek* [sic], *in the Birth of her Monstrous Offspring, the Childe of Deformation* (London, 1648), title page.
30. *The Famous Tragedie of the Life and Death of Mris. Rump . . .* (London, 1660), title page.
31. *Mistris Parliament Brought to Bed of A Monstrous Child of the Reformation . . .* (London, 1648), 4.
32. Ibid., 4–5.
33. Ibid., 5.
34. Ibid., 7.
35. Ibid.
36. Viviane Forrester, "What Woman's Eyes See," in Elaine Marks and Isabelle de Courtivron, eds., *New French Feminisms: An Anthology* (New York: Schocken Books, 1980), 182.
37. Christine Berg and Philippa Berry, "'Spiritual Whoredom': An Essay on Female Prophets in the Seventeenth Century," in Francis Barker et al., eds., *1642: Literature and Power in the Seventeenth Century: Proceedings of the Essex Conference on the Sociology of Literature, July 1980* (University of Essex, 1981), 37.
38. Diane Purkiss, "Material Girls: The Seventeenth-Century Woman Debate," in *Women, Texts and Histories 1575–1760,* eds. Claire Brant and Diane Purkiss (London: Routledge, 1992), 94.
39. Joan Kelly, "Early Feminist Theory and the *Querelle des Femmes,* 1400–1789," *Signs: Journal of Women in Culture and Society* 8 (1982), 14.
40. Berg and Berry, "'Spiritual Whoredom,'" 39.
41. Ibid.
42. James Holstun, *Ehud's Dagger: Class Struggle in the English Revolution* (London: Verso, 2000), 262.
43. Woodbridge, *Women and the English Renaissance,* 3.
44. My emphasis; ibid.
45. See Phyllis Mack, *Visionary Women: Ecstatic Prophecy in Seventeenth-Century England* (Berkeley and Los Angeles: University of California Press, 1992); Keith Thomas, "Women and the Civil War Sects," *Past and Present* 13 (1958); Susan Wiseman, "Unsilent Instruments and the Devil's Cushion: Authority in Seventeenth Century Women's Prophetic Discourse," in Isobel Armstrong, ed., *New Feminist Discourses: Critical Essays on Theories and Texts* (London: Routledge, 1992); Alfred Cohen, "Prophecy and Madness: Women Visionaries During the Puritan Revolution," *Journal of Psychohistory* 11.3 (1984), 411–30, Hilda Smith, *Reason's Disciples: Seventeenth-Century English Feminists* (Urbana: University of Illinois Press,

1982); Elaine Hobby, *Virtue of Necessity: English Women's Writing, 1646–1688* (London: Virago, 1988); Diane Purkiss, "Producing the Voice, Consuming the Body: Women Prophets of the Seventeenth Century," *Women, Writing, History, 1640–1740,* Isobel Grundy and Susan Wiseman, eds. (Athens: University of Georgia Press, 1992).

46. Woodbridge, *Women and the English Renaissance,* 16. The texts that comprise it were rather "a kind of intellectual calisthenics, a few of them . . . acrobatics of a high order, for international competition" (17).

47. Holstun, *Ehud's Dagger,* 265.

48. Cora Kaplan, "Afterword: Liberalism, Feminism, and Defect," in Helen Deutsch and Felicity Nussbaum, eds., *"defects": Engendering the Modern Body* (Ann Arbor: University of Michigan Press, 2000), 303.

49. Felicity Nussbaum, *The Brink of All We Hate: English Satires on Women, 1660–1750* (Lexington: University Press of Kentucky, 1984), 9.

50. Kernan, *Cankered Muse,* 41.

51. For a savvy discussion of the Universal Language Movement, see Sharon Achinstein, "The Politics of Babel in the English Revolution," in James Holstun, ed., *Pamphlet Wars: Prose in the English Revolution* (London: Frank Cass, 1992), 14–44.

52. Manfred Brod, "Politics and Prophesy in Seventeenth-Century England: The Case of Elizabeth Poole," *Albion* 31 (fall 1999), 303–4.

53. Ibid.

54. Kaplan, "Afterword," 304.

55. Clement Hawes, "Man is the Woman: Levelling and the Gendered Body Politic in Enthusiastic Rhetoric," *Prose Studies* 18 (April 1995), 55.

56. As Felicity Nussbaum has suggested, "The pamphlet controversy which followed the Civil War may very well have arisen in an attempt to put women back in their pre–Civil War place, to reestablish their traditional role," *Brink of All We Hate,* 13.

CHAPTER 11

ELIZABETH, GENDER, AND THE POLITICAL IMAGINARY OF SEVENTEENTH-CENTURY ENGLAND

Mihoko Suzuki

She hath wiped off th'aspersion of her sex,
That women wisdom lack to play the rex.

—Anne Bradstreet, "In Honour of that High and Mighty
Princess Queen Elizabeth of Happy Memory" (1650)

Queen Elizabeth *reigned long and happy; and though she cloathed*
her self in Sheeps skin, yet she had a Lions paw, and a Foxes head;
she strokes the Cheeks of her Subjects with Flattery, whilst she picks
their Purses; and though she seemed loth, yet she never failed to
crush to death those that disturbed her waies.

—Margaret Cavendish, The World's Olio *(1655)*

T he first extant English example of the pamphlet debate on gender, the most likely pseudonymous Jane Anger's *Her Protection for Women* (1589)—which answers a now-lost misogynist pamphlet—was published during Elizabeth Tudor's reign. And in *Esther hath hanged Haman* (1617), one of the defenses of women against Joseph

Swetnam's misogynist attack, *The Arraignment of Lewd, idle, froward, and unconstant women* (1615), the most certainly pseudo-nymous Esther Sowernam celebrates Elizabeth as "our late Sover-eign, not only the glory of our Sex, but a pattern for the best men to imitate, of whom I will say no more but that while she lived, she was the mirror of the world, so then known to be, and so still remem-bered, and ever will be."[1]

In discussing the pamphlet debate, scholars such as Linda Wood-bridge and Diane Purkiss have emphasized the formal and commer-cial aspects of the phenomenon.[2] I suggest, however, that the choice of subject matter for these purposes—attacks against and defenses of women—was nevertheless of significance, as was the historical posi-tioning of this debate in Elizabeth's reign and in that of her succes-sor James. (Similar historical circumstances were determinative in the publication of earlier defenses of women: Cornelius Agrippa's *Decla-mation on the Nobility and Preeminence of the Female Sex* [1509] led to his appointment as imperial archivist and historiographer at the court of Margaret of Austria; the English translation in 1521 by Bryan Ansley of Christine de Pizan's *The Book of the City of Ladies* as well as Vives' *Instruction of a Christian Woman* [1523; English trans. 1529] appeared when Mary Tudor was heir.)[3] James's reign was called into question by expressions of nostalgia for Elizabeth, for ex-ample by the publication of Elizabeth's Armada speech and by Shake-speare's *Antony and Cleopatra,* which celebrates Elizabeth in the guise of Cleopatra (over the colorless bureaucrat Octavian, who rep-resents James).[4] Significantly, Fulke Greville's *Life of Sidney,* with its praise of Elizabeth, could be published only in 1652, because it was too critical of James to be published during the author's lifetime.[5]

The struggle between James and his critics who promoted Eliza-beth is mirrored in the pamphlet debate between Swetnam and his critics. Beginning with the account in Genesis of Eve's role in the Fall and with Hesiod's story of Pandora, misogynist texts such as Swet-nam's have served as textual enforcers of the ideology of patriarchial subordination of women. Swetnam's critics in fact express an aware-ness that women's disempowerment was justified by the ascription of "disorder" to women.[6] Although these misogynist texts appear uni-versal and transhistorical in rehearsing depressingly similar arguments, they nevertheless arise out of particular historical circumstances, and their effect differs depending on these circumstances. For one thing, earlier such statements did not elicit the immediate and numerous de-fenses of women that Swetnam's did—pamphlets by Sowernam, Con-stantia Munda, and Rachel Speght, as well as the anonymous play

Swetnam the Woman-hater Arraigned by Women (performed 1617–18; published 1620). In *A Mouzell for Melastomus,* Speght expressed this understanding of the importance of historical difference and specificity in refuting statements justifying women's subordination that were deployed as universal and transhistorical truths; she subjected to renewed scrutiny biblical texts that were taken to authorize misogyny, by limiting the applicability and authority of the pronouncement to the specific historical context.[7] I am arguing here that Elizabeth's long reign constitutes an important historical circumstance of this debate; and that whatever the motivation in publishing the pamphlets—whether as rhetorical exercises or as the means of achieving publishing profitability—and whether or not Sowernam and Munda were males masquerading as women, they nevertheless wrote from the subject position of women and had the effect of galvanizing women's identity as a subordinate group with common interests.[8] The negative interpellation by Swetnam's pamphlet and the responses to it—whether serious or tongue-in-cheek—therefore had effects that were real, even if unintended.[9]

During her reign, however, Elizabeth was not always seen as an empowering exemplar for ordinary women; in fact, Carole Levin has unearthed statements of ordinary women that Elizabeth was promiscuous and had illegitimate children, statements that led to charges of treason.[10] We can extrapolate from Levin's findings that these women sought to bring Elizabeth down to their own level by sexualizing and hence disempowering her. These women shared with Elizabeth a subject position as women subordinate to men—for example, Elizabeth's own ambassador to France, Sir Thomas Smith, in *De Republica Anglorum* (1565), concedes that an "absolute queene" who inherits the title has the right to rule, but only because she would "never lacke the counsell of such grave and discreete men as able to supplie all other defaultes";[11] yet they did *not* agree on how to interpret that subject position. Thus Levin's research supports Allison Heisch's argument that Elizabeth's rule did not affect women's position in patriarchy.[12]

Yet I will argue here that Elizabeth's "effect" indeed had a profound influence on the ability of women to counter misogynist attacks such as Swetnam's and even to imagine political possibilities for themselves in the generations that followed her throughout the seventeenth century—a period when gender relations were in flux, as evidenced in the Swetnam debate and the pamphlets published during the Revolution satirizing women petitioners of the Long Parliament.[13] The contradiction of a woman on the throne in a strict patriarchy proved to be—at least in retrospect—an enabling condition for women who sought to overturn gender norms by asserting a woman's right to inherit titles and estates, by contesting orthodox interpretations of the Bible that justified the subordination of women, and by intervening in the public sphere and participating in political discussion.[14] In treating these concerns under the rubric of "political imaginary," I follow the example of Hilda Smith, who reminds us that "women during the seventeenth century had at once a broader and more inclusive understanding of politics than we possess today."[15]

In addition to what we might call the Elizabeth-effect in terms of the debate concerning women's participation in politics and public discourse, in this essay I will also assess the deployment of Elizabeth by those who promoted the prerogative of Parliament in its relationship with the monarch.[16] Although historians now question the Whig construction of Elizabeth as a promoter of the prerogative of Parliaments, Elizabeth's speeches to Parliament and her representation in biographies as a queen with the common touch allowed Stuart Parliamentarians to use her as an exemplar against the absolutism of James and Charles. The Parliamentarians often represented Elizabeth's gender positively in order to underline the contrast between her and the male Stuart monarchs; yet the contradiction between their celebration of Elizabeth and their excoriation of ordinary women's participation in politics confirms in this instance Heisch's observation concerning the incommeasurability between female monarch and female subjects. To trace this Elizabeth-effect in the course of the seventeenth century, my examples will necessarily be selective: I will first consider two women writers from the early Stuart period, Anne Clifford and Aemilia Lanyer, then I will turn to two promoters of the importance of the commons and the prerogatives of Parliament: Thomas Heywood from before and John Ayloffe from after the Civil War; next I will discuss two Tory women, Elizabeth Cellier and Elinor James, who nevertheless invoked Elizabeth as part of their strategy in justifying their political interventions.[17] I will conclude by considering the ongoing debate about Elizabeth in eighteenth-century and twentieth-century historiography.

In her study of women and property in early modern England, Amy Louise Erikson describes Anne Clifford as the protagonist of the most celebrated marital property dispute of the seventeenth century.[18] Clifford considered the death of Elizabeth as a formative event, for the Knole Diary, covering the years 1603 and 1616–19, begins with an account of it. The Knole Diary constitutes a detailed and vivid record of Clifford's acts and thoughts during the important years in which she contested her father's will that granted his title and estate to her uncle, Earl Francis. Clifford was presented with an agreement between her uncle and her husband that would renounce her claims to her estates in exchange for a cash payment to her husband. The archbishop of Canterbury and King James himself tried to cajole Clifford into accepting this agreement, but she remained steadfast in her refusal to do so. Clifford states in her diary that "if Queen Elizabeth had lived she intended to prefer me to be of the Privy Chamber for at that time there was much hope and expectation of me as of any other yong Ladie whatsoever."[19] She records the impact the queen's death had on herself as a young girl: although she was upset at not being allowed to be a "Mourner . . . because I was not high enough," she remembers that "I stood in the Church at Westminster to see the Solemnities performed" (22). The importance of Elizabeth for Clifford is again made evident when she refers to the queen's death in recording her mother's death many years later, precisely "13 years and 2 months after the death of Queen Elizabeth" (35n). These events of 1603 are described in retrospect, from the perspective of her dispute with her husband over her inheritance, for Clifford pointedly remarks that her father's right to "carry the Sword" in Elizabeth's funeral procession, though contested by Burleigh, "was an office by inheritance, and so is lineally descended to me" (22). Clifford evidently found an inspiring model and example in Elizabeth, who suffered years of adversity under Mary Tudor's rule and who eventually triumphed to assert the inheritance of her title and crown from Henry VIII.[20]

Later in life Clifford overtly followed Elizabeth' example in establishing and confirming her sovereignty over her Westmoreland estates. Recalling Elizabeth's royal progresses, Clifford's annual "removals" among her castles, which she recorded in detail, proclaimed her ownership of her various estates as well as created occasions for the tenants and neighbors to express their homage. Like Elizabeth, she also commissioned numerous copies of her own portrait to be given to her family, gentry officers, and neighbors, thus disseminating her image. In fact, Bishop Rainbow praised Clifford in his funeral sermon for her by comparing her to Elizabeth: "she was like herself in all things: *sibi constans, semper eadem*, the Great, Wise Queen's *Motto*."[21] Elizabeth clearly provided Clifford with a historical precedent to counter the totalizing theory of patriarchy: surely a daughter could inherit baronies if Elizabeth could inherit sovereignty over England.

Although Clifford was one of the most prominent aristocrats in her own right and through her two marriages, and Aemilia Lanyer was a middle-class daughter of a court musician, both celebrate Elizabeth in their writings. Lanyer, like Clifford, recalls how "great *Elizaes* favour blest my youth," in bidding for similar patronage from Anne of Denmark, the "Glorious Queene," one of her dedicatees.[22] Addressing Anne, she writes, "Let your Virtues in my Glasse be seen" (90), echoing Spenser's well-known exhortation to Elizabeth in *The Faerie Queene:* "Ne let his fairest *Cynthia* refuse, / In mirrours more then one her selfe to see" (III.Proem5). By referring to Anne in terms that inevitably recall Elizabeth as Gloriana, Lanyer seeks to persuade Anne to heed her predecessor's example, just as she invokes Elizabeth's memory in addressing Anne's daughter, another Elizabeth. Praising the steadfastness of Anne Clifford's mother, the duchess of Cumberland, Lanyer refers to Elizabeth's motto: "Still to remaine *the same,* and still her owne: / And what our fortunes enforce us to, / She of Devotion and meere Zeale doth do" ("To the Queenes most Excellent Majestie," 117–20).[23] In fact, Lanyer makes this connection between Elizabeth and Cumberland explicit in the opening stanzas of "Salve Deus Rex Judaeorum" itself:

> Sith *Cynthia* is ascended to that rest
> Of endlesse joy and true Eternitie,
> That glorious place that cannot be exprest
> By any wight clad in mortalitie,
> In her almightie love so highly blest,
> And crown'd with everlasting Sov'raigntie;
>   Where Saints and Angells do attend her Throne,
>   And she gives glorie unto God alone.
>
> To thee great Countesse now I will applie
> My Pen, to write thy never dying fame. (1–10)

Here and in the various dedications, Elizabeth functions as an exemplary model of a female patron and a female monarch, who represented herself as forging a special relationship with her people. In appealing to the patronage of a female readership headed by the queen, Lanyer calls upon gender interests that cut across class divisions between the aristocratic patrons on the one hand and the middle-class author and readership on the other: "vertuous Ladies" and

"Vertuous Reader." Lanyer thus writes both the prefaces and "Salve Deus" under the assumption that despite class divisions, of which she is painfully aware, women nevertheless constitute a social and political category of subjects with common collective interests.[24]

The double register of "Salve Deus" that aligned it within acceptable genres, as epideictic poetry of aristocratic patrons and as devotional poetry, gave Lanyer's text license to enter into the debate concerning women's place in the social order. Lanyer's care to justify her work and its publication, even claiming that the Latin title came to her in a dream, suggesting divine inspiration, reveals the difficulty faced by women authors seeking to publish a work, especially on the volatile issue of gender relations during this period. Following the dedicatory poems exclusively addressed to female patrons, with Elizabeth as the repeatedly invoked historical model of political empowerment and patronage, Lanyer turns in the body of "Salve Deus" to enter into the contemporary debate concerning women's place in the social order. Lanyer's poem, of course, predates the pamphlet debate on gender initiated by Joseph Swetnam in 1615. Yet it follows the publication in 1589 of Jane Anger's *Her Protection for Women,* whose strategy of assigning men vices such as lustfulness and women virtues such as wisdom effects a carnivalesque—and temporary—inversion of the traditional hierarchy between the genders. Lanyer's aim appears to be more ambitious than Anger's: she seeks to subject to renewed scrutiny the biblical stories of the Fall and Christ's Passion to question the misogynist ascription of blame to women, which justified their present subordination. To this end she calls attention to the neglected role played by women in the Bible, bringing them from the margin to the center, like Clifford, who focused on Elizabeth and her own female ancestors as models for the prominent dynastic and political role she sought to play.

In light of the positive role women played in the Passion, Lanyer reevaluates Eve's role and responsibility in the Fall. She argues that the women of the New Testament more than redeem Eve's mistake, while she believes the men responsible for Christ's Passion acted out of willful malice, and therefore considers them to be unredeemed and unregenerate. Here, Lanyer extends her critique of males as the dominant agents of history to include males as interpreters of history, interrogating the hegemonic ascription of blame for the Fall to Eve as a means to justify female subordination in patriarchy. This questioning of patriarchal and misogynist interpretations of history leads Lanyer to issue a powerful challenge to present social arrangements buttressed by that history:

Then let us have our Libertie againe,
And challendge to your selves no Sov'raintie;
You came not in the world without our paine,
Make that a barre against your crueltie;
Your fault beeing greater, why should you disdaine
Our beeing your equals, free from tyranny?
    If one weake woman simply did offend,
    This sinne of yours, hath no excuse, nor end. (825–32)

In explicitly calling for "Libertie" and claiming that women are "your equals, free from tyranny," this stanza clearly articulates the political import of Lanyer's poem.

———

Male contemporaries of Clifford and Lanyer put to different uses the iconography of Elizabeth, focusing on her celebrated relationship with her people—promoted by herself in her speeches to Parliament, and by the publication, for example, of mutually adoring letters between Elizabeth and the people of London after the discovery of the Babington Plot.[25] A good example of this aspect of the Elizabeth-effect can be seen in Thomas Heywood, *If You Know Not Me, You Know Nobody,* first published in 1605 with seven further editions before the Civil War. Part I focuses on Elizabeth's travails under Mary Tudor and ends with Elizabeth's accession, drawing a stark contrast between Catholic Mary, contemptuous of the commons, and Protestant Elizabeth, in sympathy with the people.[26] Mary callously dismisses Dodds, who petitions to practice "that faith / Which in king *Edwards* daies was held Canonicall" (A4v), even though Mary herself admits that he had earlier supported her claim to the throne. In rebuffing Dodds, Mary reasons that "Since they the lymbes, the head would seeke to sway, / Before they gouerne, they shall learne t'obay" (A4v). By contrast, Elizabeth seeks to relieve the poor through her "huswiffry" while imprisoned by her sister in the Tower (D3v); and the poor answer her concern for them by offering her "tokens of good will"—a cup of cold water and a nosegay (D4-D4v). Moreover, the townsmen salute her with a "peale of Bells" and Elizabeth "thank[s] them for their loues" (D4v)—an allusion to Elizabeth's celebrated Golden Speech to Parliament. At the conclusion of Part I, the Lord Mayor, as representative of "A thousand of your faithfull Cittizens," presents a "Purse and Bible" (G3v) to Elizabeth; she kisses and praises the Bible, while affirming her close ties to the Lord Mayor: "We thanke you all . . . / thankes my good Lord Maior, / You of our bodie and our soule haue care" (G4).[27]

Part II focuses on Thomas Gresham's building of the Royal Exchange and ends with the victory over the Spanish Armada, affirming the alliance between the queen and merchant citizens such as Gresham and Hobson, a haberdasher. Elizabeth dines with Gresham and gives the Royal Exchange its name. Hobson vauntingly states, "Knowest thou not mee Queene? then thou knowest no body: / . . . I am sure you know me," justifying his lèse-majesté on the grounds that she should know him because he had earlier lent her money at her request. Thus the title of the play that is usually assumed to describe Elizabeth "of famous memory" actually refers to the self-assessment of this "rich substantiall Citizen" (Hv). The ending of the play dramatizing the Armada victory was substantially expanded in the 1633 and 1639 editions, and represents Elizabeth "Compleately arm'd" (K), addressing her soldiers, and comparing herself to Zenobia, "An easterne Queene, who fac'd the Romaine Legions / . . . / And in the field incountred personally" (Kv). In keeping with her earlier affirmation of the middle-class citizenry, Elizabeth stresses the nonaristocratic makeup of her forces—"Me thinkes I doe not see 'mongst all my Troupes, / One with a Courtiers face" (K2)—and she personally leads her soldiers into battle: "A March, lead on, wee'le meete the worst can fall, / A mayden Queene is now your Generall" (K3v). Heywood's *Englands Elizabeth Her Life and Troubles, During Her Minoritie, from the Cradle to the Crowne* (1631) also stresses her common touch: upon her accession, "the throng of people was extraordinary, their acclamations loud as thunder, many were the expressions of loue tendred vnto her, and by her as gratefully entertained, as they were louingly presented" (227). Underscoring the close ties between Elizabeth and the London citizenry, Heywood notes in the margin: "Q. *Elizabeths* grand-fathers father was a Lord Maior of London" (232).

Heywood was only one of many Jacobean writers who celebrated Elizabeth's close relationship with her subjects.[28] In Parliament, she was often invoked as, for example, "that never-to-be forgotten excellent Queen Elizabeth," by those who sought to criticize James and Charles for their absolutist tendencies.[29] To this same end, Elizabeth's own speeches were republished, especially at flashpoints during the Civil War. In particular, her Golden Speech was reprinted in January 1642 when Charles personally went to the House of Commons to arrest his principal opponents. It was published again in March 1648 on the eve of the second Civil War.[30] In

1643 her address to Parliament from 1575 was reissued with the title page: "A most Excellent and Remarkable SPEECH delivered By that Mirrour and Miracle of Princes, Queen Elizabeth, of famous memory . . . Wherein shee fully expresseth the duty of Princes to their Subjects, and that of Subjects to their Princes: Setting forth also, the good Opinion She had of the Justice and Moderation of Our English PARLIAMENTS towards both Prince and People . . . A Discourse very suitable for these times." Here Elizabeth speaks of the "bond sealed to the people at the Coronation" and the "Covenant" that obligates the Prince "to defend them from all injuries, domesticke and forraigne," and "to institute and ordaine good and wholsome lawes" (4) that protect the people from even her own royal prerogative. She further affirms "the charter of the English Subjects liberty, which the piety of Our Royal Predecessors have granted them," and celebrates the "free people" of the English nation, opposing them to those of "other Nations, who groan under the yoak and heavy burdens laid on their servile necks by their Soveraignes" (5). Finally, Elizabeth concludes her extended praise of the "wisedome," "power," and "genius" (6) of Parliament by characterizing Parliament as "the mediator betwixt the Soveraignes of this Kingdome and the people thereof" (7). Whatever her actual practices, in this speech Elizabeth almost uncannily anticipates the position taken by Parliament in opposition to Charles I, especially concerning the contractual relationship between sovereign and people and the freedom of the English people guaranteed by the ancient constitution. This speech goes far to explain the rationale for the Parliamentarians' championing of Elizabeth throughout the seventeenth century and the continuing reissue of her speeches as late as 1693, after the Glorious Revolution.

Even after the Restoration, Elizabeth continued to function as a rallying point for republicanism, for example in John Ayloffe's "Britannia and Raleigh" (1674–75).[31] This poem represents England as the female allegorical figure Britannia in nostalgic dialogue with Raleigh, the opponent of James I, who founded a "stinking Scottish brood" (153) of tyrants. The two engage in a jeremiad lamenting the current state of England; Britannia vows to remain in exile "Till Charles loves Parliaments, till James hates Rome" (22). Raleigh suggests that Charles should be reminded of "his long-scorn'd Parliament, / The basis of his throne and government" (135–6), as well as of "his dead father's name" (137), but Britannia considers Charles's tyranny to be a disease beyond recovery: "Tyrants, like lep'rous kings, for public weal / Must be immur'd, lest their contagion steal / Over the whole" (149–51).

As an alternative to Charles, Britannia celebrates Elizabeth as the patron saint of Parliamentary preeminence—and laments the falling away from this ideal. But Elizabeth is soon revealed to be a quasi-allegorical figure based on Spenser's Gloriana—"She mounted up on a triumphal car, / Outshining Virgo and the Julian star" (57–8)—opposed by another female allegorical figure representing France: "a dame bedeck'd with spotted pride, / Fair flower-de-luces within an azure field; / Her left arm bears the ancient Gallic shield" (60–62). Britannia laments being debased as "Magna Charta whore" (110) by James and his supporters, and excoriates Charles for neglecting her:

> Frequent addresses to my Charles I send,
> And to his care did my sad state commend,
> But his fair soul, transform'd by that French dame,
> Had lost all sense of honor, justice, fame.
> Like a tame spinster in's seragl' he sits,
> Besieg'd by whores, buffoons, and bastard chits;
> Lull'd in security, rolling in lust,
> Resigns his crown to angel Carwell's trust. (115–22)

These lines make evident the popular focus on Charles's promiscuity as the cause of his political ineffectiveness and the consequent scapegoating of his mistresses. Attacking Charles by representing him as effeminate further confirms the poem's conservative gender ideology. Although both Britannia and Elizabeth as allegorical figures serve as political ideals, actual women are strenuously to be excluded from political intervention:

> Teach 'em to scorn the Carwells, Pembrokes, Nells,
> The Clevelands, Osbornes, Berties, Lauderdales:
> Poppea, Messaline, and Acte's name
> Yield to all those in lewdness, lust, and shame. (170–3)

These lines highlight the hostility to contemporary women, specifically Charles's mistresses, by juxtaposing them with notoriously monstrous women from the Roman Empire and contrasting them with exemplary men, "true sons of glory, pillars of the state," from the Elizabethan era, such as "the Sidneys, Talbots, Veres, / Blake, Cav'ndish, Drake, men void of slavish fears" (174–5). In "Britannia and Raleigh" the use of female allegorical figures as political abstractions (Britannia and France) or as ideals (Elizabeth/Gloriana) coexists with a debasement and scapegoating of actual women who encroach upon male prerogative in political affairs.

Two Restoration women who did seek to intervene in politics and public discourse and who were similarly demonized were Elizabeth Cellier, known as "the Popish midwife," and Elinor James, called the "She states-man." Cellier sought to expose the state's use of judicial torture and was prosecuted for treason and in a second trial for libel; she later advocated the licensing of midwives as professional women. James repeatedly petitioned the monarch as well as Parliament and the aldermen of London. Although both were ridiculed by contemporaries, in language reminiscent of the pamphlet debate, they sought to make reasoned contributions to the political conversation of their time.

What strikingly emerges in the 1680 trial (as recounted in *The Trial of Elizabeth Cellier, at the Kings-bench-Barr, On Friday June the 11th, 1680* [1680]) is Cellier's knowledge of and competence in the law, which she proudly underscores in her own writings.[32] She conducts her own defense—because defendants in treason trials were not permitted counsel—and proves instrumental in securing her own acquittal. Most notably she successfully challenges Thomas Dangerfield, the state's witness against her, through her own witnesses who impeach Dangerfield by testifying about his crimes; she also produces copies of records to show that he was a felon, "whipt, and transported, pilloryed, perjured, &c" (13). After her acquittal, Cellier published an account of the trial, *Malice Defeated: Or a Brief Relation of the Accusation and Deliverance of Elizabeth Cellier* (1680), a political exposé that accused the government of torturing witnesses. On the title page Cellier prominently displays her motto, "I never change," and the emblem of the anchor, both adapted from her namesake Elizabeth's motto *Semper eadem* and emblem *ancora spei*. The title of the text, I suggest, refers to John Lilburne's *Malice detected, in printing certain Informations and examinations concerning Lieut. Col. John Lilburn the morning of the Tryal . . . which were not brought into his Indictment* (1653), which sought to refute testimony by spies concerning his royalist activities.[33] Despite the apparent difference in the political positions of Lilburne and Cellier, they share a common resistance against a powerful state—in Lilburne's case the Commonwealth government of Oliver Cromwell, in Cellier's case the Restoration government of Charles II—which hired spies in order to indict its citizens. Cellier therefore finds available and useful the form of Lilburne's political exposé in order to register her political resistance.

In September of that year, she was tried again for "writing, printing, and publishing" *Malice Defeated*. While the indictment expresses the unease with women's writing, especially polemical writing on public affairs, by condemning "the virulency and Malice of this Womans Pen," it also ventriloquizes entire sections of her text and thereby calls attention to her serious charges against the government and the judicial system: that prisoners were starved and tortured "thereby to extort Perjuries and false Evidence against the Innocent" with the knowledge and consent of "the best Quality of our Nobility, Magistracy, and Clergy," and that the "Kings Evidences"—which she graphically calls "Devils Instruments" and "Hangmans Hounds"—were corrupted by bribery.[34] She was found guilty, and was sentenced to stand in pillory in "three publick Places"—the Strand, Covent Garden, and Charing Cross—and fined the large sum of a thousand pounds. A satiric account of Cellier's punishment, *Mistriss Cellier's Lamentation For the loss of her Liberty* (1681), follows earlier satires against women during the Revolution in linking Cellier's political transgression to her sexual licentiousness, and thereby seeks to negate her political agency. Cellier, however, was not silenced by such attacks. After James II's accession, she wrote *A Scheme for the Foundation of a Royal Hospital,* a proposal for the licensing of midwives as a professional society; the manuscript was found among James's papers in France, and published in 1745. Although at first Cellier's Catholicism accords ill with the almost iconic Protestantism of Elizabeth, her reference to Elizabeth in her motto and emblem as well as her allusion in the title of her tract to Leveller John Lilburne's *Malice detected,* another exposé of government abuses, suggest that these apparently unlikely models provided her with exemplars of political empowerment and intervention.[35]

Like Cellier, who addressed her proposal to James II, Elinor James, a printer's wife and later widow, fashioned herself in her numerous broadsides as a close counselor to Stuart monarchs, especially Charles II.[36] James published numerous petitions spanning the period 1682–1715, proferring political advice to England's monarchs from Charles II to George I, as well as the Parliament and the Lord Mayor and aldermen of London; at the end of her career she could declare without much exaggeration that she had been an active participant in political affairs, publishing her views on politics and the nation for forty years. She repeatedly represents herself confronting various monarchs in person, or by means of her broadsides, giving them advice; whatever the truthfulness of these scenes of familiarity, at least one monarch took notice of James's writings: one of her broadsides was found among the State Papers Domestic of James II.[37] In fact, during the Exclusion Crisis, she vigorously defended James's right to the throne and criticized William for displacing his father-in-law.

Despite her Tory allegiances, however, Elinor James surprisingly defended Elizabeth. In 1687, a Catholic pamphlet, *A New Test of the Church of England's Loyalty*, supported King James's suspension of the Test Act of 1673, which benefited Catholics; to this end, it attacked Protestant monarchs, including Elizabeth, calling her "a known *Bastard*" (4). Elinor James answered it in *Mrs James's Vindication of the Church of England, in an Answer to a Pamphlet Entituled, A New Test of the Church of England's Loyalty*. Unlike James's single-sheet broadsides, this pamphlet runs to twelve pages, and affixed to it is the imprint "London, Printed for me, Elinor James," although her husband was still living at the time. In this most sustained of her political writings, she responds to the *New Test*'s attack on Protestant monarchs, and singles out Elizabeth for spirited defense: "how dare you say, *That the Queen was a Bastard*, when all the World knows it is a great Lie?"—reminding the author of the *New Test* that James would not be king if it were not for Elizabeth's self-denial of "that blessed happiness of Marriage" (9). In this text she justifies her political intervention by recounting how Charles II granted her request to make her a godmother of the city, a symbolic role that compensates for her inability, due to her gender, to otherwise assume an effective public role: "O that I were but a Man, I would study Night and Day, and I do not doubt but I should be more than a Conqueror, and so I hope to be nevertheless"—through her writings. Anticipating criticism from those who would consider her intervention to be transgressive, she details her previous accomplishments: "but I know you will say *I am a Woman, and why should I trouble my self*? Why was I not always so, when I pleaded with the Parliament about the *Right of Succession*, and with *Shaftsbury*, and *Monmouth*, and at *Guild-Hall*, and elsewhere" (3). James's intervention, like Cellier's, drew a satiric response: *An Address of Thanks, on behalf of the Church of England, to Mris James, For Her Worthy Vindication of that Church* (1687). Like the attack on Cellier, the broadside predictably focuses on James's gender: "In this Extremity, you, Madam, are the *Pucelle de Dieu*, that *Joan of Arque* . . . the brave *Semiramis*." The satiric reference to exemplary worthies recalls the strategy used in the pamphlet debate; the comparison of James to Joan of Arc as a transgressive female recalls Shakespeare's ambivalent but, on balance, negative representation in *1 Henry VI* of Joan—debased for her witchcraft, her promiscuity, and her lowly origins that she attempts to deny—during Elizabeth's reign. Neither did the *Address of Thanks* nor the city authorities who committed James to Newgate in 1689 "for dispersing scandalous and reflecting papers"—presumably against the offer of the throne to William—achieve their goal of silencing her, for not only did she publish a response to the satiric attack, *A Short Answer to the Canting Address of Thanks* (1687), she continued to publish her numerous broadsides for another twenty-five years.

Thus even though both Elizabeth Cellier and Elinor James were considered Tories and supported Stuart monarchs, they nevertheless celebrated Elizabeth as a female monarch and, I would argue, as a model of women's right to participate in the political public sphere. Both Cellier and James sought to counteract their political disability and justify their intervention by appealing to Elizabeth as an empowering example; though characterized as "Tory," their political writings indicate that their positions were more complex and nuanced than could be accommodated by that binary category. Both writers question that classification by expressing views consistent with the provision in the Declaration of Rights (1689) that guarantees the right of a subject to petition the monarch. And it is important to remember that one of the important political legacies of Elizabeth was the construction of her as a sovereign accessible to and sympathetic to her subjects. Significantly, the critics of both Cellier and James sought to silence them by recourse to the rhetoric of the pamphlet debate, by satiric references to their gender and sexuality that purportedly disabled them from political agency.

I will conclude by turning to examples from eighteenth-century and twentieth-century historiography, in which the issue of Elizabeth's political significance continues to be debated. In volume 4 of *The History of England* (1759), David Hume contests the assessment of those Whigs who have celebrated Elizabeth as the champion of "liberty and popular government": they have "long indulged their prejudices against the succeeding race of princes, by bestowing unbounded panegyrics on the virtue and wisdom of Elizabeth. They have been extremely ignorant of the transactions of this reign, as to extol her for a quality, which, of all others, she was the least possessed of; a tender regard for the constitution, and a concern for the liberties and privileges of her people."[38] Yet Hume praises Elizabeth for being an effective ruler: "none ever conducted the government with such uniform success and felicity" (352), though faulting her for "lesser infirmities": "the rivalship of beauty, the desire of admiration, the jealousy of love, and the sallies of anger" (351). These flaws that Hume singles out are ones that are conventionally gendered feminine; in fact he makes explicit the gendered perspective he takes in assessing Elizabeth: "We may find it difficult to reconcile our fancy to her as a wife or a mistress; but her qualities as a sovereign, though with some considerable exceptions, are the object of undisputed applause and approbation" (353).

John Millar, a Scottish Whig historian and political thinker, introduces his point-by-point refutation of Hume's characterization of Elizabeth as a despot and tyrant in his *Historical View of the English Government from the Settlement of the Saxons in Britain to the Revolution in 1688* (1803): "The great historian of England, to whom the reader is indebted for the complete union of history and philosophy, appears very strongly impressed with the notion of the despotical government in the reign of Elizabeth, and of the arbitrary and tyrannical conduct displayed by that princess."[39] On the contrary, Millar credits Elizabeth and her reign with the beginnings of civil liberty and the ascendancy of Parliament: "To her the nation was indebted for the security of religions, the great forerunner of civil liberty" (446); her reign saw the advancement of the lower classes through the development of "arts, manufactures, and commerce," which entailed the alliance of the people and the crown against the "tyranny of the great barons," and encouraged the independence of "the great body of people" in defending their own privileges against both the sovereign and the nobles, eventuating in the assertion of "a spirit of liberty in the commons" through the reign of her successors.

These examples indicate the ongoing debate concerning Elizabeth's political significance in English history. Both Hume and Millar praise Elizabeth, Hume for her abilities as a monarch, and Millar as a sovereign who begins the development toward constitutional monarchy established at the Glorious Revolution, which functions as the *telos* of his historical narrative. While the republican Millar's judgment of Elizabeth takes no note of her gender, Hume focuses on Elizabeth's disability as a woman, assimilating her to the role of a "wife or mistress," assessing his own imagined relationship to her in these roles—and finding her wanting.

This debate continues in contemporary historiography of sixteenth- and seventeenth-century England, for example in Patrick Collinson's assertion in "The Monarchical Republic of Queen Elizabeth I" that "Elizabethan England was a republic which happened to be a monarchy; or vice versa."⁴⁰ Yet the Marxist historian Christopher Hill implicitly contests such a view of Elizabeth and her rule by saying of James, "[h]is ideas on the prerogative or Divine Right were no more extreme than those of Elizabeth had been," while emphasizing Elizabeth's adeptness at public relations in comparison with either James or Charles.⁴¹ Hill's view of the nature of Elizabethan sovereignty is surprisingly much closer to Hume's than to the Whig Millar's; though he, like Millar, and unlike Hume, takes no special note of her gender.

By contrast, the revisionist historian J. P. Kenyon, who affirms Stuart absolutism as following the norm in contemporary European politics, dismisses Elizabeth, in language reminiscent of Swetnam's misogynist attacks, by calling her "a sluttish housewife who swept the house but left the dust behind the door," and her reign a "petticoat government" characterized by "female tantrums, sulks and irrationality."⁴² After such a reign, according to Kenyon, the English people welcomed a male ruler, one who forthrightly insisted on the Divine Right of Kings. While Hume praised her political abilities despite her feminine "infirmities," Kenyon seeks to discredit Elizabeth by ascribing to her the political disability of ordinary women. Although Hume was able to separate his negative judgment of Elizabeth as "wife or mistress" from the positive assessment of Elizabeth as monarch, Kenyon collapses his fantasy of Elizabeth as a shrewish and slatternly wife with her actual role as ruler, thereby revealing his assumption that *no* woman is fit to rule.

Seventeenth-century women sought models for political empowerment and activism in Elizabeth—as we have seen in the cases of Clifford, Lanyer, and Cellier, to which we could add those of Anne Bradstreet and Margaret Cavendish, cited in the epigraphs; and the context of twentieth-century feminist scholarship has made possible not only a renewed assessment of Elizabeth, but also of these writers, whose own public was circumscribed and political impact limited.⁴³ While these women writers claimed political rights for themselves on the basis of the gender they shared with the sovereign Elizabeth, seventeenth-century male Parliamentarians sought to separate Elizabeth from female subjects, in constructing her as a counterexample to Stuart absolutism. Although some eighteenth- and twentieth-century male historians such as Millar, Collinson, and Hill assessed her political achievements without reference to her gender, the examples of Hume and Kenyon indicate the continuing inescapability of her gender as well as the rhetoric of the seventeenth-century gender debate. Kenyon's satiric emphasis on Elizabeth's gender, which recalls the midcentury satires of "Women in Parliament" that sought to debase women's political activity, is a vivid reminder that three centuries later we are far from being able to pronounce the early modern gender debate settled once and for all.

NOTES

An earlier version of this essay was presented at the 1999 Modern Language Association convention in a session on "Representations of Elizabeth I," sponsored by the Society for the Study of Early Modern Women. I thank the organizer, Elaine Beilin, as well as Margaret Hannay, for her interest in my topic. I also acknowledge the suggestions offered by Susan Frye, Cristina Malcolmson, Hilda Smith, and John Watkins, who shared with me unpublished work.

1. "Esther hath hanged Haman," in *Half Humankind: Contexts and Texts of the Controversy about Women in England, 1540–1640,* ed. Katherine Usher Henderson and Barbara F. McManus (Urbana: University of Illinois Press, 1985), 231.

2. Linda Woodbridge, *Women and the English Renaissance: Literature and the Nature of Womankind, 1540–1620* (Urbana: University of Illinois Press, 1984), while noting the tensions between the Swetnam debate as a "game" and "the realities of life for women," concludes: "the formal controversy was still recognizably a genre and still at heart a literary exercise" (110). Diane Purkiss, "Material Girls: The Seventeenth-Century Woman Debate," in *Women, Texts and Histories 1575–1760,* ed. Clare Brant and Diane Purkiss (London: Routledge, 1992), 69, emphasizes the debate's "production of femininity as a saleable commodity in the literary market" accomplished by "the processing of woman as a theatrical role or masquerade."

3. On Agrippa, see Albert Rabil, Jr., "Agrippa and the Feminist Tradition," the introduction to his edition of *Declamation on the Nobility and Preeminence of the Female Sex* (Chicago: University of Chicago Press, 1996), 1–36. The information concerning Margaret's patronage of Agrippa is on 10. On Vives, see Hilda L. Smith, "Humanist Education and the Renaissance Concept of Woman," in *Women and Literature in Britain, 1500–1700* (Cambridge: Cambridge University Press, 1996), 16–17.

4. On the publication of Elizabeth's Armada speech to criticize the projected match between Prince Henry and the Spanish Infanta, see Susan Frye, "The Myth of Elizabeth at Tilbury," *Sixteenth Century Journal* 23 (1992), 95–112. I discuss *Antony and Cleopatra* as a nostalgic celebration of Elizabeth at the expense of James in *Metamorphoses of Helen: Authority, Difference and the Epic* (Ithaca: Cornell University Press, 1989), 258–63. On cultural and literary nostalgia

for Elizabeth during the reign of the Stuarts, see Ann Barton, "Harking Back to Elizabeth: Ben Jonson and Caroline Nostalgia," *ELH* 48 (1981), 706–31.

5. Christopher Hill characterizes praise of Elizabeth as "a favourite method of political denigration within acceptable limits," listing numerous authors who deployed this means to avoid censorship. "Censorship and English Literature," *The Collected Essays of Christopher Hill* (Amherst: University of Massachusetts Press, 1985), 1:57.

6. See Carole Pateman, "'The Disorder of Women': Women, Love, and the Sense of Justice," in *The Disorder of Women: Democracy, Feminism, and Political Theory* (Cambridge, UK: Polity Press, 1989), 18.

7. For example, she takes St. Paul's pronouncement to the Corinthians "It is good for a man not to touch a woman" to have been motivated by the specific situation of the Corinthians then under persecution: "the Apostle doth not heerby forbid marriage, but only adviseth the *Corinths* to forbeare a while, till God in mercie should curbe the fury of their adversaries" (*The Polemics and Poems of Rachel Speght*, ed. Barbara Kiefer Lewalski [New York: Oxford University Press, 1996], 16). On Speght's "historical relativism," see Woodbridge, 90.

8. Ann Rosalind Jones argues that Swetnam's diatribe made possible the responses from women-voiced writers, and that "the public space opened up by popular printing legitimates new roles for women." "From Polemical Prose to the Red Bull: The Swetnam Controversy in Women-Voiced Pamphlets and the Public Theater," *The Project of Prose in Early Modern Europe and the New World*, ed. Elizabeth Fowler and Roland Greene (Cambridge: Cambridge University Press, 1997), 127.

9. On the "failure of interpellation" brought about by the "disidentification" on the part of the interpellated, see Judith Butler, "Competing Universalities," in Judith Butler, Ernesto Laclau, and Slavoj Žižek, *Contingency, Hegemony, Universality: Contemporary Dialogues on the Left* (London: Verso, 2000), 158: "As an instrument of non-intentional effects, discourse can produce the possibility of identities that it means to foreclose. . . . the articulation [of foreclosure] can become rearticulated and countered . . . unmoored from the intentions by which it is animated."

10. Carole Levin, *The Heart and Stomach of a King: Elizabeth I and the Politics of Sex and Power* (Philadelphia: University of Pennsylvania Press, 1994), 66–90.

11. Sir Thomas Smith, *De Republica Anglorum*, ed. Mary Dewar (Cambridge: Cambridge University Press, 1982), 65.

12. Allison Heisch, "Queen Elizabeth I and the Persistence of Patriarchy," *Feminist Review* 4 (February 1980), 45–56.

13. On women petitioners and satires directed against them, see my *Subordinate Subjects: Gender, the Political Nation, and Literary Form in*

England, 1588–1688, forthcoming, Ashgate Publishing, 2002, chapter 4.

14. See Lisa Gim, "'Faire *Eliza's* Chaine': Two Female Writers' Literary Links to Queen Elizabeth I," in Susan Frye and Karen Robertson, eds., *Maids and Mistresses, Cousins and Queens: Women's Alliances in Early Modern England* (New York: Oxford University Press, 1999), 183–98, for a discussion of Elizabeth as a "a provocative gender model" for writers such as Bathsua Makin and Diana Primrose, who "might seek to emulate her education and abilities even though they could not attain her political position" (183).

15. Hilda L. Smith, "Introduction: Women, Intellect, and Politics: Their Intersection in Seventeenth-Century England," in *Women Writers and the Early Modern British Political Tradition* (Cambridge: Cambridge University Press, 1998), 4.

16. John Watkins, "Old Bess in the Ruff: Remembering Elizabeth I, 1625–1660," *English Literary Renaissance* 30.1 (winter 2000), 95–116, argues for the multiplicity of the appropriations by rival political perspectives. See also his forthcoming *Representing Elizabeth in Stuart England: Literature, History, Sovereignty,* Cambridge University Press, 2002.

17. For a fuller discussion of Lanyer, Cellier, and James, see *Subordinate Subjects,* chapters 3 and 7.

18. Amy Louise Erikson, *Women and Property in Early Modern England* (London and New York: Routledge, 1993), 111.

19. D. J. H. Clifford, ed., *The Diaries of Lady Anne Clifford* (Phoenix Mill, Gloucestershire, UK: Alan Sutton, 1990), 21.

20. Mary Ellen Lamb, "The Agency of the Split Subject: Lady Anne Clifford and the Uses of Reading," *ELR* 22 (1992), 350, has argued that Clifford inserted herself into the "gendered or even male-gendered subject position as reader of a patriarchal canon." On the importance of Clifford's matrilineal heritage and kinship network, see Barbara Lewalski, *Writing Women in Jacobean England* (Cambridge: Harvard University Press, 1993), 125. On Clifford's reading and writing of history from a female subject position, see my "Anne Clifford and the Gendering of History," *Clio: A Journal of Literature, History and the Philosophy of History* 30.2 (winter 2001), 195–229.

21. Edward Rainbow, *A Sermon Preached at the Funeral of the Right Honorable Anne Countess of Pembroke, Dorset, and Montgomery . . .* (1677), 53.

22. *The Poems of Aemilia Lanyer: Salve Deus Rex Judaeorum,* ed. Susanne Woods (New York: Oxford University Press, 1993), "To the Queenes Most Excellent Majestie," 110, 126.

23. For a different reading of these lines, see Susanne Woods, *Lanyer: A Renaissance Poet* (New York: Oxford University Press, 1999), 51. Woods points out that "Queen Elizabeth was a poet as well as the

supreme model of piety, which makes her a complex exemplar for Lanyer, who is here a poet mediating between one queen and another" (Elizabeth and Anne).

24. I am arguing here that through these texts Lanyer seeks to forge tactical and strategic alliances in order to legitimate her work and herself as a writer, by contrast to recent criticism of Lanyer, which has divided between those who emphasize Lanyer's solidarity with a community of women and those who stress Lanyer's "resentment" toward aristocratic women. Examples of the former include Lewalski, 213–41; Elaine V. Beilin, *Redeeming Eve: Women Writers of the English Renaissance* (Princeton: Princeton University Press, 1987), 117–207; Wendy Wall, *The Imprint of Gender: Authorship and Publication in the English Renaissance* (Ithaca: Cornell University Press, 1993), 319–30. The latter include Anne Baynes Coiro, "Writing in Service: Sexual Politics and Class Position in the Poetry of Aemilia Lanyer and Ben Jonson," *Criticism* 35.3 (1993), 357–76; and Lisa Schnell, "'So Great a Diffrence is There in Degree': Aemilia Lanyer and the Aims of Feminist Criticism," *Modern Language Quarterly* 57.1 (March 1996), 23–35. The split itself between the two schools indicates the difficulty of simultaneously attending to *both* gender and class: if the former critics de-emphasize class differences, then the latter, in emphasizing class divisions, do not give sufficient importance to the common experience of women in patriarchy to which Lanyer clearly appeals.

25. *The True copie of a Letter from The Queenes Majestie, to the Lord Maior of London* . . . (1586).

26. In *Historiography and Ideology in Stuart Drama* (Cambridge: Cambridge University Press, 1995), Ivo Kamps focuses on the play's championing of Elizabeth's Protestantism over Mary's Catholicism. He considers an important historical context of the play to be the negotiations for a match between Prince Henry and the Spanish Infanta and hence an "anxiety about a perceived growth in Catholic power" during James's reign (72–3).

27. Many of these details—for example, the presentation of the nosegay and the Bible—are taken from Richard Mulcaster's contemporary account in *The Quene's Majestie's passage* (1559).

28. See, for example, Thomas Dekker's *The Whore of Babylon* (1607), which has Plain Dealing—a satirist who represents the commons—defect from the Empress of Babylon (the papacy) to Titania (Elizabeth); and Edmund Bolton's *The Cities Advocate* (1629), a work that promotes the link between Elizabeth and the London citizenry made up of artisans and tradesmen. On Bolton, see *Subordinate Subjects,* chapter 1.

29. *Commons Debates, 1628,* 4:62. Qtd in Christopher Hill, "Parliament and People in Seventeenth-Century England," *The Collected Essays of Christopher Hill* (Amherst: University of Massachusetts Press, 1986), 3:34.

30. C. V. Wedgwood, *Oliver Cromwell and the Elizabethan Inheritance* (London: Jonathan Cape, 1970), 5–6.

31. *Poems on Affairs of State*, ed. George deF. Lord (New Haven: Yale University Press, 1963), 1:228–36.

32. On the background of Cellier's treason trial for the "Meal Tub Plot," see Anne Barbeau Gardiner, "Introduction," *Malice Defeated and The Matchless Rogue*, The Augustan Reprint Society, 249–50 (Los Angeles: William Andrews Clark Memorial Library, 1988), iii–vii.

33. See Pauline Gregg, *Free-Born John: A Biography of John Lilburne* (London: Harrap, 1961), 330.

34. *The Tryal and Sentence of Elizabeth Cellier; For writing, Printing, and Publishing, a Scandalous Libel, called Malice Defeated, &c* (1680), 14.

35. For another recent account of Cellier, see Frances Dolan, *Whores of Babylon: Catholicism, Gender, and Seventeenth-Century Print Culture* (Ithaca: Cornell University Press, 1999), chapter 4. Dolan focuses on the disabling force of anti-Catholic discourse at the time of the Popish Plot both in the satiric representations of Cellier and in her self-representations. My account differs from hers in stressing the importance for Cellier's writings of republican political discourse from the English revolution. On the relationship between Cellier's status as a midwife and her credibility as a witness, see Rachel Weill, "'If I did say so, I lyed': Elizabeth Cellier and the Construction of Credibility in the Popish Plot Crisis," in *Political Culture and Cultural Politics in Early Modern England*, ed. Susan D. Amussen and Mark A. Kishlansky (Manchester and New York: Manchester University Press, 1995), 199–200.

36. On James, see the recent study on women and print culture by Paula McDowell, *The Women of Grub Street: Press, Politics, and Gender in the London Literary Marketplace, 1678–1730* (Oxford: Clarendon Press, 1998), esp. 46–51, 128–45, 201–13. McDowell places James's broadsides in the contexts of "street ballad, satirical political song, [and] public political speech (140–1). In claiming the importance of gender for James's discursive self-construction, I diverge from McDowell, who considers James's "scattered and momentary irruptions of a gendered consciousness" to occupy a "strikingly minor place" in James's writings (202).

37. Lois G. Schwoerer, "Women of the Glorious Revolution," *Albion* 18.2 (summer 1986), 208, cites *CSPD*, June 1687–February 1689, #2032.

38. David Hume, *The History of England* (Indianapolis: Liberty Classics, 1983), 4:354.

39. John Millar, *An Historical View of the English Government from the Settlement of the Saxons in Britain to the Revolution in 1688* (1803), 457.

40. Patrick Collinson, "The Monarchical Republic of Queen Elizabeth I," in *Elizabethan Essays* (London: Hambledon Press, 1994), 43.

41. Christopher Hill, *The Century of Revolution, 1603–1714* (London: Cardinal, 1974), 63; "Governments and Public Relations: Reformation to 'Glorious Revolution,'" in *A Nation of Change and Novelty: Radical Politics, Religion and Literature in Seventeenth-Century England* (London: Routledge, 1990), 105.

42. J. P. Kenyon, *Stuart England* (1978; sec. ed. Harmondsworth: Penguin, 1985), 19, 57.

43. On Bradstreet, see Frye, *Elizabeth I,* 146–7, and Ivy Schweitzer, "Anne Bradstreet Wrestles with the Renaissance," *Early American Literature* 23.2 (1988), 291–32. On Cavendish, see my "The Essay Form as Critique: Reading Cavendish's *The World's Olio* through Montaigne and Bacon (and Adorno)," *Prose Studies: History, Theory, Criticism* 22.3 (December 1999), 1–16.

INDEX

mermaids, 154–5
middle class, 59, 62, 68–9, 91, 125
midwifery, 186, 201
    and political rhetoric, 213, 215,
        218
    licensing of, 200–1, 242
Mill, Humphrey, 49
Millar, John, 246–7
misogyny, 21, 39, 41, 44, 48, 59,
        60, 92, 148, 210, 217,
        224–6
    commodification of, 39, 62
*Mistris Parliament Presented in her
    Bed*, 217
Montagu, Ann, 50
Montaigne, Michel, 84
Mordecai, 198
Moss, Anne, 39, 42
mothers / motherhood, 163, 185,
        191, 202–3
    authority of, 160
    concept of "natural mother,"
        185–8, 191, 201, 203
    England as mother country, 194,
        202
    "invention of motherhood,"
        186, 188, 199
    malevolent, 196
    see also maternity
Moundford, Mary, 68, 150
mourning 149–52
    see also ars moriendi, death
Mulcaster, Richard, 251
Munda, Constantia, 6, 47–9, 51,
        63, 69, 71, 172, 175,
        178–81, 210, 232–3
    Worming of a madde Dog, 37,
        48, 50, 58

Nashe, Thomas, 121
nationhood, 186–7, 215
nationalism, 2, 189, 193–5, 202–3
Neville, Henry, 39
"Newes from the Court," 39
"Newes from the Sea," 39

Newstead, Christopher, 130
Niccholes, Alexander, 165
North, Sir Thomas, 85
Northren Mother's Blessing, 168–9
Nynges, William, 104

Orgel, Stephen, 185
Overbury scandal, 42
    *A Wife, now the Widow of Sir
        Thomas Overbury*, 5, 38,
        40–1
Overbury, Sir Thomas, 38, 44, 47
    "The Wife," 40–1
Ovid, 49

pamphlets, 58, 84, 131, 210,
        224–5, 232, 237, 244–5
    costs of, 129–30
    female readers of, 133–4
    gendered female, 122
    and the middle class, 7, 59–63
    Mris Parliament pamphlets,
        216–8
    and print entertainment, 62
    and street ballad genre, 105
    Samuel Rowland's gossip
        pamphlets, 7, 121–134
    see also print
paradise, *see* Eden, garden
Parker, Martin, 106
    Taylor's Lamentation, 112
    Wiving Age, 106, 113
Parkhurst, William, 41
Parliament
    Elizabeth's praise of, 240
    as female, 217–18
Pateman, Carole, 249
patriarchy, 201–2, 213–14, 220–1,
        223–4, 232, 237
    language of, 213, 219–21
    not monolithic, 105, 124, 134,
        142
patrons / patronage
    Anne of Denmark, 7, 83, 86,
        91, 236